Intending and Acting

⨆ Bradford Books

Edward C. T. Walker, Editor. Explorations in THE BIOLOGY OF LANGUAGE. 1979.

Daniel C. Dennett. BRAINSTORMS. 1979.

Charles E. Marks. COMMISSUROTOMY, CONSCIOUSNESS AND UNITY OF MIND. 1980.

John Haugeland, Editor. MIND DESIGN. 1981.

Fred I. Dretske. KNOWLEDGE AND THE FLOW OF INFORMATION. 1981.

Jerry A. Fodor. REPRESENTATIONS. 1981.

Ned Block, Editor. IMAGERY. 1981.

Roger N. Shepard and Lynn A. Cooper. MENTAL IMAGES AND THEIR TRANSFORMATIONS. 1982.

Hubert L. Dreyfus, Editor, in collaboration with Harrison Hall. HUSSERL, INTENTIONALITY AND COGNITIVE SCIENCE. 1982.

John Macnamara. NAMES FOR THINGS. 1982.

Natalie Abrams and Michael D. Buckner, Editors. MEDICAL ETHICS. 1982.

Morris Halle and G. N. Clements. PROBLEM BOOK IN PHONOLOGY. 1983.

George D. Romanos. QUINE AND ANALYTIC PHILOSOPHY. 1983.

Jerry A. Fodor. MODULARITY OF MIND. 1983.

Robert Cummins. THE NATURE OF PSYCHOLOGICAL EXPLANATION. 1983.

Stephen Stich. FOLK PSYCHOLOGY AND COGNITIVE SCIENCE. 1983.

Irvin Rock. THE LOGIC OF PERCEPTION. 1983.

Jon Barwise and John Perry. SITUATIONS AND ATTITUDES. 1983.

Elliot Sober, Editor. CONCEPTUAL ISSUES IN EVOLUTIONARY BIOLOGY. 1983.

Norbert Hornstein. LOGIC AS GRAMMAR. 1984.

Paul A. Churchland. MATTER AND CONSCIOUSNESS. 1984.

Owen J. Flanagan. THE SCIENCE OF THE MIND. 1984.

Myles Brand. INTENDING AND ACTING. 1984.

Intending and Acting

Toward a Naturalized Action Theory

Myles Brand

A Bradford Book
The MIT Press
Cambridge, Massachusetts
London, England

This book was set in Palatino by Village Typographers, Inc., and printed and bound by The Murray Printing Company in the United States of America.

Library of Congress Cataloging in Publication Data

Brand, Myles.
    Intending and acting.

    "A Bradford book."
    Bibliography: p.
    Includes index.
    1. Act (Philosophy)   2. Intentionality (Philosophy)
I. Title.
B105.A35B73   1984   128'.4   83-24817
ISBN 0-262-02202-8

Contents

Preface

Philosophers have long been concerned with human action. Some of the most penetrating remarks, for example, are to be found in Aristotle's *Ethica Nicomachea*. But to a very significant degree this concern has been subservient to concerns with other philosophical issues, such as the nature of moral and legal responsibility, the apparent conflict between human freedom and causal determinism, and the possibility of a physicalistic explanation for all that there is. In the modern era Locke, Hume, Kant, and Bentham, to name a few, developed views about human action, but only in the service of broader metaphysical, epistemological, and moral concerns.

In the first half of this century philosophers dealing with action tended to follow the traditional pattern. For instance, Prichard developed an influential account, within the context of his moral theory, that identified actions with a species of mental events. However, Gilbert Ryle's *Concept of Mind* (1949) and J. L. Austin's papers of the same period altered the pattern. Although there was continued interest in using the results of action theory to resolve (or dissolve) long-standing philosophical problems, the focus shifted to the nature of action itself. With this shift attention to problems about action grew rapidly. In the three decades following the publication of the *Concept of Mind*, a spate of books and a deluge of articles on action theory appeared.

Philosophical action theory has evolved through several stages since the early 1950s. The first stage, which lasted until approximately 1970, was in some ways a continuation of earlier work. It was piecemeal; there was little attempt to provide a systematic theory. And although human action itself was the focus, action theory was still seen as an instrument to deal with other issues. Characteristic of this stage is that many of the best efforts were contained in articles. These have been collected in several anthologies: Brand (1970), Care and Landesman (1968), Lehrer (1966), and White (1968). Among the more influential books of this period are Anscombe's *Intention* (1963), Melden's *Free Action* (1961), Charles Taylor's *The Explanation of Behavior* (1964), Richard Taylor's *Action and Purpose* (1966), and von Wright's *Norm and Action* (1963). The most influential and the most significant work of this period was Davidson's, especially his "Actions, Reasons, and Causes" (1963) and "The Logical Form of Action Sentences" (1966).

The second stage in the recent development of philosophical action theory is characterized by systematization and a relative lack of concern with associated issues. Goldman's *A Theory of Human Action* (1970) marked the emergence of this stage. Action theory began to flourish and achieve the status of an independent area of investigation. Among the more important books, in addition to Goldman's, are: Castañeda's *Thinking and Doing* (1975), Chisholm's *Person and Object* (1976b), Danto's *Analytical Philosophy of Action* (1973), Davis's *Theory of Action* (1979), Hornsby's *Actions* (1980), Thalberg's *Enigmas of Agency* (1972), and Thomson's *Acts and Other Events* (1977).

But stagnation set in. The philosophical lines were drawn: positions hardened, epicycles were added, and progress was slowed. Interest waned. Work on action theory derivative of that begun in the 1970's continues, but, it seems, without enthusiasm. To be sure, these projects are worthy ones and ought not to be abandoned. But it has become clear that their ability to explain the nature of human action is limited.

The goal of this book is to usher in the next—and third—stage of philosophical action theory. This stage is similar to the second in that the focus is systematic theorizing about human action. But it differs from its predecessors in being continuous with *non*philosophical work on human action. Through the second stage philosophers generally ignored the scientific study of action. Of course, passing mention of related psychological theories was made; but there was no serious attempt to integrate philosophical action theory with the relevant scientific theories. My contention is that future progress in action theory depends on the integration of the philosophical with the scientific. Put another way, I advocate the naturalization of philosophical action theory.

This idea is not new. William James's view in the *Principles* (1890) was that philosophical and psychological concerns about action are intermingled. But James seemed to have held this position inadvertently, since he tended to confuse the philosophical with the psychological. There is nothing inadvertent about the position advocated here: I want to argue that philosophical and scientific theories about action are continuous. This line of development for action theory, it is well to note, coheres with some recent developments in epistemology, the philosophy of mind, the philosophy of language, and value theory. It is no longer heresy to see the philosophical enterprise as continuous with the scientific one: one dogma of empiricism is finally giving way. Probably the most significant work of this type has dealt with the philosophical foundations of psychology (see, especially, Fodor (1975, 1981b, 1983), Dennett (1969, 1978)). Those efforts have focused on cognitive psychology, on the input and central systems, as it were. One of my goals is to focus attention on the philosophical foundations of the human output system.

Let me say at the outset that this book is limited in scope. And that in two ways. It is not the definitive statement on the naturalization of action theory. I view it, rather, as the first—tentative—steps in this direction. It is intended to make a contribution to the resolution (or dissolution) of certain conceptual problems about human action. It is a part of an ongoing literature, not the last word. It is a step in the dialectic. Second, I have not attempted to provide an exhaustive account of human action. For example, I have said nothing helpful about the affective influences on action. My target is intention. But even here there are lacunae. I do not discuss conditional intentions, nor the way in which intentions can be reasons. It is not because these topics are unimportant or philosophically uninteresting. They are important and interesting. Rather I have focused my arguments on one crucial, central claim: an understanding of human action depends on a scientific reading of intention. If I have succeeded, the next step will be to take up these additional problems.

I have used two methodological guidelines. First, approach from philosophy. I am attempting to move *philosophical* action theory toward the scientific study of action. Philosophical action theory is the foundation on which I build. Thus, I have taken pains to be thorough and careful on this part of the project. For the tastes of some I might have been too thorough. Naturalized action theory can be approached from, say, psychology, artificial intelligence, or even robotonics. In those cases there would be less emphasis on conceptual issues and more emphasis on empirical ones. Readers whose interests are primarily scientific might want to skim part II, in which detailed conceptual analysis dominates. It is my considered opinion, however, that this philosophical spadework is essential and must be done thoroughly and with care. My goal is to build from the bottom up.

Second, point directions on empirical issues. I contend that philosophical action theory is continuous with the scientific study of action. As we move from philosophical foundations to empirical issues, the account depends more and more on results in psychology and related disciplines. Since the models used in these disciplines are evolving and, sometimes, changing radically, it would be a mistake to inexorably tie an account of action to specific models. Rather, it should be shown how the most promising lines of current research in the cognate scientific disciplines interface with the results of conceptual analysis. It is also vital to see that research within its recent historical context. I make some attempt to do this in part IV.

There is one difficulty about which the reader should be warned. An account of human action, I will argue, must make contact with both cognitive psychology and motivational psychology. Cognitive psychology, broadly understood to include some work in artificial intelligence, has undergone rapid recent development. Promising lines of research are emerging. But motivational psychology, once the focus of attention and pride, is currently in disarray. The best that can be done at this time is review the major contributions to the motivational literature that bear on human action, assess the degree to which plausible empirical models are being proposed, and suggest, briefly at least, future directions for research.

That part of the project that discusses the cognate scientific disciplines is programmatic and incomplete. But that is as it should be. I am not arguing that some extant empirical models are entrenched to the extent that disconfirmation is unlikely, nor am I proposing any new empirical models. Rather, I am attempting to ascertain the extent to which empirical models increase our understanding of human action.

Richard Taylor introduced me to the problems and puzzles about human action almost twenty years ago. For that, I am indebted to him. Our solutions, however, have tended to go in different directions. I began thinking about the continuity of philosophical action theory and the scientific study of action a number of years ago. I am not, though, the only one to have recently thought along these lines; Bach (1978) and Brandt (1979), for instance, hold programmatic views that are not altogether different.

I have tried my proposals on many colleagues, colloquia audiences, and students. I thank them all sincerely for their patience and efforts to correct my errors; I have certainly benefited from this help. I hope that I will be forgiven for not mentioning these many, many people by name. I must, however, mention Daniel Berger, with whom I discussed the first parts of this manuscript, Mike Harnish, with whom I discussed much of the book, and Kent Bach, who gave the penultimate draft a thorough and helpful reading. I have learned from Hector Castañeda and his work, and I owe various philosophical debts to Donald Davidson, Roderick Chisholm, and Wilfrid Sellars. I also want to thank J-C. Smith who prepared the index and made suggestions for a final revision, and Ann Hickman who expertly word-processed several versions of the manuscript. Last, but certainly not least, I want to express my overwhelming gratitude to my wife, Peggy, and my son, Josh, who picked up the slack when I worked on this book and did not do my chores, and who tolerated my moods when all did not go well.

Earlier versions of some of the material in this volume have appeared previously. In a number of instances the views defended here are contrary to those in the earlier papers. Chapters 1 and 2 derive from "The Fundamental Question in Action Theory" (1979c). Chapter 3 is based on "Particulars, Events, and Actions" (1976) and "Identity Conditions for Events" (1977). Chapter 4 is a development of "Intending and Believing" (1983b). Parts of chapters 6, 7, and 8 are based on "Cognition and Intention" (1982)† and "The Human Output System" (forthcoming). And parts of chapter 9 are derived from "Philosophical Action Theory and the Foundations of Motivational Psychology" (1980b).

†Copyright © 1982 by D. Reidel Publishing Company, Dordrecht, Holland.

Part I

THE NATURE OF HUMAN ACTION

1
Philosophical Action Theory

In the first section of this chapter I delineate in an intuitive way the subject matter of our inquiry—human action. There are several types of theories about the nature of human action that can be labeled, broadly speaking, causal. In the second section I provide a taxonomy for these causal theories, and in the following three sections I discuss them, emphasizing the difficulties they face. A plausibility argument is given for one of these types, for which I reserve the label 'the Causal Theory of Action.' According to the Causal Theory, a person acts when what he does is caused by a certain type of mental event, say, a complex of wanting and believing, or an intending.

Though plausible, indeed more plausible than its competitors, the Causal Theory is not without difficulties. One alleged difficulty is that action cannot be defined by reference to causal chains because these chains are not structurally uniform, that is, they sometimes contain wayward or deviant segments. In the sixth and seventh sections I provide a strategy for dealing with this problem. This chapter does not deal with all the difficulties facing a Causal Theory. A fundamental one—one, in fact, that is a problem for any philosophical theory about human action—will be broached in the next chapter.

1. Human Action

There is an intuitive distinction between what people do and what happens to them. Some of what happens to persons concerns their relationships to other persons, institutions, or the environment, such as becoming orphaned, being drafted or being knighted, and becoming sunburned. And some of what happens to persons depends primarily on themselves, either on their bodily or mental states and processes, such as their hair growing, their kidneys cleaning blood, or their having nightmares. There are some cases that do not fall clearly on one side or the other; perhaps an interesting example is being victimized in a love affair. But the general distinction between what we do and what happens to us has strong intuitive support.

Consider the following lists of particular events.

List A	*List B*
Richard's walking into a restaurant	Richard's putting his hands forward to break his fall
Richard's reading the menu	Richard's grimacing with pain
Richard's raising his arm in order to attract the waiter's attention	Richard's taking a deep breath
Richard's chewing his food	Richard's looking at his knee.

Both are lists of things Richard does, not things that happen to him. Suppose that Richard does these things in an ordinary way, the way most of us do things of these sorts most of the time. Our interest, initially at least, concerns which of these events are *actions*. Is Richard's chewing his food an action? Is his putting his hands forward when falling, or his grimacing actions, when done in ordinary ways?

One proposal is that the events on list A are actions but the events on list B are *mere doings* (cf. Taylor, 1966, chapter 8). That is, there is a tripartite distinction between actions, mere doings, and what happens to us. No doubt there is a distinction between the events on lists A and B, but it is far from clear that it is a difference between actions and events that are not actions. Contrary to this proposal, I take it that the events on both lists A and B are actions. This view is preferable in that it emphasizes the similarities between the events on both lists and contrasts them with what happens to us.

Admittedly, labeling the events on both lists 'actions' is at least partially stipulative. The word 'action' is far from common in ordinary usage; it tends to be reserved for portentous occasions. It might be closer to ordinary usage to label these events 'acts.' But 'acts' has been given broad scope in the philosophical literature, sometimes including such mental events as believings and entertainings, as well as events like those on lists A and B. In the end I trust that no one will be misled by the terminology: after all, it matters little what we label events on these lists, provided that their nature is made clear. It is the conceptual issues with which we are concerned.[1]

Allowing that the events on lists A and B are all actions, what then is the distinction between the lists? The 'Wittgensteinian answer' is this (cf. Anscombe, 1963, pp. 8 ff.). When Richard chews his food, he knows what he is doing, and his knowledge does not depend on his observing, directly or indirectly, his mouth's moving. But when Richard grimaces, he does not know what he is doing unless he observes himself doing it, for instance, by looking in a mirror or being told by someone else that he is doing it. In general the distinction between lists A and B is that between actions in which the agent knows what he is doing without observation and actions in which the agent does not know what he is doing without observation.

The operative notion of observation needs clarification. Do kinesthetic sensations yield observational knowledge, for instance? However, even putting aside this qualm, the distinction between the lists cannot be explicated in this way. Consider Richard's raising his arm in order to attract the waiter's attention. Clearly, observation is necessary for him to know what he is doing: he must see the waiter if he is to attract his attention. It is controversial whether Richard must see the waiter if he merely *tries* to attract his attention; but it is clear that he will succeed in attracting his attention only if he sees him, or observes him in some way. In the normal case a person knows what he is doing without observation when what he is doing involves only the movement of his body, such as raising his arm, or when his action is mental, such as solving a chess puzzle 'in his head.' Whenever an action includes the causal consequences of the agent's bodily movements, observation is necessary for him to know what he is doing. Thus, the distinction between actions on lists A and B is not that between those in which the agent requires observation to know what he is doing and those in which he does not require observation to know what he is doing.

Although the Wittgensteinian answer does not succeed in providing a basis for the distinction between the actions listed on A and B, it does point the way toward an explanation. The proposal was correct to the extent that the distinction reflects a difference in the antecedent cognitive states of the agent. Under the assumption that there is nothing extraordinary in these cases, the actions on list A are intentional and those on list B are not intentional. There is a cognitive feature in intentional action, which is lacking in action that is not intentional. That additional cognitive feature consists in the action's being planned prior to execution. I will discuss this feature of intentional action at length.

Distinctions among actions that are not intentional can be drawn. There are several parameters, apparently orthogonal to each other. Under normal conditions some actions are performed rotely, habitually, automatically, or routinely. Presumably those on list B are not intentional for this reason. Sometimes actions are performed involuntarily, which include those done from strong emotion or instinct, or while drugged, drunk, or hypnotized. Some actions are performed in a state of ignorance, by accident, or by mistake. From the viewpoint of the ascription or diminution of responsibility, legal or moral, the manner in which these distinctions are drawn is crucial. For example, in many circumstances moral responsibility for what we do is diminished to the degree to which an action is involuntary. But I shall not be concerned with these distinctions; I leave that important and difficult task to the legal and moral philosophers. My interest is more foundational. I am concerned with the underlying nature of human action, with special emphasis on intentional action.

2. Four Types of Theories about the Nature of Human Action

It is highly plausible that a human action is associated with a sequence of causally related events. Consider the simple bodily action of Richard's raising his arm. It is reasonable to think that there is a mental event of Richard's which causes some events in Richard's nervous system, which in turn cause some muscular and skeletal events, and which then cause Richard's arm to rise. This claim is also highly plausible in the case of mental actions. Consider the simple one of Pat's thinking of her favorite color. Here there is a mental event of Pat's which causes another mental event, described perhaps as Pat's favorite color being thought of by her. In cases of complex actions, whether bodily ones, such as Richard's signaling by waving his arm, or mental ones, such as Pat's recalling her neighbor's name by using the mnemonic device of reciting the letters of the alphabet, it is again highly plausible that there is an associated sequence of causally related events. In cases of complex bodily action the sequence extends beyond the person and into the world, as it were.[2]

In all these cases the question arises: Which part of the causal sequence is to be identified as the action? Historically three types of answers have been defended. According to one, which I label 'the Oldtime Volitional Theory,' the action is to be identified with the entire causal sequence. Richard's raising his arm *is* a mental event of a specified sort causing his arm's rising. According to another, which I label 'the Mental Action Theory,' the action is to be identified with the initial mental event in the sequence. Richard's arm rising is an effect of some special mental action. And according to the third, for which I reserve the label 'the Causal Theory,' the action is to be identified with the bodily or mental effect of the antecedent mental event. There is another type of theory that locates action in the causal sequence, though no one to my knowledge has defended it. Richard's raising his arm actually consists of two actions, one of which is mental and the other of which is bodily. I label this last view 'the

Double Action Theory.' No one has defended the Double Action Theory in its bald form because it multiplies actions beyond necessity. The account of human action I will defend might be thought to contain some features of a Double Action Theory, though I think it would be best classified as a Causal Theory.

A more careful formulation of these types of theories is in order. Let S range over persons, A over event types, and t over durations. There are, then, sentences of the form 'S As at t,' for example, 'Richard raises his arm at noon' and 'Pat thinks of her favorite color at midnight,' as well as grammatical variations of this form. These sentences report particular events or occurrences. For simplicity, however, let us delete the temporal specification, and assume that 'S As' and its variants report particular events. Also let B range over types of behaviors, including covert (mental) behaviors, which are *not* actions. Thus substitution-instances of 'S's Bing' are 'Richard's arm rising' and 'Pat's neighbor being thought of by her.' Let M stand for some unspecified mental actions; and let $\overline{M}$ stand for some unspecified *non*actional mental events. It is a matter of deepest concern how M and $\overline{M}$ are to be explicated. For the sake of argument and to make contact with the historical tradition, M can be imagined to be a willing and $\overline{M}$ a wanting plus believing. Assuming universal closure these four generic theories of human action can be stated as follows:

> *The Oldtime Volitional Theory:* S's Aing is an action *iff* there is a $\overline{M}$ of S such that (i) $\overline{M}$ caused S's Bing, (ii) $\overline{M}$ is appropriate to S's Aing, and (iii) S's Bing is associated with S's Aing.

> *The Mental Action Theory:* S's Aing is an action *iff* there is a M of S such that (i) M caused S's Bing and (ii) S's Bing is associated with S's Aing.

> *The Causal Theory:* S's Aing is an action *iff* there is a $\overline{M}$ of S such that (i) $\overline{M}$ caused S's Aing and (ii) $\overline{M}$ is appropriate to S's Aing.

> *The Double Action Theory:* S's Aing is an action *iff* there is a M of S such that M caused S's Aing.

The Oldtime Volitional Theory is a reductive account. Human action consists in causally related nonactional events. This type of theory appeals to those with strong nominalistic inclinations: our ontology need contain only categories of events and relations between them (in addition to persons), and not an additional category of actions. Linguistically it holds out the promise of translating action talk into nonaction talk. The other three types of theories provide no basis for translating action sentences into nonaction sentences.

The Oldtime Volitional Theory was well regarded in the eighteenth and nineteenth centuries. John Stuart Mill, for example, says:

> Now what is an action? Not one thing, but a series of two things: the state of mind called a volition, followed by an effect. The volition or intention to produce the effect, is one thing: the effect produced in consequence of the intention, is another thing: the two together constitute the action. I form the purpose of instantly moving my arm; that is a state of my mind: my arm (not being tied or paralytic) moves in obedience to my purpose; that is a physical fact, consequent on a state of mind. The intention followed by the fact, or (if we prefer the expression) the fact when preceded and caused by the intention, is called the action of moving my arm. (*Logic*, Bk. 1, chap. iii, sec. 5)

And John Austin, the nineteenth-century jurist, says "a voluntary movement of my body, or a movement which follows a volition, is an *act*" (1873, vol. 1, p. 427). This theory continues to be favored by contemporary jurists. H. L. A. Hart (1968, pp. 90 ff.) argues that it is currently the orthodox view in Anglo-Saxon law. The theory, however, appears not to be attractive to contemporary philosophers, at least when developed along the lines suggested by Mill. But Judith Jarvis Thomson (1977) argues for a view that on one interpretation might be classified as an Oldtime Volitional Theory (cf. Brand, 1981). Thomson argues, first, that causal sequences are themselves events and then claims that an action is a causing of a bodily event. It is the entire sequence, the causing, that constitutes the action, not the mental antecedent nor the bodily effect.[3]

Berkeley appears to be an advocate of the Mental Action Theory. In the "First Dialogue" Philonous says, "The Mind therefore is to be accounted *active* in . . . so far forth as *volition* is included in them. . . . In plucking this flower I am active, because I do it by the motion of my hand, which was consequent upon my volition. . . . I act, too, in drawing the air through my nose, because my breathing so rather than otherwise is the effect of my volition" (*Three Dialogues*). Note that Berkeley uses 'volition' to refer to a mental *action*, in contrast to Mill who uses it to refer to a nonactional mental event. Much confusion, no doubt, has been engendered because 'volition' has not been assigned a uniform sense. To avoid this confusion, it would be best, where possible, not to use this term.

In this century the Mental Action Theory is associated with H. A. Prichard. He says at one point, "to act is really to will something" (1945, p. 190). But because of Ryle's (1949) attacks, the view lost favor. However, it has recently been revived. Aune (1977), Davis

(1979), and Hornsby (1980) advocate versions of the Mental Action Theory. Hornsby, for instance, identifies an action with an agent's mentally trying: "Every action is an event of *trying* or attempting to act, and every attempt that is an action precedes and causes a contraction of muscles and a movement of the body" (1980, p. 33).

The Causal Theory is probably the most widely held view. It was held by Hobbes, Locke, and Hume, for example. Locke says:

> *Volition* or *willing* is an act of the mind directing its thought to the production of any action, and thereby exerting its power to produce it. . . . He that shall turn his thoughts inwards upon what passes in his mind when he wills, shall see that the will or power of volition is conversant about nothing but our own *actions;* terminates there; and reaches no further; and that volition is nothing but that particular determination of the mind, whereby, barely by a thought, the mind endeavors to give rise, continuation, or stop, to any action which it takes to be in its power. (*Essay*, Bk. 11, chap. xxi, 28, 30)

Recently the Causal Theory has been advocated by Davidson (1963, 1978), Goldman (1970, 1976), Sellars (1966, 1973), Castañeda (1975, 1980), and Searle (1979, 1981). Impetus for the current interest in the Causal Theory can be traced to Davidson's "Actions, Reasons, and Causes" (1963). Although his main concern in that paper was to provide plausibility arguments for the Causal Theory, he has often been interpreted as defending the view that a complex mental event consisting of a person's desire to do something and his belief that he can do it causes his action. Actually the view that actions are caused by desires (or wants) plus beliefs is best associated with Goldman's *A Theory of Human Action* (1970).

Mental Action and Causal theories can be viewed as functional accounts of action. No attempt is made to specify a nonrelational essential property of actions: rather an action is defined by the role it plays in a causal sequence. On the Mental Action Theory an action is the cause of certain types of behavior, and on the Causal Theory an action is the effect of certain types of (mental) behavior.

These four types of theories do not exhaust the possible accounts of human action (cf. Brand, 1970). Another type is the Agency Theory. This type resembles the Causal Theory in that an action is defined as an effect of a certain sort, though now the cause is a substantial self or agent, not a mental event. Something is an action, that is, only if an agent makes it happen. Chisholm (1976, 1976b) and Richard Taylor (1966, 1974) have been prominent in the defense of the Agency Theory. Thomas Reid (*Active Powers*) is often read as holding this view and Berkeley might also be best interpreted as defending it, rather than a Causal Theory. There are, however, some serious criticisms of this theory. It is unclear what an agent is and what causal-like relationship an agent, which is a substance, bears to his behavior, which is an event (see Thalberg, 1976). It is also unclear how an agent can be influenced by ongoing mental events and external happenings without being necessitated (that is, caused) to act. It cannot be claimed, for instance, that an agent is influenced when there are external conditions necessary but not sufficient for his acting. For the relation 'is causally necessary for' takes events as arguments in both places; but on the Agency Theory, the required relation must take substances in the second place.

Another type of theory, further removed than the Agency Theory from the four causal theories, is one that defines an action as behavior within a social context. According to one version of this view, held by Melden (1956), an action is a bit of behavior in which a person follows a rule. My moving a chess piece, for example, is an action in virtue of my being aware of the rules of the game and my following those rules in moving the piece. However, when someone moves a chess piece, say moving a knight two spaces forward and one to the left, he performs an action even if he knows nothing at all about chess. His action would not be properly described as a chess move, but nevertheless he would have done something: he would have brought about a change in the world. Moreover, this version of the theory may suffer from vicious circularity. Rule following seems to be actional, and hence cannot straightforwardly be used to illuminate the nature of action (cf. Kripke, 1982). Another version of this type of theory, defended at one time by H. L. A. Hart (1948–1949), says that an action is a bit of behavior for which the agent can be ascribed responsibility. One difficulty, however, is that the issue of responsibility, legal or moral, does not arise in all cases of action. For instance, my scratching my ear while alone at night in my bedroom raises no questions of legal or moral responsibility. (Also cf. Geach, 1960.) In general these types of theories define 'action' too narrowly, since not all actions are performed in social contexts.

It would be an interesting historical and critical exercise to detail the particular versions of all the types of theories about action held by modern philosophers, and to compare and contrast their views with those of contemporary writers. Few authors, for instance, hold in bald form one of the four causal theories, but rather propound subtle variations and sometimes combinations. It would also be interesting to catalogue and discuss the criticisms and rejoinders that have been made on behalf of each type of theory. Carried out properly, these projects are monumental. Here I want only to review briefly some of the key objections to the four causal theories. I do this in order to provide background for the constructive discussion to follow, and not to offer a summary or history, even a greatly abbreviated one, of philosophical action theory.

3. The Oldtime Volitional Theory

Clause (ii) in the specification of the Oldtime Volitional Theory says that the content of the nonactional mental event relates to the performance of an action. Suppose that the nonactional mental event is a desire plus belief and suppose that the action type is winking. Then clause (ii) says that the content of the agent's mental event is his winking. Put colloquially, the person desires to wink and believes that he is able to do so. This clause seems to result in some oddity. On the Oldtime Volitional Theory an action is identified with the entire act sequence, including the desire and belief. However, the content of these mental events is the entire act sequence. Persons desire *to wink,* not have their eyelid close. But winking includes desiring on this theory. Thus, the content of the desire is in part itself. But that is counterintuitive: the content of desiring is a *future* event type. The same oddity obtains in the case of belief. Notice that clause (ii) is also included in the specification of the Causal Theory. However, this oddity does not attach to the Causal Theory, since the action is there identified with the effect of the desire and belief, *not* the entire act sequence.

Clause (iii), 'S's Bing is associated with S's Aing,' is also required for an explication of the Oldtime Volitional Theory since without this clause, counterexamples can be generated. Suppose that 'S's Aing' is 'Richard's raising his arm.' Suppose also that Richard wants to raise his arm and he believes that he can do so. But now imagine that his arm is suddenly paralyzed. He becomes alarmed, and a nervous reaction develops, causing his eye to twitch. It is not the case that Richard raised his arm; but the right-hand side of the definition without clause (iii) would be satisfied, since there is a bit of Richard's overt behavior, his eye twitching, that is a causal consequence of his wanting and believing.

Clause (iii) is intended to capture the idea that S's Bing is the nonactional, behaviorial component of S's Aing. Richard's arm rising is the nonactional, overt behavioral part of Richard's raising his arm. The most natural explication of this clause is the following.

(D1.1) For every person S, action type A and type of behavior B, S's Bing is associated with S's Aing *iff:* (i) it is necessary if S's Aing occurs, S's Bing occurs; and (ii) for any type of behavior B^*, if it is necessary that S's Aing occurs only if S's B^*ing occurs and if it is necessary that S's B^*ing occurs only if S's Bing occurs, then S's B^*ing $= S$'s Bing.

(The temporal parameters are again suppressed for simplicity.) Clause (ii) of (D1.1) is a maximal condition. If it were not included, there would be an infinite number of bits of behavior correlated with each action. Without that clause, Richard's arm rising halfway, his arm rising quarterway, and so on, in addition to his arm rising all the way, would be associated with Richard's raising his arm.

Given this definition of 'S's Bing is associated with S's Aing,' the Oldtime Volitional Theory fails to be a reductive account. The definiens of (D1.1) makes essential use of action terms. There might be another explication of 'S's Bing is associated with S's Aing' that preserves the reductive status of the Oldtime Volitional Theory while retaining its plausibility, though I cannot think of one.[4] If the Oldtime Volitional Theory is not reductive upon analysis, then there appears to be nothing to recommend it over the Mental Action Theory or the Causal Theory, since each of these types is simpler than the Oldtime Volitional Theory. The Mental Action Theory also contains the clause 'S's Bing is associated with S's Aing'; but unlike the Oldtime Volitional Theory, the Mental Action Theory does not purport to be reductive.

Other difficulties can be and have been raised for Oldtime Volitional theories, such as the charge of obscurantism with regard to the mental antecedent. But these difficulties are not unique to the Oldtime Volitional Theory, and given the failure of the theory to retain its reductive status, it is better to discuss these difficulties in the context of the other causal theories.

4. The Mental Action Theory

A common objection to Mental Action theories is that they are subject to vicious regresses (see, e.g., Ryle, 1949). An action is performed only if there is a willing (or some such mental action) in the causal sequence. Since willings are themselves actions, there must be a willing to will, and a willing to will to will, and so on *ad infinitum.* The regress is vicious, it is alleged, because each willing takes time, thus requiring an impossibly long time for the performance of a single action. There are several ways to short-circuit this objection. The most plausible one is that the regress collapses because willing to will is identical to willing: there is nothing beyond willing that one must do in order to will to will. Another response is that willing need not precede every action; in particular, willings need not be willed (McCann, 1974), though this response has the appearance of being *ad hoc*.

Another objection that has received wide currency, though its target has not been limited to Mental Action theories, is the logical relatedness argument (see, e.g., Melden, 1961, Winch, 1958, Taylor, 1966). The heart of the argument is this. Logical relations preclude causal relations. Willings are logically related to their correlated behavior, since there is no way to identify or refer to willings without identifying or making reference to that behavior. Therefore, willings do not cause their correlated behavior. This argument has been strongly attacked (see, e.g., Davidson, 1963, Stoutland, 1970; but cf. Browne, 1975). The premise stating that willings cannot be identified or referred to without identifying or referring to the correlated behavior is false. Willings are mental events. Events can be identified or referred to in numerous ways, only one of which is by means of their effects; they can, for example, be identified and referred to through their spatiotemporal location or through their noncausal relations with other events. Richard can refer to some particular willing as 'the willing that caused my arm to go up'; but he can also refer to it as 'the first willing I had after noon while sitting in my office chair' or as 'my favorite willing of the day.' Even if this premise were true, moreover, it would not follow that willings are logically related to their correlated behavior. For willings and bits of behavior are events, and events cannot stand in logical relations. Linguistic items, or perhaps quasi-linguistic items such as propositions, enter into logical relations; events, which are spatiotemporal objects, do not. Again, sentences about events, including sentences about willings, stand in logical relations, but not the events described.

Unlike the previous two objections, there is another one that is at least prima facie serious. This one concerns the attribution of moral responsibility. From a commonsense viewpoint persons are primarily morally responsible for their actions. Though someone might be responsible for the consequences of his actions, he is responsible in a reduced or mediated way. Thus, if the action is identified with the mental component of the causal sequence, a person is primarily morally responsible for that mental event, and not the physical effect of it. But the physical component of the causal sequence normally determines moral responsibility. Suppose that Gordon wills to stab John and that in fact he is successful. We would hold Gordon responsible for the physical act of stabbing, not what occurred in his head. It is the stabbing that is normally taken to be morally wrong.

Mental Action theories, however, are not without a defense. Such theories can be coupled with a deontological account in which moral responsibility accrues to the mental component of the causal sequence. Such nonconsequentialist views may be difficult to defend, though perhaps not impossible (see Prichard, 1949 and Aune, 1977). A more attractive route is to offer an account of moral responsibility in which persons are primarily responsible not for their actions but the intended consequences of them. Gordon's action is his willing to stab John; but he is primarily responsible for its intended physical consequences. In any case the Mental Action theorist must supplement his view in a way that accounts for our strongly held intuitions about moral responsibility.

This last objection suggests the general criticism that Mental Action theories are counter to common sense. From the commonsense, pre-theoretical viewpoint, we observe other persons performing actions. What we observe are physical events, not ones happening in someone's head. We request, cajole, command, and compel persons to act. Again, we are usually concerned with their physical activity, not something that happens in their heads. We criticize and correct what other persons do. What we criticize and correct are most often physical activities, not mental ones. We fear and admire the actions of others. What we fear or admire are overt physical events, not, usually, mental ones. We teach persons how to perform actions, and they gain the ability to do so. What we teach them, and what they have the ability to do, is not to will, or to try, or to choose, but to actually perform these actions. We say that some persons are good mimics, and can replicate what others do. We mean that they can act in the same physical ways. Much the same obtains for other commonsensical features of human action.

In the same way that the Mental Action theorist might attempt to supplement his account to explain (or explain away) ordinary intuitions about the attribution of moral responsibility, so too he might attempt to supplement his account to explain (or explain away) these pronouncements of common sense. The Mental Action theories are at least *prima facie* unnatural; it remains to be seen whether they are irretrievably counterintuitive.

The most serious problem for Mental Action theories is providing an account of willing, or whatever mental action is taken to initiate the causal sequence. Ryle, for one, found this an impossible task.

[Volition] is an artificial concept. We have to study certain specialist theories in order to find out how it is to be manipulated. It does not, of course, follow from its being a technical concept that it is an illegitimate or useless concept. 'Ionisation' and 'off-side' are technical concepts, but both are legitimate and useful. 'Phlogiston' and 'animal spirits' were technical concepts, though they have now no utility. . . . The concept of volition belongs to the latter tribe. (1949, p. 62)

In order to respond adequately, the Mental Action theorist must provide an account of willing (or some such initiating mental action) that assigns it a real explanatory role and that makes clear its nature. Recent Mental Action theorists have recognized this problem, though I would not say that to date they have successfully solved it. For example, Hornsby (1980) attempts to remove some of the mystery by identifying the mental action with trying. But 'trying' in her account remains a technical, undefined locution. For ordinarily, trying involves physical, overt activity. To try to do something is to complete one activity in order to do another (see Taylor, 1966, chapter 6). When I try to clear the highbar, I perform some overt actions, putting myself in the proper position and running to the bar, in order to leap it. But this ordinary notion of trying is not available to Hornsby, since for her trying cannot be overt activity.

In sum, there are real difficulties facing the Mental Action Theory: it is counter to common sense, especially with regard to the attribution of moral responsibility; and it leaves mysterious the nature of the mental action that initiates the causal sequence. These difficulties may not be insurmountable, but they do make the Mental Action Theory unattractive.

5. The Causal Theory

The Causal Theory says that all and only actions are caused by a certain type of nonactional mental event. This claim is consistent with various detailed pictures, the most plausible of which seems to be the following (cf. Thalberg, 1977). Suppose that, on a particular occasion, Richard clapped his hands. Thus the following two events occurred:

(1) Richard's clapping his hands;

(2) Richard's hands moving together.

These events are distinct, since (2) includes only the spatiotemporal region in which his hands move, a region that stops at the shoulders, whereas (1) includes a spatiotemporal region greater than that. Event (2) is associated with the action (1). The relationship between (2) and (1) is that of part to whole (cf. Thomson, 1977, chapters V–VII). Richard's clapping his hands is an event consisting of a causal sequence, part of which happens inside Richard's body, such as events in his nervous system, and part of which is publicly observable, namely, his hands moving together. That entire complex causal chain is an action, according to the Causal Theory, in virtue of being caused by a nonactional mental event, say a desire plus belief. This rendition of the Causal Theory presupposes that causal sequences are themselves events and that causal sequences can be initiated by an event, both reasonable assumptions. A chain reaction consisting of several billiard balls moving is itself an event and one that might be caused by the cue stick striking the first ball. In short an action is a causal sequence, which in the case of bodily action includes overt behavior and which was in turn initiated by a nonactional mental event of a specified sort.

Richard's hands can move together without his clapping his hands if, for instance, someone else has hold of them and pushes them together. But can the causal sequence that is Richard's clapping his hands occur without Richard performing an action? Suppose that an electrode were implanted in poor Richard's brain, and that when a current passes through it, a causal sequence occurs consisting of certain events in his nervous system causing events in his muscular and skeletal systems, and finally causing his hands moving together. The mental antecedent normally initiating this action does not occur. Did Richard clap his hands? No, according to the Causal Theory. Without Richard's wanting to clap his hands and believing that he will (or some such complex mental antecedent), something happened to Richard; he did not *do* anything, in the sense of performing an action.

Note incidentally that the Causal Theory is not committed to the view that all actions are free. Richard's wanting to clap his hand might be the result of coercion or compulsion, and need not issue from Richard's own deliberations. Richard might have been confronted with irresistible incentives that induced him to want to clap his hands, or he might have some pathological disorder that leads him to constantly want to move his hands. The source of the wanting (and believing) does not affect whether an action has been performed.

The Mental Action Theory, by way of contrast, presents a different picture. There is some mental action, say (following Hornsby, 1980) Richard's 'trying' to clap his hands, such that this action causes the entire physiological sequence, ending with the publicly observable event of his hands moving together. There is no bodily *action* of Richard's clapping his hands. There is, rather, the *mental* action of his trying to clap his hands and the physical effects of his hands moving together.

The Causal Theory is more plausible than the Oldtime Volitional Theory or the Mental Action Theory. It does not attempt to provide a reductionist account, which it seems clear cannot be sustained; and it neither hypothesizes a special type of mental event (a 'willing') nor conflicts with common sense. Of the two alternatives to the Causal Theory, the Mental Action Theory is the main competitor. It might in the end be supplemented by an account of this special type of mental event and by a means for explaining away its apparent conflict with common sense. Philosophical theories sometimes have a way of rising from the ashes. But as matters now stand, the Causal Theory is the most plausible.

Although the Causal Theory is the most plausible framework in which to explain human action, it is not without problems. A persistent one concerns causal waywardness or deviance. (This problem is not unique to the Causal Theory; it arises for any theory that identifies an action with part or whole of a causal sequence.) There are actually two problems of waywardness, which have not always been distinguished. For the moment let us suppose that the mental antecedent to action is a desire (or want) plus a belief. Consider the following cases.

Case 1. Abel, who is attending a party, wants to spill his drink because he wants to signal to his confederates to begin the robbery and he believes, in virtue of their prearrangements, that spilling his drink will accomplish that. But Abel is inexperienced in crime and this leads him to be very anxious. His anxiety makes his hand tremble, and so his glass spills. (See Frankfurt, 1978, p. 157.)

Case 2. Bob finds himself in a difficult position while climbing. He is supporting another man on the rope. He wants to rid himself of the danger of holding that man, and he thinks that he can do so by loosening his grip. His belief and want unnerve him, and as a result cause him to loosen his hold. (See Davidson, 1973, p. 153.)

Case 3. Carl wants to kill his rich uncle because he wants to inherit the family fortune. He believes that his uncle is home and drives toward his house. His desire to kill his uncle agitates him and he drives recklessly. On the way he hits and kills a pedestrian, who, as luck would have it, is his uncle. (See Chisholm, 1966, pp. 29–30.)

Case 4. Dan, the sheriff, sees the bank robber riding down Mainstreet. He wants to shoot him and believes that by taking careful aim, the bullet from his gun will directly hit the robber. Dan, however, is a terrible shot. The bullet goes in the wrong direction; but as luck would have it, the bullet hits a spittoon and ricochets, hitting the bank robber.

These cases raise two issues. In cases 1 and 2 there is interference between the mental antecedent and the resultant bodily behavior. The want and belief cause their behavioral object, but the person did not perform the action. Abel, the party-going robber, did not perform the action of signaling to his confederates; and Bob, the mountaineer, did not perform the action of loosening his hold on the rope. Since these cases raise an issue about the connection between the antecedent mental events and the resultant behavior, I call it *'the problem of antecedential waywardness.'* In cases 3 and 4 complex activities are involved. The agents begin the activities in the appropriate ways; there is no problem about the connection between the antecedent mental events and the initiation of the behavior. The activities, however, are not completed as expected. Carl, the hostile nephew, did not expect to kill his uncle by running him down; and Dan, the inept sheriff, did not expect to hit the bank robber by means of a ricochet. The issue in these last cases concerns the consequences of the activity once begun, and thus I label it *'the problem of consequential waywardness.'*

From the viewpoint of the Causal Theory the problem of antecedential waywardness is a problem about the definition of 'action.' An action is the effect of the antecedent mental event; but the first two cases purport to show that the antecedent mental event can cause the overt behavior without there being an action. The problem of consequential waywardness does not concern the definition of 'action.' In cases 3 and 4 the agents performed actions, for example, driving toward the uncle's house, firing the sixshooter; but these actions did not bring about the results in the expected way. The problem of consequential waywardness concerns the definition of 'intentional action.' Carl did not kill his uncle intentionally and Dan did not hit the bank robber intentionally. I will deal with the problem of antecedential waywardness first and then return to the problem of consequential waywardness.

6. Action and Antecedential Waywardness

One proposal to resolve the problem of antecedential waywardness is to argue that the causal connection between the antecedent mental event and the resultant behavior must be normal, and that specifying causal normalcy is a scientific matter. In cases 1 and 2 the want and belief caused the behavior in some empirically irregular fashion. This proposal has been favored by Davidson (1973) and at one time by Goldman (1970), among others. Goldman has said, for instance, that the desire must cause the overt behavior "in the characteristic way." With respect to this characteristic or normal way, he adds:

> To this question, I confess, I do not have a fully detailed answer. But neither do I think that it is incumbent on me, *qua* philosopher, to give an answer to this question. A complete explanation of how wants and beliefs lead to intentional acts would require extensive neurophysiological information, and I do not think it is fair to demand of a *philosophical* analysis that it provide this information. (1970, p. 62)

The problem of antecedential waywardness accordingly is a problem for the special sciences, not for philosophy.

However, this purported solution misconstrues the function of scientific explanation. Psychologists, neurophysiologists, and other scientists studying human behavior record causal series as they find them. Their work yields information about the details and intermediate steps in these complex sequences. But it does not yield a criterion for normalcy. That is a normative task, and a philosophical one. At best the special sciences can tell us whether some type of causal series is statistically prevalent, but that is different from providing a criterion for normalcy. It is possible that for certain types of cases abnormalcy is statistically predominant. Indeed that situation might in fact obtain when the activity evinces extreme anxiety or fear. No doubt answers to scientific questions are presupposed by the Causal Theory: nevertheless the problem of antecedential waywardness is not a scientific one, since it concerns the analysis of the concept of human action.

The cases of the robbery accomplice and the mountain climber defeat those Causal Theories, such as Davidson's (1963) and Goldman's (1970), in which there is causal space, as it were, between the mental antecedent and the beginning of the neurophysiological chain leading to the overt behavior. The robbery accomplice spills his drink because of his wants and beliefs, but only through the roundabout causal route in which his anxiety intervenes. Similarly the climber loosens his hold on the rope because of his wants and beliefs, but only through the roundabout causal route in which his fear intervenes. An adequate Causal Theory must preclude the possibility of these types of interventions: there can be no causal space between the mental antecedent and the beginning of the physiological chain. That is, on an adequate Causal Theory, the mental antecedent must *proximately* cause the physiological chain leading to overt behavior.

I will resist the temptation to discuss causation.[5] A word about proximate causation is necessary, however. This notion is definable as follows:

(D1.2) e proximately causes f iff (i) e causes f and (ii) there are no events, $g_1, g_2, ..., g_n$ (where $n \geqslant 1$) such that e causes g_1 and g_1 causes g_2 and ... and g_n causes f.

Assume universal closure and let e and f range over events. '(Event) e remotely causes (event) f' is defined by saying that e causes f and there are causally intervening events $g_1, g_2, ..., g_n$ ($n \geqslant 1$). Note that (D1.2) does not exclude the possibility that the effect f is overdetermined. Indeed f might be overdetermined in part remotely and in part proximately.

The Causal Theory can now be restated as follows.

(D1.3) S's Aing during t is an action *iff* there is a nonactional mental event $\overline{M}$ of S such that (i) $\overline{M}$ proximately causes S's Aing during t and (ii) $\overline{M}$ is appropriate to S's Aing during t.

In the case of Richard's clapping his hands, the action begins spatially and temporally at that point where the mental antecedent ends.[6] Assuming that mental events are locatable in part of the brain, the action of Richard's clapping his hands begins in the brain. Statement (D1.3) is actually a *schema*, not a definition of 'action.' A definition of 'action' results when, first, the mental antecedent $\overline{M}$ is specified and, second, its conditions of appropriateness are given. The first issue concerns the attitude type to which the antecedent belongs and the second concerns the content of the mental antecedent.

The critic of the Causal Theory might not be satisfied. Although antecedential waywardness has been precluded, there remains the possibility that causally deviant chains can occur between the onset of brain activity and overt bodily movement. When that occurs, the agent has not performed an action, even though the causal chain beginning with the mental event is initiated in the right way. Thus, the critic might say, a criterion of causal normalcy is required and schema (D1.3) will not suffice to define 'action.'

My response is that an action has occurred, provided only that the causal chain has been initiated in the right way and the bodily movement has taken place. With a qualification to be discussed momentarily, the route from the initial neurological events to the bodily movement is irrelevant. Schema (D1.3) remains intact.

To test this response, consider a series of cases. Suppose that Richard wants to clap his hands, believes that he is able to do so, and that this mental event, let us assume, proximately causes a sequence of events, the initial one being an event in his central nervous system. Suppose in addition that Richard previously had some neurological damage and some of his nerves near the shoulder were replaced with lengths of artificial filament. Now if Richard's want and belief cause his hands to move together, I am fully prepared to say that he clapped his hands, even though the causal sequence from the initial central nervous system event to the hands moving together includes causal connections that are not ordinary. The precise causal connections are not relevant to whether Richard acted.

Suppose that in this case Richard's neurological damage was such that an artificial nerve could not be implanted, but rather it was necessary to detour the impulse through a device outside Richard's body. Assume further that Richard is ignorant of the precise causal mechanism involved: he knows no more about this device than most of us know about the precise internal neurophysiological connections when we clap our hands in the ordinary way. Although the causal chain is highly irregular in this case, I am again fully prepared to say that Richard clapped his hands, provided that his want and belief proximately caused the initial central nervous system event and that his hands in fact moved together. Again the exact causal connections are irrelevant, even if they involve detours external to the person's body.

Modify the previous case so that the device through which the impulse passes contains a randomizing mechanism such that the neurological circuit is completed only some of the time. Suppose again that Richard's want and belief proximately caused the initial neurological events. Also suppose on this occasion that the circuit is completed and Richard's hands move together. Did he perform the action of clapping his hands? This case is science fiction. We have reached the limits of our ordinary intuitions and there is no definitive answer. However, I would be strongly inclined to say that he did clap his hands. If the randomizing mechanism had not completed the circuit, and thus Richard's hands had not moved together, then he would not have clapped his hands. But that situation is not different from other breakdowns in the connections between the initial neurological events and the resultant bodily movements. I would continue to be inclined to maintain this view even if the intermediate stages were more bizarre than the ones in this case. But there is no final, knockdown argument for or against that position, since, as I said, we are at the limits of the ordinary concept of human action.

The final type of case bears superficial similarity to the previous ones: but it is importantly different. Imagine that rather than a randomizing mechanism there is another person, say the surgeon, who must press a button in order to close the circuit. Assume also that the subject is ignorant of this fact. On the occasion in question Richard's want and belief proximately cause the initial stage of the neurological chain; the surgeon presses the button, and Richard's hands move together. Although this too is a science fiction case, we do not appear to have a great deal of difficulty in applying our ordinary concept of action. *Richard* did not clap his hands; rather, the surgeon moved Richard's hands for him. Richard did something—brought about certain neurological events—but he did not perform the action of clapping his hands. The reason we are inclined to treat this case differently is that, loosely put, a person must perform his own action: no one can perform someone else's action. A person can be guided, cajoled, commanded, coerced, even hypnotized, into acting; but nevertheless, if he acts, it is *his* action.

Although this treatment of the last case is not entirely uncontroversial, it is highly plausible. Thus repair of (D1.3) is required: namely, (i) is to be replaced by

(i') $\overline{M}$ proximately causes S's Aing during t, where S's Aing during t is a continuous causal chain.

S's Aing during t is a *continuous causal chain,* in the technical sense required here, *iff* there is a chain of causally related events, $e_1, e_2, \ldots,$ e_n such that (i) S's Aing during t is identical with this causal chain and (ii) there is no S^*, distinct from S, nonactional mental event $\overline{M}^*$, and duration t^*, where $t^* \geq t$, such that S^*'s having $\overline{M}^*$ during t^* is identical with e_i, an event in the causal chain. Thus, the surgeon's intervention precludes Richard's clapping his hands, since the surgeon's wants and beliefs play a role in the chain leading to Richard's hands moving together. Note that this amended definition does not exclude the possibility that the subject himself interjects additional mental events into the causal chain. If, for instance, Richard had control over the button, then when he presses it, *he* claps his hands—though in that case it is an action performed *by* doing something else. Or consider the following variation on the theme. Richard now knows that he is not able to move his hands himself, that his wants and beliefs initiate a causal chain resulting in the light's going on, and that the surgeon presses the button only when the light is on. It might appear that in this case Richard can clap his hands despite the chain detouring through another person's action. That, however, is the wrong way to see the situation. Richard does not clap his hands; rather he brings about his hands moving together by signaling the surgeon, and *that* is not the same as his clapping his hands. The situation remains the same even when the method by which Richard gets the surgeon to press the button is more complex. Suppose that the surgeon initially does not want to press the button when signaled, but agrees to do so only after a great deal of persuasion by Richard. Richard now signals by setting off the light; and the surgeon, somewhat reluctantly, presses the button. Here too Richard did not clap his hands. Rather he brought it about that his hands moved together by cajoling someone else to do it. Richard performed an action; but it was not one of clapping his hands.[7]

7. Intentional Action and Consequential Waywardness

Consequential waywardness concerns not the initiatory stage of activity nor the intermediate stages leading to the bodily movements, but the effects of the bodily action. Consequential waywardness raises the issue of intentional action. As illustrated in cases 3 and 4, Carl, the hostile nephew, achieved his goal of killing his uncle by accident, not intentionally; and Dan, the inept sheriff, also achieved his goal of hitting the bank robber by accident, not intentionally.

I contend that an intentional action is an action performed following a plan. Carl's killing his uncle was not intentional because his plan was to shoot him at home, not run him down in the street. The actions of getting into the car and driving toward his uncle's house were intentional because they followed his plan. But at that point intentionality stops: the events occurring after this time were unplanned causal consequences of Carl's intentional actions. Similar views about intentional action and plans have been held by Goldman (1970, chapter 3), Toumela (1977, chapters 7 ff.), and Castañeda (1979, 1983).

Let me provide substance to this contention. A first approximation is this. The initial step is to define 'action plan':

(D1.4) P is an action plan for Aing *iff* P is an ordered n-tuple, $\langle A_1, ..., A_n, A \rangle$, where n $\geq$ 1 and where each A_{i+1} is causally dependent on A_i.[8]

Causal dependency between action types is to be explained as follows: for any event types F and G, F is causally dependent on G *iff*
there is a causal law that entails that it is causally necessary that, for
every event x if x is of type F, then there is an event y such that y is of
type G. That is, loosely, one action type is causally dependent on
another when instances of the latter are causally necessary for instances of the former. Thus a plan for hitting the bull's-eye consists
in loading the gun, aiming, holding one's breath, and so on. An action plan according to (D1.4) is an abstract entity, an ordered set.
This is the sense of 'plan' that makes intelligible talk of there being
plans yet to be devised or there being plans that are long forgotten.

A person *has* a plan for doing something when he thinks that there
is a plan for accomplishing his goal. That is,

> (D1.5) S has an action plan P to A during t *iff* S believes that P is
> an action plan for Aing and that if he instantiates P during t, he
> will A.

Several points of clarification are needed. First, (D1.5) defines a relatively weak notion. According to it a person can have a plan even if
there is in fact no plan for accomplishing his goal. Roger might have
a plan to run a 3:30 mile—he will train every day, eat healthy foods,
and so on—when in fact, given his present and future physiological
states, he *cannot* run a 3:30 mile. There is a stronger notion in the
offing. Let us say that P is an action plan of S to A during t just in
case there is an action plan P for Aing and S believes that he will
instantiate P during t. This stronger notion has limited applicability
because most persons at least some of the time do not have sufficient
background causal knowledge to generate a true belief that they will
instantiate some particular plan. A related second point is that (D1.5)
leaves it open how much of the causal route to A is known or believed by S. The norm, it would appear, is that persons have a reasonably good idea about the primary causal dependencies between
parts of their plans, even if the details escape them. But the ordinary
or folk concept of having a plan seems not to require any minimal
causal knowledge. Third, notice that (D1.5) says nothing about *planning*, that is, the psychological process by which persons construct
plans. Planning might be modeled by a series of practical syllogisms
or more plausibly, by complex hierarchical structures, as some recent
computer simulation suggests (e.g., Byrne, 1977): but that is a topic
requiring extended treatment, and not one I shall discuss.

We are now in a position to define 'intentional action.'

(D1.6) S's Aing during t is an intentional action *iff*
(i) S's Aing during t is an action; and
(ii) S has an action plan P to A during t such that his Aing is included in P and he follows P in Aing.

Clause (i) refers back to (D1.3), the Causal Theory of Action. Definition (D1.6) captures the intuition that Carl's driving toward his uncle's house is intentional but his killing his uncle by running him down is not, since the former but not the latter is part of Carl's plan. Similarly Dan's shooting the bank robber is not intentional, since Dan planned to hit him directly, not by means of a lucky ricochet. (There is some temptation to say that Dan did shoot the bank robber intentionally. This temptation probably results from imagining that Dan's plan did not include information about the flight of the bullet. But that is not the case described here. Although Dan does not have a precise idea about what path the bullet will take, he does plan to hit the robber directly and not by means of a 'lucky bounce.')

Special mention needs to be made of the claim that S acts intentionally only when he *follows* a plan. It is possible that a person believe that a sequence of actions will lead to his Aing, not attend to this belief, but nonetheless this belief play a causal role in his Aing. Suppose that Carl believes that his uncle takes a walk each night at 9:00 and that he could kill him by running him down during that walk. But Carl thinks that there is less chance of detection if he shoots his uncle at home, so he puts that plan aside. As a result of his belief that his uncle walks at 9:00, Carl sets out for his house at midnight. And you know the rest of the story: his uncle takes his evening constitutional later than usual; and Carl hits and kills his uncle while driving to his house. His killing his uncle was inadvertent, not intentional, despite his having in some sense a plan that included his killing his uncle by running him down. The reason why the killing was not intentional was that the plan did not play the appropriate causal role in the action. It is crucial then to specify the appropriate causal role of plans. I will deal with this issue in later chapters, in part by transforming this folk psychological picture of intentional action into a scientific one. For the moment we can mark this causal role by saying that the agent does not merely act in accordance with his plan, but follows it.[9]

There are, however, problems for the proposal. Consider a variation of case 3. On this version Carl's goal is to orphan his cousin. In order to achieve that goal, he formulates a dastardly plan, the highlights of which are the following:

(i) I load my pistol;

(ii) I get in my car at midnight and drive north on Mainstreet;

(iii) I park in the alley behind my uncle's house;

(iv) I enter the house either through the back door or the front door;

(v) I go to his bedroom, either through the kitchen or the living room;

(vi) I shoot and kill my uncle while he is asleep;

(vii) I orphan my cousin;

(viii) I leave the house the way I entered;

(ix) I drive south until arriving home;

(x) I park the car in the garage and hide my pistol.

This plan contains several features not captured by definition (D1.4). First, according to (D1.4) a plan is a linear structure. But Carl's dastardly plan is a branching structure. He leaves it open whether he will enter through the back door, thus crossing the kitchen, or the front door, thereby crossing the living room. Second, this plan is hierarchically ordered. The goal of the plan, orphaning his cousin, does not occupy the temporally terminal point in the plan. Third, and interestingly, the action (vii) is not causally dependent on other actions in the plan. Notice that Carl's killing his uncle does not include that spatial region. Events e and f are identical only if e and f occupy the same spatial region. Thus Carl's killing his uncle and his orphaning his cousin are not identical. Nor are they causally related. Carl's cousin is orphaned exactly when his uncle dies. Suppose that his cousin is miles away from the scene of the crime. Since there is no simultaneous causation at a distance, the relation between Carl's uncle dying and his cousin becoming an orphan cannot be causal.[10]

Following Goldman (1970, chapter 2) we can say that Carl's killing his uncle generates his orphaning his cousin. Goldman recognizes several species of generation: causal, conventional, and simple.[11] Causal generation is causation. Conventional generation involves social or conventional rules and circumstances; simple generation makes reference only to circumstances, not rules. An example of simple generation is Richard's breaking his promise by coming home late. For our purposes it is not necessary to distinguish between these latter two kinds of generation, if indeed there are two distinct kinds.[12] Let us call generation that involves circumstances, with or without rules, 'conventional generation.' Thus Carl's killing his uncle conventionally generates his orphaning his cousin. In short, there are two kinds of relationships among proposed actions in a plan, causal and conventional.

These considerations lead to altering (D1.4) to read:

(D1.4') P is an action plan for Aing *iff* P is a tree structure constructed from $(A_1, A_2, \ldots, A_n, A)$, where $n \geq 1$ and where each
A_{i+1} is dependent on A_i.

This notion of action plan is to be used in (D1.5). 'Dependency' here
is wider than 'causal dependency.' In particular for any event types F
and G, F is *dependent on* G *iff either* there is a causal law that entails
that it is causally necessary that, for every event x, if x is of type F,
then there is an event y such that y is of type G or that it is causally
necessary that, for every event x, if x is of type G, then there is an
event y such that y is of type F *or* there is a convention such that, for
every event x, if x is of type F, then there is an event y such that y is
of type G. That is, this dependency relation includes causal necessity, causal sufficiency, and conventionality. A great deal can be
said about the tree structures in action plans: Goldman (1970) and
Toumela (1977) have made a reasonable start on that project.

The admission that parts of some actions are not causally related
also necessitates further revision of the schema for the Causal Theory. Namely, (i) of (D1.3) is to be replaced by

(i*) $\overline{M}$ proximately causes S's Aing during t, where S's Aing
during t is a continuous chain.

Using the notion of dependency defined above, we can say that S's
Aing during t is a *continuous chain*, in the technical sense required
here, *iff* there is a tree structure F constructed from the set of event
types $(F_1, F_2, \ldots, F_n)$, where $n \geq 1$ and where each F_{i+1} is dependent
on F_i, such that (i) S's Aing during t is identical with an instance of F
and (ii) there is no S^*, distinct from S, nonactional mental event $\overline{M}^*$,
and duration t^*, where $t^* \leq t$, such that S^*'s having $\overline{M}^*$ during t^* is
identical with an instance of F_i (contained in F). For simplicity
Causal Theories can be taken to have the form of the original (D1.3),
coupled with the implicit understanding that parts of an action can
be conventionally generated but cannot include actions of other
persons.

There is an additional and more important problem for the definition of 'intentional action.' The definition says, approximately, that
an action is intentional just in case the agent follows a plan and that
action is included in his plan. But sometimes actions are intentional
without being explicitly part of a preconceived plan. It would take an
extraordinary degree of foresight for someone to anticipate all the
obstacles, alternatives, and details of intentional action in advance.
The solution is to broaden the definition, so that some intentional

actions are not explicitly part of a preconceived plan. The main insight of the proposed definition remains: intentional action is, at its core, planned action. The intentionality of an action, however, can be inherited from the overall *pattern* of activity and need not be explicitly preconceived. That is the main point. Although actions are intentional in virtue of being part of a plan, each intentional action need not itself be planned. Intentionality accrues to 'focal' actions in a plan. These focal actions taken together form a pattern of activity and other actions are intentional in virtue of being part of this pattern of activity. (Cf. Castañeda, 1979, 1983, and Bratman, 1983.)

Let us make this general observation precise. The way to achieve this precision is to codify in principles the specific types of actions that according to our commonsense viewpoint inherit their intentionality from the overall pattern of activity. Consider Carl's dastardly plan again. First, suppose that he arrives at his uncle's house and finds the front and rear doors locked. He tries the window, finds that it is open, and enters that way. After that, all continues according to plan. Carl substituted one action for another. This substituted action is intentional. Second, Carl's dastardly plan is relatively complete; but it certainly does not include all the steps that Carl will in fact take while orphaning his cousin. The plan, for instance, says nothing about starting the car before driving to his uncle's house, or aiming the gun before shooting. These actions were not part of the plan when originally conceived, but were rather improvised as the plan progressed. Third, suppose that on the way to his uncle's house, Carl decides to stop in a restaurant for a late night snack; and after that he proceeds with his plan to orphan his cousin. His eating at that time is not part of his plan, nor is it necessary to carry out his original plan. The original plan is interrupted, and hence there are not continuous dependency relations among the actions in the plan.

Let us amend definition (D1.6) as follows:

> (D1.6') S's Aing during t is an intentional action *iff*
> (i) S's Aing during t is an action; and
> (ii) *either* S has an action plan P to A during t such that his Aing is included in P and he follows P in Aing *or* S's Aing during t satisfies (Prin. S), (Prin. Im), or (Prin. In).

The principle for action substitution is this.

> (Prin. S) *If* (i) S's A^*ing is an action, (ii) S's A^*ing is a substitutive action for S's Aing with respect to S's action plan P, and (iii) S is not able to A, *then* S's A^*ing is an intentional action.

(Temporal parameters are suppressed for simplicity.) Let us add that S's A^*ing is a substitutive action for S's Aing with respect to his action plan P *iff* S forms an action plan P^* that differs from his action plan P only in containing his A^*ing where P contains S's Aing. This principle can be reiterated so that more than one action per plan can be substituted. Suppose, for example, Carl attempts to enter his uncle's house first through the doors and then through the windows, but finds them all locked. He quickly forms a new plan, differing minimally from the original one, in which he breaks the kitchen window. His breaking the window is intentional. Plans involving minimal changes from those already set in motion can be formed rapidly and easily.

With regard to improvisation, the following principle obtains:

> (Prin. Im) *If* (i) S's A^*ing is an action, (ii) S does not have an action plan that includes his A^*ing, but (iii) S does have an action plan that includes his $A_i$ing and his A_{i+1}ing depends on his A^*ing and his A^*ing depends on his $A_i$ing, *then* S's A^*ing is an intentional action.

Thus, for example, Carl's aiming the gun before shooting his uncle is intentional. It was not part of the original plan, but was a necessary intermediary for completing the plan.

And with regard to plan interruption:

> (Prin. In) *If* (i) S has an action plan P such that his $A_i$ing and his A_{i+1}ing are contained in P but his A^*ing is not contained in P, (ii) S's A^*ing occurs between S's $A_i$ing and S's A_{i+1}ing or during S's $A_i$ing or S's A_{i+1}ing and (iii) S's A^*ing is not dependent on either S's $A_i$ing or S's A_{i+1}ing, or conversely, *then* S's $A_i$ing and S's A_{i+1}ing are intentional actions.

That is, an action retains its status as intentional provided only that it is part of an action plan, even if that plan is not instantiated in the manner originally conceived. Of course, the interrupting action can be intentional, since nothing prevents it from belonging to another plan. Carl might well have formulated another plan, to stop at the local greasy spoon for a cheeseburger, while carrying out his original dastardly plan. Driving to his uncle's house, which occurs prior to his eating the cheeseburger, and climbing through the window, which occurs after his snack, are intentional despite not being performed in the serial order originally envisioned.

Notice that (Prin. In) is liberal. Provided that the planned actions are completed within the allotted time period, no interruption overrides the intentionality of the actions. In cases of minor inserted plans such as Carl's stopping for a snack, this is obvious. But I also contend that major interruptions, including those not under the subject's control, leave intact the intentionality of the completed actions. To take a bizarre case, suppose that Carl was kidnapped by aliens as he began to enter his uncle's house, that is, during step (iv). After studying their specimen, the aliens induce a space-time warp and replace Carl in his uncle's bedroom at approximately the moment he would have arrived there. Though severely shaken by the experience, Carl regains his senses and continues with step (vi) of the plan, shooting his uncle. I am strongly inclined to say that the completed actions in this plan, (i)–(iv) and (vi)–(x), are intentional. Of course, step (v), walking through the house, is not an intentional action; indeed given that Carl was moved by the aliens from the door to the bedroom, it is not an action of his at all. But here again we are at the limits of our ordinary concept of intentional action, and it could be that these intuitions are not shared by everyone.

Definitions (D1.4') and (D1.6'), supplemented by (Prin. S), (Prin. Im) and (Prin. In), provide a second approximation to an explication of 'intentional action.' It may be that further refinements or amendments are required. For example, someone might object to (Prin. S). This principle says that in order to substitute within a plan, the subject must be unable to perform the planned action—where the sense of 'able' (or 'can') is that of ability or opportunity. In the example discussed in connection with (Prin. S), Carl was unable to enter through the doors because they were locked. But suppose that the doors were unlocked and Carl merely preferred to enter through the window. He could have used either door but did not. My inclination is to say that his entering through the window was not an intentional action; it was no part of his plan, but completely spontaneous. For those who have the contrary inclination, (iii) of the antecedent of (Prin. S) could be replaced by

(iii') S is not able to A or S prefers not to A,

or some such revision. No doubt there are other modifications and fine tuning of these principles that will be appealing. Such modifications might lead to a closer approximation to an explication of 'intentional action.' The main point, however, is that there is a strategy for explicating the ordinary, folk concept of intentional action and at least a good start toward realizing this strategy. An action is intentional if it is part of a pattern of planned activity. The problem of consequential waywardness, the problem presented by 'happy accident' cases, is thereby resolved.

8. The Intentionality Thesis

As a way of bringing together some of the issues discussed in this chapter, consider the following important and controversial claim, which I label the 'Intentionality Thesis.'

> (IT) S's Aing during t is an action only if S's Aing during t is an intentional action.

That is, (IT) says that all action is intentional. (Note that the converse of (IT) is clearly true, since an intentional action is an action.) The Intentionality Thesis has had a checkered past in the philosophical literature. Sometimes it is assumed obviously true and not in need of support; sometimes it is assumed obviously false and not in need of refutation. Rarely are arguments for or against it adduced.[13] My contention is that the Intentionality Thesis is false.

'Action,' I argued, is to be defined by the Causal Theory. In developing that argument, I temporarily followed Davidson (1963) and Goldman (1970), among others, in taking the mental antecedent to action to be a complex event consisting of a want and belief. The problem of antecedential waywardness required for its resolution that the mental antecedent proximately cause action. Wanting plus believing, I shall argue in later chapters, is not a good candidate for the proximate cause of action. Although wanting and believing appear to play some role in the initiation of action, they are not the kinds of events that directly cause action. The forcefulness of the anxious robber and nervous climber cases derived in part from the identification of the antecedent to action with wanting plus believing. Rather the best candidate for the proximate cause of action—to anticipate—is intending. The version of the Causal Theory I will be advocating, then, differs from Davidson's and Goldman's in regard to the mental antecedent to action. If I am correct about the mental antecedent, the Intentionality Thesis has the force of saying that every intending directly causes an intentional action.

In the previous section I claimed that intentional action is action performed in following a plan. There are serious complications in this claim, though for the moment we can bracket them. Thus if (IT) is true, all action is planned. Also, then, every intending directly causes a planned action. *But* some actions are not planned and some intendings do not cause planned action. In the first section of this chapter list B consisted of actions that are not planned, and hence not intentional actions. In these cases an intending causes action, despite the action being automatic.

One vital issue not directly discussed in this chapter is the extent of planned activity: that is, how much of what we do is planned. I will argue that a great deal is planned, more than might be initially supposed. Common sense or folk psychology appears to recommend a notion of planned activity in which conscious deliberation is necessary. But there is another, more liberal notion of planned activity, one that is rooted in cognitive psychology and related disciplines, that does not require conscious deliberation. It is this latter notion that I shall use. It is a consequence of this view that, although not all action is planned, a great deal is. And thus while not all action is intentional, much of it is.

The concept of intentional action is a key one in our conceptual framework. Intentional action is the highest level behavior undertaken by persons. It is the kind of activity for which persons are primarily legally and morally responsible. It is also the type of action for which the question of freedom arises. I shall thus devote special attention to intentional action. I will be attempting to articulate the nature of human action through the development of a plausible Causal Theory; but I shall also be concerned to specify the characteristics defining the important subclass intentional action.

2

A Fundamental Problem

According to the Causal Theory an event is an action just in case it is proximately caused by a mental event of a certain sort. I take it that a fundamental problem—possibly, *the* fundamental problem—in philosophical action theory is to adequately specify the nature of the proximate cause of action. The objective of this chapter is to set the stage for a resolution of this fundamental problem.

In section 1 this fundamental problem is raised in the context of recent action theory literature. Although this problem is discussed in terms of the Causal Theory, it is not restricted to it, but arises for all types of action theories. Section 2 deals with Wilfrid Sellars's response to the problem. In the previous chapter it was assumed that the initiating cause of action is a complex event consisting of a desiring (or wanting) and believing. This view is widely held by those defending the Causal Theory. Beginning in this chapter, however, I shall call that into question. I will follow Sellars in taking the initiating cause of action to be an intending. In later chapters I will argue that intending is not reducible to desiring (or wanting) plus believing.

I contend that an adequate account of intending, the proximate cause of action, involves specifying its internal structure. Sellars, on one reading, maintains that no such specification is forthcoming, since nothing other than the causal roles of intending can be known. In section 3 I consider this strong functionalistic response and argue against it. The final section outlines the program to be followed in the remainder of this book for resolving this fundamental problem about human action.

1. A Fundamental Problem in Philosophical Action Theory

In his well-known and classical paper "Actions, Reasons, and Causes" (1963), Donald Davidson suggests that primary reasons are causes of actions. Under a natural interpretation of the text, he holds that a primary reason is a combination of a pro-attitude toward actions of a certain kind and a belief that that kind of action can be performed. With regard to pro-attitudes, Davidson says they include "desires, wantings, urges, promptings, and a great variety of moral views, aesthetic principles, economic prejudices, social conventions and public and private goals and values" (1963, p. 68). He then adds, "The word 'attitude' does yeoman service here, for it must cover not only permanent character traits that show themselves in a lifetime of behavior, like love of children or a taste for loud company, but also the most passing fancy that prompts a unique action, like a sudden desire to touch a woman's elbow" (1963, p. 68). Davidson, that is, suggests a Causal Theory in which the antecedent to action is a complex mental event specified in terms of a pro-attitude plus a belief.

Wilfrid Sellars also holds a Causal Theory. But he is dissatisfied with Davidson's version. In particular he charges that Davidson has failed to specify the mental antecedent adequately. Sellars says, "The main source of my discomfort is the expression 'pro-attitude.' Davidson is well aware that this is an omnibus term and lists, in the course of his discussion, some of the specific mental states in which this term applies. Yet he has little to say about this, and the total effect is that when it comes to the mental *episodes* involved in the causation of action, what he stresses are episodic *beliefs* about *matters of fact*" (1973, p. 190). He adds, "what disturbs me about Davidson's account is that in his examples he tends to stress the onslaught of factual thoughts and leaves the relevant pro-attitudes to be relatively long term dispositions which constitute the mental background of the functioning of reasons" (1973, p. 190). In fairness to Davidson, he does say that the term 'pro-attitude' will be used to refer to immediate promptings as well as long-term dispositions. But Sellars's objection remains: actions are caused by a certain kind of mental event, and by specifying the mental antecedent in the most general terms as a pro-attitude, Davidson has failed to clarify the nature of the mental antecedent causing action.

There is a reply to this charge implicit in Davidson's "Actions, Reasons, and Causes." It is a mistake to think that there is a peculiar kind of mental event that causes action; rather there are many kinds of such events, all of which in given circumstances can cause actions. In response to a similar objection by Melden, Davidson says, "Melden asks the causal theorists to find an event that is common and peculiar to all cases where a man intentionally raises his arm, and this, it must be admitted, cannot be produced. But then neither can a common and unique cause of bridge failures, plane crashes, or plate breakings be produced" (1963, p. 74). In the same way that plane crashes can have many kinds of causes, such as pilot incompetence, stormy weather, or faulty tower equipment, so too actions can have many different kinds of causes.

But Sellars's objection cuts deeper than this. Although there are any number of kinds of events that might precede the mental antecedent to action, including various attitudes and beliefs, there must be one type of event that is the proximate cause of action. Returning to the analogy of plane crashes, the proximate cause of a crash is the plane's heading for another body. The plane may have entered into that situation because of the weather, the pilot, some hijackers, or what not; but the proximate event causing every plane crash is the plane's heading toward another body. Similarly there are diverse causal chains leading to the peculiar kind of mental event that causes action; but there is one kind of mental event that proximately causes action. In stating that a pro-attitude, understood in a wide sense, causes action, Davidson has not specified the proximate cause; he has, in Sellars's terms, only given us the "mental background" preceding the proximate mental event causing the action.

Sellars's view is that the proximate cause of an action is an intention to do something here and now. In more detail Sellars holds that background attitudes and beliefs yield a piece of reasoning and this reasoning in turn causes an intention. An intention to perform an action A is a thinking to oneself 'I shall do A.' If the opportunity to perform A is in the future, say ten minutes from now, then the thought is of the form 'I shall do A in ten minutes.' As the time to do A approaches, the thought changes, for example, to the form 'I shall do A here and now.' A thought of this specific kind is called a 'volition' by Sellars, though I shall not follow him in this usage.

Sellars has pointed to a specific type of mental event that is the proximate cause of action, a here and now intention. That is a step in the right direction. But it does not solve all the problems: indeed it leaves unanswered a fundamental one. An adequate account of the proximate cause of action must specify the nature of this type of mental event. It must say what properties mental events of this type have, and which others lack, such that only they initiate action. Again, why does one type of mental event proximately cause action, while others do not, no matter how fully they occupy consciousness? This problem is a fundamental one in action theory.

I will follow Sellars in taking the proximate cause of action to be an intending to do something here and now. Let me call this 'immediate intention.' But caution is required. The fundamental problem is to specify the nature of this event type. Classifying it as an intention provides *some* information: but precious little. We need to know the properties of this event. The way to look at the issue is this. There is a type of mental event that proximately causes action: let us designate it 'immediate intention.' That is, *whatever* mental event type proximately causes action is to be labeled 'immediate intention.' The fundamental problem is to specify the nature of the proximate cause of action, the immediate intention.

Although this fundamental problem was raised in the context of the Causal Theory, it recurs for other theories of action. For an Agency theorist, such as Chisholm (1976b), the issue focuses on the peculiar properties of persons so that they, and (perhaps, but doubtfully) they alone, initiate actions. In regard to the Oldtime Volitional Theory, the question closely resembles the form of it facing the Causal Theory: What are the properties of the nonactional mental event that cause the correlated behavior? Nor can the Mental Action theorist escape the problem. The Mental Action theorist can claim either that there is some nonactional mental event proximately causing the mental action or there is not. If he claims the former, the theory seems to require an inordinate amount of covert activity in bringing about a physical movement. But in either case the problem about the nature of the unique mental element arises. In the former case the issue closely resembles that confronting the Causal Theory: What are the properties of this mental event such that it proximately causes the mental action? In the latter case the issue concerns the nature of the mental action: What distinguishes these special mental actions from other mental events? There is no plausible action theory for which some form of this fundamental problem does not arise.

Somewhat surprisingly this fundamental problem has not been explicitly considered by most of the recent writers on action theory, even those advocating the Causal Theory. Davidson (1963) does not raise it, though this is understandable in light of his concern to establish the general thesis that a Causal Theory is the correct approach, and not to detail any particular version of it. Goldman (1970) similarly does not explicitly raise this question (though cf. Goldman 1976). Goldman (1970) says that wants and beliefs cause actions; but when he characterizes wants, he argues that they are pro-attitudes. Like Davidson, he has not singled out a specific event-type that proximately causes action. And because he has not taken that first step, he has nor broached the question of what properties this event type has in virtue of which it alone initiates action.

Sellars is in a better position than Davidson or Goldman to deal with this fundamental question because he has isolated the event type, intending here and now, that proximately causes action. Although Sellars does not directly raise the question, he is on my reading aware of it. I shall discuss Sellars's treatment of this issue in the next section. Another exception is Castañeda (1975, chapters 6 and 10 and 1980), who recognizes the importance of this fundamental question. He says (1975, p. 6): "The Causational dimension [of action] is the most profound mystery in the nature of practical thinking." Castañeda's answer, which is original and intriguing, is intimately tied to his views about the contents of mental attitudes. I will delay discussion of it until chapter 4.[1]

2. Sellars on the Fundamental Problem

Sellars, as I mentioned, holds that the proximate cause of action is an intention to do something here and now. He advocates a version of the Causal Theory that can be restated as follows:

(D2.1) S's Aing during t is an action *iff*:
(i) S immediately intends to A during t; and
(ii) S's immediately intending to A during t proximately causes S's Aing during t.

This definition provides an unpacking of the schema (D1.3). (The clause saying that intending to A is appropriate to Aing has been suppressed.) As I observed, the Intentionality Thesis (IT) is false; that is, not every action is intentional. Definition (D2.1) does not commit one to the claim that all intendings cause intentional actions. An action is intentional only if it is planned; but an intending can cause spontaneous, reflexive, or automatic actions, none of which is planned. (We should not, of course, be misled because the word 'intentional' contains the word 'intention.') Now I propose that we accept Sellars's (D2.1) as the correct version of the Causal Theory. But this is only the initial step in articulating the theory. The next and more important step is to provide an account of intention.

Sellars uses two methods for clarifying the notion of intention: he locates intentions within the nexus of other related types of mental events; and he provides a logic for statements about intention. (See Sellars, 1966, 1966b, 1967, 1976; cf. Aune, 1975, Castañeda, 1975b.) With regard to the first method, Sellars takes intention to be primitive, and analyzes other types of mental events in terms of it. Desires are construed as dispositions to have intentions. Hence there is a logical connection between desires and immediate intentions (Sellarsian volitions) in that they are both species of intentions. Decisions are intentions to do something at a future specific time. Preferring one course of action to another is having the disposition to form intentions to do the former and not the latter, when both courses are believed to be available. And so on. With regard to the second method, Sellars holds that there is no special logic of intention sentences. The logic of intention sentences is assimilable to first-order logic in virtue of the reduction principle: 'shall [p]' implies 'shall [q]' iff 'p' implies 'q'. ('Shall [p]' is Sellars's expression for an intention to bring about p.) The force of this principle is essentially to treat practical reasoning as a special case of theoretical reasoning (cf. Aune, 1977). A great deal more can be said in regard to each method, but from our vantage point the main ideas have been given.

Immediate intention initiates action, and only immediate intention does so. What are the properties of this mental event in virtue of which this claim is true? Assuming that Sellars is correct about the relationships between intending, deciding, preferring, and so on, and that he is correct about the logic of intention sentences—both *highly* controversial assumptions—we nevertheless remain without an answer to this key question. No information has been provided that tells us the properties of immediate intentions such that they, and they alone, are efficacious in bringing about action. The conceptual connections between intending and other types of mental events, as well as the logic of intention sentences, concern relational properties of intention; but we need to know about the structural properties of intention. In making 'intention' primitive, Sellars has failed to resolve our fundamental problem. Castañeda (1975), as I read him, also accepts (D2.1). However, he correctly recognizes that this definition, even when supplemented with Sellars's remarks on the logic of intention sentences and the conceptual relationships between types of mental attitudes, does not conclude the matter. Castañeda (1975, pp. 280–284) argues, correctly, that unless intention has some special internal features, action would be impossible. Neither the content of the intention nor the belief by the agent that he will perform the action in the immediate future nor anything similar initiates action; it must be some property of the intention itself that is responsible for its special status.

Although Sellars does not make any explicit suggestions for supplementing (D2.1) with an account of the nature of intention, his writings lend themselves to such an interpretation. In any case these suggestions are worth considering, even if not entirely textually accurate, because they are natural and plausible ways to supplement (D2.1). One such suggestion is that immediate intentions result from the agent's practical reasoning; and it is this property of resulting from practical reasoning that is sufficient for being the proximate cause of action. However, this suggestion presupposes that all actions are the outcome of practical reasoning, and that surely is not the case. Some actions are impulsive, automatic, thoughtless, reckless;

and some actions are compulsive, commanded, or coerced. If all actions are caused by immediate intendings and some actions are not the result of practical reasoning, then some immediate intendings are not the result of practical reasoning.[2]

One response is that all *genuine* or *full-bodied* actions result from deliberation or practical reasoning, and that is the only interesting notion of action. This response is tantamount to restricting action to intentional action; that is, to accepting (IT), since practical reasoning can be thought of as a form of planning. Thus this response construes action too narrowly. There are unplanned actions, actions not preceded by practical reasoning, such as impulsive actions, spontaneous actions, thoughtless actions, compelled actions, and so on. It may well be advantageous to concentrate on intentional action when dealing with certain philosophical problems, such as moral responsibility, the free will issue, or *akrasia*, but that should not lead to the false claim that there are only intentional actions.

A second reading of Sellars is that immediate intention is to be understood in terms of a learned response (see, e.g., Sellars, 1966, pp. 109 ff.; cf. Aune, 1975). A child learns that 'I shall do *A*,' whether said in public or thought to oneself, is to be followed by the doing of *A*. He has learned this relationship when he has gained the propensity to perform actions of type *A* while having a thought whose content is 'I shall do *A* here and now.' The child has a genuine intention to do *A* only when this propensity has been acquired.

But again we remain without a resolution to our fundamental problem. Specifying the manner in which we acquire propensities to immediately intend does not indicate what properties immediate intention has in virtue of which it alone proximately causes action. Finding out how children internalize causal laws, or how their behavior comes to conform to causal laws, does not tell us what properties the event types referred to in these laws have. An answer to the epistemological question of how thought and language is acquired and used is not an answer to the question of the structure of immediate intention.

3. The Functionalistic Response

At this point it might be wondered whether the request to 'get inside' intention is legitimate. It is a request for specifying the nature of intention by describing its internal structure. But that type of description, it might be thought, cannot be given: intending is a mental event and mental events can only be characterized functionally. A functional characterization of a mental event consists in citing its causal relations to input stimuli, output responses, and causal interactions with other mental events. Definition (2.1), in short, cannot be supplemented in the way requested, though it can be conjoined with a functionalistic account of intention (cf. Toumela, 1977, chapters 3–5).

The above second reading of Sellars might well be interpreted as making this functionalistic response. The notion of intention is made intelligible by locating intending within the causal networks of language and thought acquisition and use. According to Sellars thinking is, in a way, internal speech (cf. Sellars, 1981). A covert episode of saying to oneself 'I shall do A here and now' proximately causes the doing of A. Given this, the only remaining issue to discuss is how this causal connection is established. Nothing can be known about the internal structure of the proximate cause of action, except, it seems, the form of the inner piece of speech.

However, there is a major difficulty with this functionalistic response. This difficulty can be seen more clearly by considering Lawrence Davis's (1979) action theory, since it is explicitly and unabashedly functionalistic. Davis opts for a Mental Action Theory, in contrast to the Causal Theory (D2.1). Davis labels the mental action a 'volition': "An agent," he says, "has done an A, and his doing an A is an action, just in case an E_A [that is, the associated behavioral event] occurred as the result of a volition of the agent's" (1979, p. 15). Nothing can be known about volitions except their causal role in action. Davis's abbreviated statement of this role is: "A volition is an event which is normally a cause of the agent's belief that he is acting in a certain way, *and* which normally causes such doing-related events as make it true that he *is* acting in that way" (1979, p. 16; cf. pp. 20–22).

There is a preliminary difficulty for Davis's view, leaving aside issues that arise from his taking a Mental Action Theory stance. It is odd to think that a single mental event causes *both* the associated behavior and the belief that the associated behavior is being brought about. The belief that the associated behavior is occurring, it would appear, results from perceptual stimuli, including afferent feedback. These perceptual stimuli occur after the bodily movement has begun. But the cause of the movement—Davis's volitions—must occur prior to the onset of the movement. Davis, that is, has assigned an impossible causal role to the mental action.

The major difficulty with Davis's view is that it trivializes the account of the mental aspect of action. Essentially we are told only that a volition is that mental event which initiates the associated behavior of an action. Given that Davis is mistaken about the connection between volitions and the belief that an action is occurring, we are not even informed how volitions connect with other mental events. This type of functionalistic account is threatened by Ryle's charge of obscurantism. We need more information about the mental aspect of action. Sellars's functionalistic account is more interesting than Davis's. If Sellars is correct, we know the role intention plays in language and thought acquisition and use. But in the end Sellars's account suffers from the same difficulty as Davis's. It trivializes the account of intention. Intention is treated as a black box, as it were: we are told about its function and how it is acquired, but not its internal structure. The account is insufficiently informative.

Let us make some distinctions. Functionalism is the general doctrine that mental events are to be characterized in terms of their actual and counterfactual causal relations to input events, output events, and other mental events (cf. Block, 1980, Fodor, 1981). Within this general framework there are different types of functionalism. One division concerns the way in which the causal connections are specified. Folk psychological functionalism is the view that the causal relations between input, output, and other mental events are to be specified in folk psychological terms. Scientific functionalism is the view that the causal relations between input, output, and other mental events are to be specified in terms of the best available scientific psychological theories. One version of scientific functionalism identifies the best available psychological theories as computational ones. A computational theory is basically one that says that psychological processes can be modeled by a computer program. A program, essentially, is a method of representing complex operations in terms of simple, primitive ones, where the primitive operations are stated in formal or syntactic terms. This version of scientific functionalism has sometimes been called 'machine functionalism.'

Orthogonal to the distinction between folk psychological and scientific functionalism is a distinction between what I shall call surface and depth functionalism. Surface functionalism is the view that all that is knowable about a mental event is its causal relations to input events, output events, and other mental events. Depth functionalism is the view that not all that is knowable about a mental event is the causal relations in which it stands; rather something can also be known about the internal structure of some mental events.

Davis and Sellars hold a surface, folk psychological functionalism, at least with respect to the mental aspect of action. Davis holds that nothing can be known about volitions except their causal roles; and Sellars holds that nothing can be known about intentions except the way they are acquired and function in action. Moreover, for both

Davis and Sellars these causal roles are to be understood in the context of folk psychology. Although each attempts to reinforce the conceptional foundations of folk psychology by means of philosophical analysis, folk psychology is nevertheless the basis for explaining these causal roles.

Folk psychological functionalism, however, is less plausible than scientific functionalism; and surface functionalism is less plausible than depth functionalism. Folk psychological functionalism lacks the conceptual and empirical resources to provide informative explanations. As I will argue later, folk psychology, speaking generally, characterizes mental events too grossly. A finer grained and better defined taxonomy of mental events is needed in order to generate lawlike generalizations and useful models. Simply put, a functionalism based on folk psychology loses information about mental processes.

According to surface functionalism, all that can be known about a mental event is its causal role. Surface functionalism, as defined, disallows decompositional analyses of mental events. But sometimes complex mental events must be decomposed in order to be adequately explained. Intention, in particular, is an event of this kind. It must be decomposed into constituent mental events. Decompositional analysis is not antifunctionalistic. The point rather is that complex mental events must be *first* decomposed into constituents *and then* analyzed functionally (see Cummins, 1977). In the case of intention its internal structure must first be made apparent and then the constituents can be treated functionally.

In sum Sellars's and Davis's manner of dealing with the mental aspect of action is unattractive. In a way they attempt to avoid providing an account of the mental aspect. They argue, essentially, that no account of the mental aspect of action is forthcoming because surface folk psychological functionalism obtains and surface folk psychological functionalism yields little information about the mental aspect of action. But this form of functionalism is implausible, or at least not as plausible as depth scientific functionalism; and depth scientific functionalism does yield information about the structure of the mental antecedent to action.

Sellars's and Davis's views direct attention to the claim that a theory of action is dependent on a general account of the nature of the mental events. However, to a great extent this claim is unfounded. While there are some views about the nature of mental events that affect a theory of action—such as Sellars's surface folk psychological functionalism—a theory of action is largely independent of a general account of mental events. There are two related focal problems about the nature of mental events: the *first* concerns the ontological status of mental events and the *second* concerns the relationship between mental and physical events, especially brain events and others occurring in the central nervous system. There are a number of competing and overlapping theories that offer solutions to these problems; among the more interesting are eliminative materialism, functionalism, the type-type identity theory, the token-token identity theory, and dualism. (For a concise review, see Fodor, 1981.) Despite the fact that an adequate theory of action contains talk about intending as well as other mental events, action theory on the whole is neutral with respect to these views about the nature of mental events.

Eliminative materialism offers an answer to the first problem: there are no mental events, only physical ones. According to a moderate version of this doctrine, talk about mental events is meaningful and can be translated without loss into talk about physical events. Talk about mental events is a convenient though misleading mode of speaking, since expressions do not literally refer to mental events. This translation version of eliminative materialism is analogous to linguistic phenomenalism (as defended, for example, by C. I. Lewis, 1946). There are no physical objects; but we can talk as if there are physical objects for convenience, provided that in our reflective, philosophical moments we realize that this talk can be translated without loss into a language only containing expressions that refer to sensings. I strongly suspect that the translation version of eliminative materialism is as unsatisfactory as linguistic phenomenalism. An adequate science of the mind cannot be formulated wholly in physical terms. Physiology does not cut nature at the same joints as psychology, and hence lawlike generalizations about mental processes cannot be captured by physiology (see Fodor, 1975, chapter 1). But be that as it may, *if* the translation version of eliminative materialism is true, all talk about mental events within the context of action theory should be taken as mere convenience, which in principle can be translated into physical talk. A theory of action is not *logically* committed to the ontological claim that there are mental events: that is the main point. I should add, however, that an adequate action theory is committed to the claim that talk about mental events is meaningful. As a consequence a theory of action is not compatible with radical versions of eliminative materialism that entail that such talk is meaningless. I take it that these extreme versions of eliminative materialism are highly implausible (though cf. Churchland, 1979).

Unlike eliminative materialism, functionalism entails that there are mental events. But functionalism in any of its forms does not offer a specific answer to the second problem about the nature of mental events. Functionalism says that mental events are to be characterized by their causal relations to input and output events and to other mental events; but it does not say how mental events are related to brain events. Functionalism is logically compatible with, for instance, a type-type identity theory, a token-token identity theory, and even with dualism. A type-type identity theory says that every type, or kind, of mental event is identical with some type of physical event; similarly a token-token identity theory says that every particular mental event is identical with some particular physical event. Type-type identity theories have an untoward consequence. If each type of mental event is identical with some type of biological or physical process or event in humans, then something that differs markedly from us, such as a silicon alien or an IBM computer, cannot undergo mental processes. It is not relevant whether in fact aliens or computers undergo mental processes: rather this possibility should not be precluded *a priori*. A token-token identity theory does not have this consequence because it does not equate the law-governed sortals under which mental events fall with the biological and physical sortals applicable to humans. Functionalism in any of its forms is also logically compatible with dualism. Functionalism says that mental events are characterized by their causal relations to other events, but leaves open whether mental events are identical with physical events. Dualism entails that mental events are not identical with physical ones, but leaves open whether mental events can be characterized by their relations to other events. The major problem for dualism, as is well known, is explaining the interaction between mental and physical events. Dualism is plausible only if causation is not analyzed by a push-pull model, that is, a model based on the idea of energy transfer. Such an analysis of causation is now unavailable; it remains to be seen whether one is forthcoming.

It is in short reasonable to think that mental events can be characterized by their functional roles and that the specific relationship between mental and brain events is token-token identity. This view about the nature of mental events does not generate an action theory, nor is it generated by an action theory. Rather it results from independent considerations. Even if functionalism is on final analysis untenable, and with it the token-token identity theory, and even if contrary to expectation some other view about the mental and the physical is tenable, even the translation version of eliminative materialism, all our claims about action and intention would nevertheless remain intact. Of course not every view about the nature of mental events would leave these action-theoretic claims intact, but many would and, most important, the plausible ones would. From a systematic vantage point it would be nice to fit action theory into a general theory of mental events. But there appears to be no necessity for doing so: by and large, action theory can proceed without resolving the outstanding issues about the nature of the mental.

4. A Program for a Solution

A fundamental problem about action concerns the nature of the mental antecedent. What are the features of the mental antecedent to action such that only events of this type initiate action? William James (1890) held that voluntary actions are initiated by a *fiat*. A fiat, according to him, is a focusing of attention on a memory trace of the action type to be performed. For example, Richard's waving his arm is caused by his attending to a memory trace of his past arm wavings. A natural and widely held view of attention, both to external events and to inner happenings, is that it is a cognitive process. Thus James is committed to the position that the mental antecedent is purely cognitive.

James, however, is mistaken about the mental antecedent to action. Cognitive features are clearly part of the proximate cause of action; indeed, cognitive features are an essential element in the causal history of an action: but they are not the whole of it. Consider someone who is deciding between alternative courses of action. He first focuses on, attends to, one course, then another, and finally he acts. Attending to a kind of action is, at best, necessary for acting. It is not sufficient. The person must also be *moved to act*. Suppose that I now have the opportunity to jump up and touch the ceiling. I might focus my attention on jumping and touching the ceiling; and I might do so to the extent that my attending to this course of action fully occupies consciousness: but unless I am moved to act, I will not jump and touch the ceiling. Representing to oneself a future course of action, no matter the centrality and persistence of this representation, will not by itself initiate action. There must also be a noncognitive feature—a *conative* feature, to revive some old-style terminology— to the mental event initiating action.

I take it to be a deep insight of folk psychology that the initiating mental event has both cognitive and conative features. Without conative features, action could not begin. Having a representation of a future action is compatible with not acting, even if the world is completely friendly toward that action. The proximate cause of action involves *both* a representation of the future course of action and the motivation to undertake that course. Thus an adequate answer to our fundamental problem involves articulating both the cognitive and conative features of the proximate cause. It might be thought that certain types of cognitive representations can function in a manner that motivates behavior. I take this claim to be fundamentally mistaken. But even if I am wrong and purely cognitive representations can move someone to act, the main point remains. The motivational aspect of the proximate cause to action must be explained—or explained away. It cannot be ignored.

According to (D2.1), the proximate cause of action is an immediate intention. Thus immediate intention has both cognitive and conative features. Or to say it another way, immediate intending is a complex mental event that is to be decomposed into cognitive and conative events. I have opted for (D2.1) as the point of departure in resolving our fundamental problem. In addition to (D2.1) a theory about intention is required; without it, little more than naming the proximate cause has been accomplished.

A theory of intention, I take it, has two parts: a conceptual or philosophical part and a psychological or empirical one. These parts of the theory are interconnected and interdependent. A philosophical account of intention that ignores psychological reality is like a foundation built without regard for the house that is to be constructed on it; and conversely, a psychological account of intention that is not based on tenable philosophical positions is like a building made without attention to the foundation on which it is to stand. Philosophical considerations, in addition to adding clarity, provide constraints on psychological theorizing. Systematic data and successful local psychological theories, in turn, help determine choices among competing philosophical strategies.

My approach in this book is to start with a philosophical theory of action. That theory is to be modified and developed in accordance with theoretical and experimental results in psychology and cognate disciplines, including artificial intelligence ('AI'). The final goal, toward which only initial steps will be taken, is to provide a naturalized action theory.

To outline this approach in a bit more detail, part I has presented the philosophical action-theoretic background. In chapter 1 I argued for the plausibility of a Causal Theory of action, that is, a theory saying that actions are the proximate effect of a specific type of mental event. In this chapter I labeled that mental event 'an immediate intention.' It was observed that being caused by an intention is not sufficient for being an intentional action. Intentional actions are

planned actions, and in the previous chapter I presented a folk psychological account of planned action.

In part II I begin the task of presenting a theory of intention that is
both philosophically and psychologically adequate. This part is concerned with ontological issues. Actions and intentions are events,
and thus an account of the ontological status of events is required. I
argue that events are particulars, bearing important resemblance to
physical objects. Intention is a mental attitude with a content; and
thus an account of the status of contents is required. In chapter 4, I
argue, following Lewis (1979) and Chisholm (1980), that the objects
of attitudes are properties and that all attitudes are at their cores
self-referential.

In part III I focus on the folk or commonsense psychology of the key
attitudes believing, desiring, and intending. I argue that these attitudes are irreducibly different from each other. Chapter 5 deals with
desiring and intending and chapter 6 with believing and intending.
Folk psychology provides a first approximation: but it does not contain a well-developed theory of the mental attitudes; in particular, it
does not contain a theory of intending that sheds a great deal of light
on the structure of this attitude. For that information we need to look
toward recent work in scientific psychology and related areas.

In part IV I begin the attempt to understand the proximate cause of
action in scientific terms. Intention, as I have said, is complex in that
it has a cognitive component and a conative component. Each component in turn is itself complex. I distinguish two parts of the cognitive component, one concerned with monitoring and guidance and
another concerned with the prior representation of a complex activity: the former is discussed in chapter 7 and the latter in chapter 8.
The latter is the distinctive feature of intentional action. Many—but
not all—psychologists concerned with action have often concentrated on simple, habitual or reflex action and put aside complex
activity. Representation of complex activity has recently been discussed in AI, with, I believe, some interesting results. I shall also
take up that discussion in chapter 8.

The conative component of intention is more difficult to clarify
than the cognitive component. Unlike the cognitive aspect, there is
no clear nor obvious way to transform the folk psychological notion
into a scientific one. This is true even when a crucial simplifying
assumption is made: namely, that the agent is affectively neutral,
that his emotional state does not dictate his action. Without this assumption the problem would be unmanageable, since there is little
scientific understanding of the emotions. But even granting this assumption, the current prospect for understanding motivation is not

good. In chapter 9 I discuss whether the conative aspect of intention can be understood in terms of some extant motivational theory. That chapter is largely negative. A partial understanding of causation can be gained by assimilating certain aspects of it to the computational model. For the remainder I speculate about the additional theoretical apparatus that must be developed. In sum, our fundamental question will be mostly, though not completely, answered by explaining the nature of intention in terms of extant scientific psychological theory.

Part II

THE ONTOLOGICAL FOUNDATIONS
FOR ACTION THEORY

3

Events as Spatiotemporal Particulars

A person performing a bodily action is a physical event; and similarly, a person intending to do something is a mental event. In this chapter I discuss the nature of events. The view that I defend is that events are particulars. A particular is something that is spatiotemporally locatable and not, literally, repeatable.

Section 1 is an informal discussion of the ontological status of events. Basically I contend that events are relevantly similar to physical objects, differing from physical objects in that they do not fully occupy the spatiotemporal region in which they occur. In section 2, I develop the machinery for formal statements of ontological status. This machinery consists in stating identity conditions. I discuss the function and form of these statements. In section 3, I provide identity conditions for events. These identity conditions are compared and contrasted with Davidson's and Kim's, which also presuppose that events are particulars. In section 4, I discuss the semantical implications of this view. The ontological status of events is given by identity conditions; determination of whether two singular terms name one event is given by a semantical criterion. In section 5, I discuss some of the ramifications of this theory for issues about mental events, in particular, the truth conditions for identity sentences containing references to mental events.

1. The Informal Picture

Philosophers of language and logic distinguish between three broad categories of linguistic items:

(i) singular terms;
(ii) predicates;
(iii) sentences.

Parallel ontological distinctions can be made:

(i') particulars;
(ii') properties;
(iii') propositions.

Paradigm members of (i') are physical objects, such as balls, tables, and automobiles. Persons and other animate objects are included in (i'). Properties and propositions are abstract entities, a mark of which is not being spatiotemporally locatable. Many types of objects in (i'), by contrast, are concrete, though not all are. Sets and numbers (if they exist) are particulars, but not spatiotemporally locatable. Properties are attributes of objects, usually objects of category (i'), but not necessarily, since there are, for example, properties of properties. Propositions are the least well understood of these entities. On one widely held view, propositions are abstract bearers of truth and falsity whose structure reflects relationships between particulars and properties.

This tripartite ontological distinction may ultimately break down. Some philosophers have argued that properties are collections of particulars; and some have argued that propositions can be eliminated from any categorization. Others have argued that there is only one kind of abstract entity, possible worlds, and that properties and propositions are derivative of these. Be that as it may, the distinction marked by (i')–(iii') is a plausible working hypothesis and one that I will accept.

It is not clear into which category events fall. Indeed there have been theories associating events with each of these categories. Chisholm (1976b) has defended the view that events are propositional. Excluding details that do not concern us here, events are the same as propositions, except that they are time-bound; that is, they occur (or are exemplified) on some occasions but not others. Goldman (1970, chapter 1) has argued that actions are properties of persons; and Kim (1970, 1973, 1976) has extended this view to the claim that all events are property exemplifications of concrete particulars. The Kim-Goldman view might well be associated with category (ii') since properties are constitutive of events, though, strictly speaking, events are a kind of particular on it. Davidson (1967, 1970a, 1970b, 1971) has argued forcefully for the view that events are concrete particulars. Although I agree with Davidson in placing events in category (i'), I disagree with much of the development he gives to this perspective, as will be seen.

There are several prima facie reasons for the particularist view, though I doubt that any of them are decisive. First, it appears that particularism is ontologically more parsimonious than the property-exemplification or propositional views. On the property-exemplification view there are properties and particulars. On the propositional view entities from each of the three categories are required: there are propositional events; there are exemplifications of these propositional events, which are particulars; and there is at least one property, exemplifying. For example, on Chisholm's theory there is the propositional event (or state of affairs) of Nixon's resigning and there is the occasion on January 20, 1973 of his resigning, where this spatiotemporal happening *exemplifies* the abstract state of affairs. On the particularist view only entities from category (i') seem to be needed.

However, this advantage of a particularist view is illusory. "Any theory of events," Chisholm once said (1970, p. 15), "should be adequate to the fact of recurrence, to the fact that there are some things that recur, or happen more than once." On Chisholm's theory there is a single thing, a state of affairs, that recurs; that is, it occurs, and then does not occur, and then *it* occurs again. But if events are concrete particulars, they do not literally recur. The solution to this problem on a particularist event theory consists in saying that an event recurs just in case at least two events of the same *type* occur. Thus Pat's kissing Richard recurred if she kissed him on Monday and did the same type of thing on Tuesday. But types are properties. Hence a particularist theory solves the problem of recurrence at the cost of committing itself to properties.[1] Moreover in order to account for persons having certain types of mental attitudes—so-called *de dicto* attitudes, I will argue later—a particularist theory of events must be supplemented with objects from the category of propositions. Thus, a theory capable of dealing with the full range of issues about events requires commitment to objects from all three categories (i'), (ii'), and (iii').

The second apparent reason for particularism is that the machinery of extensional first-order logic is sufficient to parse event sentences if events are particulars. The advantage in parsing event sentences in terms of extensional first-order logic is that it is an important step toward completing the program of showing that the logical form of all natural language sentences is fully captured by extensional first-order logic. This program is attractive because, if completed, it would provide a ready-made formal semantics for natural language, including a Tarski-like truth definition. In particular, Davidson (1967) argues that an event sentence such as

(1) Richard crossed the street,

can be parsed by

(2) $(\exists x)$[Crossed (Richard, the street, x)],

which in quasi-English says, approximately,

(3) There is something x such that x was a crossing by Richard of the street.

Sentence (2) is stated in extensional first-order logic.

However, matters are not unproblematic. It is not clear whether extensional first-order logic is adequate to parse all event sentences. Standardly, predicate modification is treated as a case of conjunction (see Davidson, 1967). Although this method seems to work for adjectival modification, it is not adequate for adverbial modification. Consider

(4) Richard almost crossed the street.

On the standard interpretation, (4) becomes

(5) $(\exists x)$[Crossed (Richard, the street, x) & Almost (x)].

But (5) entails (2), which is equivalent to (1), whereas (4) does not entail (1). Some authors draw the conclusion that extensional first-order logic is not adequate to translate event sentences; Clark (1970), for instance, suggests a logic that uses sentence-operators, on the model of alethic modal logic. This conclusion may not be warranted because the natural language entailments of sentences such as (4) might be preserved without abandoning extensional first-order logic, perhaps by adding to it special rules governing predicate modifiers. In any case this apparent attractive feature of particularism is not straightforward: at best, extensional first-order predicate logic must be seriously complicated in order to parse all event sentences.

The third reason is that our ordinary way of thinking about events seems to suggest a particularist viewpoint. Events are in the world; they are part of the booming, buzzing confusion that confronts us. Events are concrete: a shooting or a birth is something to which we attribute spatial and temporal location. As evidence for this claim, we ordinarily think that events can be recorded on film or video tape: it is difficult to conceive of recording something abstract (that is, nonspatiotemporal) on film or video tape.

Common sense apparently sanctions the view that events are extended spatiotemporal objects. In contrast, physicists and philosophers of science sometimes think of events as nonextended spatiotemporal particulars, that is, as points. Another view, intermediate between the physicist's idealization and the ordinary one, is that, though spatially extended, events are temporally pointal; they are time slices of a spatial region (cf. Pollock, 1976, pp. 145 ff). Neither of these last two views corresponds to ordinary thinking. We think of a wedding as an event, not as consisting of infinitely many pointal events somehow connected.

The dictates of ordinary thinking are not necessarily decisive. The tenability of a philosophical account of events rests on its ability to provide a foundation for related philosophical theories, for example, theories about action, causation, and explanation, and its ability to deal with puzzles, for instance, the problem about recurrence. It might be that when all is said and done, there will be competing accounts of events, each being equally satisfactory for these tasks. There is no conclusive reason to think that exactly one event theory will meet these requirements, or even that one theory will do it better than others. But I will not defend this metaphilosophical thesis here.[2] Rather I will defend one substantive theory that construes events as particulars. It is a version that meets these criteria for adequacy and that accords well with commonsense intuitions. Fundamental to this particularist theory is the claim that there is significant similarity between events and physical objects.

We often talk about events and physical objects in the same way (Davidson, 1971). We use definite and indefinite descriptions simi- larly: we speak about the spy, about a spy, about there being many spies; and we speak about the escape by the spy, an escape by the spy, there being many escapes by the spy. We count escapes just as well as we count spies. We assign proper names to physical objects, conventionally to all persons, but also to other physical objects, for instance, 'The Sears Tower,' 'Mt. Everest,' 'The Titanic.' Similarly proper names are assigned to events, for example, 'Hurricane Carl,' 'Super Bowl XVII,' 'The Battle of Waterloo.' This similarity between talk about events and physical objects is an important factor in mak- ing plausible Davidson's parsing of event sentences into first-order form.

Physical objects have parts that are themselves physical objects; for example, an automobile has parts, such as tires and a carburetor, that are physical objects. Similarly events have parts that are themselves events. The Battle of Waterloo, for instance, consists of a number of separate clashes, and each of these in turn consists of separable events. Some philosophers have thought that when a complex phys- ical object is dismantled into parts, it becomes a 'scattered object,' though it retains its type identity. An automobile engine, when dis- mantled, remains an automobile engine. Similarly some complex events, when separated into parts, become 'scattered,' though retain their type identity. A baseball game, if disrupted by rain, remains a baseball game: this is so even if the disruptions are many and involve completion of the game on another day at another place.

Physical objects occupy spatiotemporal regions, and so do events: they are both types of concrete particulars. However, there is one crucial difference between physical objects and events. Physical objects fully occupy the spatiotemporal region in which they exist; but events do not fully occupy the spatiotemporal region in which they occur.

More carefully, consider the following principle:

(P1) For any spatiotemporal region r and any x, if x occupies all of r, then, for any y, if y occupies all of r, y is x.

Principle (P1) is true when the range of x and y are physical objects. It is in this sense that physical objects fully occupy spatiotemporal regions. Clearly there are spatiotemporal regions fully occupied by a lead ball; and similarly there are regions fully occupied by an automobile, though these regions are irregular, allowing for the unoccupied spaces in the interior and under the hood.

No doubt it is sometimes difficult to make judgments about the precise regions occupied by a physical object. Consider the difficulty of ascertaining the precise region fully occupied by a tree, train, or house. In some instances the background principles needed to make these judgments are unclear or arbitrary. For example, does the region occupied by my house include the detached garage? Does the region occupied by the train include the empty spaces in the dining car? These background principles are epistemic and pragmatic. The difficulty in ascertaining these principles does not affect the ontological point that physical objects fully occupy spatiotemporal regions.

Some events are easily located; for example, the event of a billiard ball moving occupies the spatiotemporal region occupied by the ball from the time it begins to move until it comes to rest. But as in the case of physical objects, it is sometimes difficult to make judgments about the precise regions occupied by events. These judgments also depend on epistemic and pragmatic background principles that are sometimes vague and arbitrary. Where, for instance, are we to locate Richard's long-distance telephone call to New York? It includes the region occupied by Richard and the person with whom he is talking. But does it also include the region occupied by the phone lines? The switching terminal in Kansas City? These questions do not have completely nonarbitrary answers. But as in the case of physical objects, the lack of a full complement of epistemic and pragmatic principles for location does not vitiate the ontological point that events occupy spatiotemporal regions.

In contrast to physical objects, events do not fully occupy spatio-temporal regions. That is, (P1) is false when the range of x and y is restricted to events. As a consequence, more than one event can occupy a spatiotemporal region. The events of Esther Williams swimming the channel and Esther Williams catching a cold, we can take it, each wholly occur within the same spatiotemporal region. Other pairs of spatiotemporally coincidental events are: its raining in Chicago (now) and its growing dark in Chicago (now); Richard's taking a shower (now) and Richard's humming "Here Comes the Chief" (now); Pat's saluting the flag (now) and Pat's daydreaming about a vacation (now). Another example (cited by Lombard, 1979), which involves events of longer duration, is an adolescent boy's voice becoming lower over a number of years and his facial hair growth developing during that same period.

Davidson appears to agree that more than one event can occur in a single spatiotemporal region, though he suggests an argument against this view (1970, pp. 230–231). Consider:

(6) this metal sphere's rotating (now);
(7) this metal sphere's becoming warm (now).

Though spatiotemporally coincidental on the macro-level, it might be claimed that (6) and (7) are not distinct, since each is identical with molecular motion. However, the identities required by this argument do not obtain. Macroscopic events are on some accounts supervenient on microscopic ones. Whether that is true or not, it is highly implausible to claim that macroscopic events are identical with microscopic ones. But moreover, even if (6) and (7) were identical with molecular events, they would not be identical with the same molecular events. The molecular activity that appears macroscopically as rotation is different from the molecular activity that appears macroscopically as the sphere's being warmer.

In the examples so far considered, the events involved physical objects. An event e involves a physical object o just in case there is a spatiotemporal region r such that e occupies all of r and o occupies all or part of r. Not all events involve physical objects. For example, there can be spatiotemporal regions devoid of physical objects in which a magnetic field or a gravitational field changes strength. Another type of case is one in which the temperature changes or a sound increases in intensity or an odor subsides in a region not containing physical objects. It might be said that in this type of case there must be physical objects in the region, because a change in temperature, odor, or so on, is supervenient on a molecular change. But there being micro-level particulars in a region does not entail that there are physical objects in that region. Physical objects, the objects that we commonly sense, are macroscopic; molecules and atoms, not to mention subatomic particles, are not physical objects.

An important consequence of there being events not involving physical objects is that the existence of some events does not depend on there being physical objects. Likewise there can be physical objects where there are no events. Suppose that for a period of time our metal ball remains unchanged on the macro-level. It neither expands nor contracts, neither becomes warmer nor cooler, nor so on. There is no event occurring in the spatiotemporal region fully occupied by the metal ball. The ball is in an equilibrium state and being in an equilibrium state is not a case in which something is happening to the ball.

As compared with physical objects, events seem evanescent. One can touch, bite, kick, or kiss many physical objects; but it is not possible to do the same to an event. The reason for this difference is that an event occurs within a spatiotemporal region without fully occupying that region. Indeed there can be indefinitely many events within a region. The seeming intangibility of events is due to their lack of fully occupying a region.

Observe moreover that (P1) is false if the range of either x or y is an event. Suppose that the metal ball becomes warmer at a constant rate throughout its entire lifespan. Then, letting x be the ball and y the event of the ball's becoming warmer, (P1) is false. Both the ball and its becoming warmer occupy the same spatiotemporal region, but the ball itself is not identical with the event of its becoming warmer. To say that physical objects fully occupy spatiotemporal regions is not to say that they *solely* occupy these regions.

In sum, the picture is this. Physical objects and events are both concrete, spatiotemporal particulars. The crucial difference between physical objects and events is that physical objects fully occupy the spatiotemporal regions in which they exist but events do not fully occupy the spatiotemporal regions in which they occur. Events and physical objects, moreover, are ontologically independent: some events do not involve physical objects and some physical objects exist for a time without being involved in an event. It is time now to present this picture more formally.

2. Identity Conditions

Our problem is to specify the nature of events: one good way to resolve this problem is to provide identity conditions. In general,
identity conditions are statements that encode the nature of an ontological kind. Identity conditions do this by specifying conceptually
significant properties of objects of that kind.[3]

One true statement of identity conditions is that sets are identical
just in case they have the same members; that is,

(8) $(A)(B)$[if A and B are sets, then $A = B$ iff $(x)(x \epsilon A \equiv x \epsilon B)$].

Quine expresses this common view about sets when he says:
"Classes raise no perplexities over identity, being identical if and
only if their members are identical" (1960, p. 209). Another true
statement of identity conditions, and one central to our concerns, is
that physical objects are identical just in case they occupy the same
spatiotemporal regions; that is

(D3.1) $(o_1)(o_2)$[if o_1 and o_2 are physical objects, then $o_1 = o_2$ iff
$(r)(o_1 0r \equiv o_2 0r)$],

where r ranges over spatiotemporal regions and 0 is '...occupies---.'
It is important to be clear about these identity conditions for physical
objects. Sometimes it is argued that spatiotemporal continuity will
not provide identity conditions, since physical objects might have
discontinuous histories. Notice, however, that (D3.1) is not stated in
terms of spatiotemporal continuity; rather it says that o_1 and o_2 are
the same just in case they occupy all and only the same regions. If
physical object o_1 is spatiotemporally discontinuous, then it is the
same object as o_2 only if o_2 has exactly the same discontinuities. Ab-
stracting the form of these statements of identity conditions yields:

(IC) $(x)(y)$(if x and y are Ks, then $x = y$ iff Fxy).

In the case of sets, F is the dyadic property of having the same members as; and in the case of physical objects, F is the dyadic property of
occupying the same spatiotemporal regions as.

Identity conditions are often confounded with *identifying conditions*.[4] Identifying conditions are criteria for judging or telling how
many of a certain kind of object there are, or for reidentifying a single, enduring object of a kind. Identifying conditions serve epistemological or pragmatic functions. Consider, for instance, the claim
that S and S' are the same person just in case S and S' have the same
parents and siblings. This is a rule for counting persons, and for
reidentifying persons over time. It is useful in law courts and in

psychoanalysts' offices. But it does not specify the nature of persons: since parents and siblings are themselves persons, it is circular when taken to be a characterization of persons. A true statement about the nature of persons, it seems reasonable to expect, will be unique in that no other nonequivalent statement would also specify the nature of persons. But identifying conditions for persons are not unique; there can be many nonequivalent, true such statements. In addition to sameness of parents and siblings, identifying conditions for persons can be given in terms of sameness of fingerprints, sameness of actions performed, sameness of causal histories, or so on. Identifying conditions are true, general statements about the kind of evidence that provides good support for identity claims. But since they are evidential statements, identifying conditions are not infallible guides to identity. Although sameness of fingerprints, for example, is very strong evidence for sameness of persons, it is possible— indeed it appears physically possible—that two persons produce the same fingerprints. By contrast, true identity conditions have no counterinstances.

It is not always easy to decide whether criteria should be interpreted as identity conditions or identifying conditions or both. Consider the claim

(9) For any persons S and S', S and S' are the same person just in case S and S' have bodies and their bodies occupy the same spatiotemporal regions.

This claim can be interpreted as providing identifying conditions. Suppose that we are concerned with whether the man on the witness stand is the same man who lied for Richard. According to (9) the matter can be settled by establishing whether there is spatiotemporal coincidence between the man on the witness stand and the man who lied for Richard. But (9) can also be interpreted as a statement of identity conditions. Rewritten in the form (IC), it would say that personal identity consists in sameness of body. No doubt, interpreted as identity conditions, (9) is highly controversial: since Locke, many philosophers have argued that personal identity consists in sameness of mental states, in particular, memories, and not sameness of body. Be that as it may, the point is that sometimes a single statement is ambiguous between identity conditions and identifying conditions. However, this type of ambiguity does not vitiate the distinction between identity conditions and identifying conditions: the former encodes the nature of an ontological kind of object; and the latter provides a criterion for making judgments about sameness and difference for a kind of object.

Sometimes identity conditions are thought to be prerequisites for using the machinery of quantificational logic. In order to quantify over a domain, there must be a criterion for distinguishing one individual from another within the domain. But this objective can be gained by a very general criterion of individuation that is not relativized to ontological types; in particular, Leibniz's Law, $(x)(y)[x = y$ iff $(F)(Fx \equiv Fy)]$, that is, for any x and any y, x and y are identical just in case they have all and only the same properties.[5] Thus, for example, Leibniz's Law is sufficient for quantification over both sets and physical objects—and indeed any ontological type—since it establishes the formal requirements for distinguishing among members of domains. Leibniz's Law is not a statement that specifies the nature of sets or physical objects, or any ontological type. It is far too general; unlike (8) and (D3.1), it fails to indicate a conceptually significant property of an ontological kind. To make this last point another way, identity conditions pick out properties of an ontological kind such that having these properties in common is sufficient for having all properties in common. For instance, it follows from (D3.1) and Leibniz's Law that

(10) $(o_1)(o_2)$[if o_1 and o_2 are physical objects, then if $(r)(o_1 0 r \equiv o_2 0 r)$, then $(F)(Fo_1 \equiv Fo_2)$];

that is, in the case of physical objects, occupying the same spatiotemporal regions is sufficient for having all properties in common. That is not the case for Leibniz's Law: it does not pick out key properties on the basis of which identity follows.

Recently Brody (1980) argued that Leibniz's Law provides identity conditions. He summarizes his view in the following way. "For all . . . objects, indiscernibility (understood in a sufficiently broad fashion) [that is, Leibniz's Law] is both a necessary and sufficient condition for identity. This is a perfectly general condition for identity, and involves no conditions that vary according to the type of object involved" (p. 43). His view is that Leibniz's Law is all that we need to know, or can know, about identity between objects (see pp. 3–10). Brody is correct in pointing out that Leibniz's Law provides the machinery necessary for understanding identity between pairs of objects,[6] and that the relation of identity does not change when the ontological type to which the pairs belong changes. But he is incorrect about a fundamental point: that identity conditions explicate the relation of identity. The function of identity conditions is to specify conceptually significant properties of ontological types, not to define 'identity' or to introduce relativistic identity relations. True identity conditions indicate the nature of persons, or the nature of physical objects, or the nature of events, or so on.

Return to

(IC) $(x)(y)$(if x and y are Ks, then $x = y$ iff Fxy).

Here K stands for an ontological kind. Sets, propositions, properties, physical objects, persons, and events are ontological kinds; unicorns, possible fat men, and saints are not, nor are self-identical objects, objects that exist, or objects identical with Socrates. Although it is not clear exactly how to define 'ontological kind', some necessary conditions can be stated. Ontological kinds are kinds, and kinds are not universal and have at least several instances. Thus self-identical objects and objects identical with Socrates are not ontological kinds. Moreover instances of an ontological kind are so necessarily; that is, if something is an instance of an ontological kind K, then it is necessary that if that thing exists, then it is an instance of K. Thus saints do not constitute an ontological kind: something that is a saint can exist and not be a saint. By contrast, if something is a physical object, it is not possible that it exist and not be a physical object. These two conditions, clearly, are not sufficient: the kind *sets with three members* satisfies these conditions without being an ontological kind. But I shall not attempt to provide the additional necessary conditions: it suffices to say that the intuitive notion of an ontological kind is reasonably well understood.[7]

It is important to be clear about the property F in statements of the form (IC). It is a property of pairs of objects that belong to the ontological kind K. It is not a property of each object of this sort, not one such that an object belongs to kind K in virtue of having it. This latter type of property, which is ordinarily monadic, is related to the dyadic property F in (IC), but not as a matter of logic alone. The dyadic property F in (8) is having the same members as; and the monadic property associated with it is having members. 'A has members' does not follow from 'A has the same members as B,' since it might be that $A = B = \Lambda$. Identity conditions specify the nature of an ontological kind in the roundabout way of indicating a relational property that is sufficient for identity of object pairs of that kind.

There is no mechanical procedure for finding the dyadic property F, given an ontological kind K, which results in a true, nontrivial instance of (IC). For each K, it is a substantial issue what F is. Although there is no algorithm for determining F given a K, there are several constraints on the property F. One obvious constraint is

(C1) F is nontautological.

A tautological dyadic property is one that every pair of objects share. Such properties clearly do not characterize any ontological kind.

Another constraint, not so obvious, is that for a given K, F is the widest property that would make a statement of the form (IC) true. Suppose that for the sake of argument the following statement of personal identity were true:

(11) For every S and S', if S and S' are persons, then $S = S'$ iff $(e)(SRe \equiv S'Re)$,

where e ranges over events and R is '...veridically remembers---.' Consider now

(12) For every S and S', if S and S' are persons, then $S = S'$ iff $(r)(S0r \equiv S'0r)$ & $(e)(SRe \equiv S'Re)$;

that is, personal identity consists in spatiotemporal coincidence *and* sameness of memories. If (11) is true, sameness of memories is sufficient for personal identity for any S and S'; and thus by Leibniz's Law, S and S' share all properties. From this it follows that (12) is also true. But although true, (12) is misleading if construed as identity conditions. Statement (12) indicates a feature of persons, spatiotemporal coincidence, that is irrelevant, that is not part of the nature of persons (on the assumption that (11) is true). Statements (11) and (12) cannot both provide adequate identity conditions for persons; and since (11) by hypothesis does, (12) does not.

This constraint can be paraphrased by

(C2) F is maximal with respect to K.

Given a K, (C2) obtains just in case: (i) substitution of F into (IC) yields a true sentence; and (ii) there is no other property F^* such that substitution into (IC) yields a true sentence and F^* is wider than F. A dyadic property, say G, is wider than another dyadic property, say H, just in case, necessarily, for any x and y, if x bears H to y, then x bears G to y, but not conversely. This constraint can also be stated in the following way: identity conditions I for K are maximal just in case, for every I^*, if I^* are identity conditions for K and I entails I^*, then I is I^*. This latter formulation, though more intuitive, is less explicit. Constraint (C2) rules out (12) providing identity conditions for persons on the assumption that (11) does. The property being spatiotemporally coincidental and having the same memories is not maximal with respect to persons. There is another property, having the same memories, that yields a true instance of (IC)—namely, (11)—and which is wider than the conjunctive property of spatiotemporal coincidence plus sameness of memories.

A related constraint is

(C3) F is minimal with respect to K.

Suppose again that (11) is the correct view about personal identity. Consider now

(13) For every S and S', if S and S' are persons, $S = S'$ iff $(e)(SRe \equiv S'Re) \vee p$,

where p is any irrelevant disjunct. Clearly (13) is not adequate: the disjunctive property of having the same memories as or p does not specify the nature of persons. (Observe that this disjunctive property satisfies the maximality constraint (C2). There is no property wider than it that yields a true sentence of the form (IC) when K is persons.) Let us say, then, that the minimality constraint, (C3), obtains, given a K, just in case: (i) substitution of F into (IC) yields a true sentence; and (ii) there is no other property F^* such that substitution into (IC) yields a true sentence and F is wider than F^*. Alleged identity conditions (13) fail to satisfy this constraint because there is a property, having the same memories as, such that it makes a sentence of the form (IC) true (by hypothesis) and it is wider than the disjunctive property. As before, this constraint can be restated directly in terms of identity conditions: identity conditions I for K are minimal just in case, for every I^*, if I^* are identity conditions for K and I^* entails I, then I is I^*.

Identity conditions indicate the nature of an ontological kind. Each ontological kind, it is safe to suppose, has a different nature. It is impossible that there be two such kinds with the same nature. If they had the same nature, in what sense would there be two ontological kinds? Suppose that personal identity consisted in spatiotemporal coincidence of bodies, as (9) says under one interpretation. Persons, then, would be a subclass of physical objects, since according to (D3.1) identity conditions for physical objects is in terms of spatiotemporal coincidence. But suppose further that reference to a person having a body were eliminated, that personal identity was just spatiotemporal coincidence. In that case there would be no difference at all between persons and physical objects: there would not be an ontological kind persons. If there is to be an ontological kind persons, there must be something distinctive about the nature of persons. This constraint is given by

(C4) K is unique with respect to F.

Constraint (C4) obtains just in case, for a given F, if there is a K such that a statement of the form (IC) provides adequate identity conditions for K, then for any K^*, if a statement of the form (IC) also provides adequate identity conditions for K^*, then K^* is K.

It is possible that more than one property satisfies these constraints for a given K. But it would seem that an ontological kind has one best characterization. Consider once more the debate about personal identity. It would seem that personal identity consists in sameness of body, or sameness of mental states, or so on, but not several of these. I do not know of any proof that there will always be one best characterization of an ontological kind: rather it appears to be a reasonable presumption.[8] With some hesitation, then, I suggest the additional constraint

(C5) F is unique with respect to K.

This constraint means that, for a given K, if there is an F such that a statement of the form (IC) provides adequate identity conditions for K, then for every F^*, if a statement of the form (IC) provides adequate identity conditions for K, then F^* is F.

To emphasize the main point, there is no mechanical procedure for determining adequate identity conditions for an ontological kind. Constraints (C1)–(C4), and perhaps (C5), will eliminate some mistaken proposals; but for a given K, they will not generate a specific dyadic property F that provides adequate identity conditions. That is a substantive matter.

3. Identity Conditions for Events

Recall the identity conditions for physical objects,

(D3.1) $(o_1)(o_2)$[if o_1 and o_2 are physical objects, then $o_1 = o_2$ iff $(r)(o_1 0 r \equiv o_2 0 r)$],

where r ranges over spatiotemporal regions and 0 is '...occupies---.' Informally I argued that physical objects and events are relevantly similar: they both are concrete particulars occupying spatiotemporal regions. They differ in that a spatiotemporal region cannot be occupied by more than one physical object at a time but can be occupied by more than one event at a time. These similarities and differences are reflected in the following identity conditions for events:

(D3.2) $(e)(f)$[if e and f are events, then $e = f$ iff $\Box(r)(e0r \equiv f0r)$].

Identity conditions for events, that is, consist in *necessary* spatio-temporal coincidence.

Identity conditions (D3.2) permit the occurrence of distinct events in one spatiotemporal region. Esther Williams swimming the channel and Esther Williams catching a cold, despite being spatiotemporally coincidental, are distinct. For it is possible that Esther Williams swim the channel and not catch a cold at that time; and it is possible that she catch a cold and not swim the channel then. Similarly the metal sphere's rotating and its becoming warmer are distinct, since it is possible that the sphere rotate at that time and not become warmer and it is possible that it become warmer and not rotate.

Specifying the sense of necessity in (D3.2) is a complex matter, and a satisfying discussion of it would take us too far afield. Briefly, it seems clear that the kind of necessity is stronger than physical necessity. To say that p is physically necessary is to say, informally, that p is true in all possible worlds that have the same laws of nature as the actual world. If the necessity operator in (D3.2) were interpreted as expressing physical necessity, then (D3.2) would give the wrong result for some cases of distinct events that are lawfully connected. For instance, suppose that e is this pendulum's increasing in length during an interval and f is the pendulum's decreasing in period during the same temporal interval. These events are distinct, yet they co-occur in the same spatiotemporal regions in worlds having the same natural laws (and objects) as the actual world. A problem also arises in cases of lawful common effects. Suppose that a piston on top of a closed cylinder containing a gas is depressed. Two effects of that event are the volume of the gas decreasing and its temperature increasing. The volume of the gas decreasing and the temperature of the gas increasing are spatiotemporally coincident in the actual world, and in any world with the same physical laws, yet these events are distinct. Rather the necessity operator in (D3.2) should be interpreted as expressing logical necessity. Under this interpretation, (D3.2) yields that the pendulum's increasing in length and its decreasing in period are distinct, as is the gas decreasing in volume and increasing in temperature. It seems reasonable to take the underlying logic of this alethic operator to be Fey's system T (or equivalently, von Wright's M). However, it might well be that some weaker system better captures the sense of this necessity operator.[9]

These identity conditions for events satisfy constraints (C1) to (C5). Necessary spatiotemporal coincidence is uniquely matched with the ontological kind events; and it meets both the minimality and maximality requirements with respect to the kind events. In this regard it is worth observing that the following statement of identity conditions for physical objects, though true, fails to satisfy (C2), the maximality constraint:

(14) $(o_1)(o_2)$[if o_1 and o_2 are physical objects, then $o_1 = o_2$ iff $\Box(r)(o_1 0r \equiv o_2 0r)$].

There is another true statement of the form (IC) for the ontological kind physical objects; namely (D3.1), such that the dyadic property expressed in it, spatiotemporal coincidence, is wider than the dyadic property used in (14), necessary spatiotemporal coincidence.

Generally speaking, our intuitions about physical objects are clearer than our intuitions about events. Thus a spinoff advantage of the relationship between physical objects and events given by (D3.1) and (D3.2) is that solutions for problems about events can be sought in solutions for parallel problems about physical objects. For instance, are there 'conjunctive' events, 'negative' events, 'disjunctive' events? It seems that there are 'conjunctive' physical objects. There are objects made of parts, such as a watch or an auto. Similarly there are 'conjunctive' events. These are events consisting of parts that are themselves events. Of course not any group of disparate physical objects can be taken as a single object: my watch and Socrates' mug do not make a single physical object. Similarly not all groups of events can be conjoined: there is no single event of my watch's running and Socrates' drinking from his mug (but cf. Thomson, 1977, and Brand, 1981). There is, however, no clear sense to be given to 'negative' or 'disjunctive' physical objects—although some artificial sense can be devised. And similarly there are not, literally, 'negative' or 'disjunctive' events—although some artificial sense can be devised (cf. Suppes, 1970).[10]

According to (D3.2), events are particulars. This proposal, however, is not the only one that places events in the category of particulars. Two others are Davidson's and, on one reading, Kim's. Davidson (1970) holds that identity conditions for events can be given in terms of sameness of causes and effects. Restating this view in the form (IC):

(D) For any e and any f, if e and f are events, then $e = f$ iff $(g)(gCe \equiv gCf)$ & $(h)(eCh \equiv fCh)$,

where the ranges of g and h are restricted to events and where C is '...causes---'. Thus for example, Richard's waving his arms (now) is the same event as Richard's giving the victory sign (now) just in case there is no difference in causes and effects.

There is an important point of agreement between (D3.2) and (D). They both state identity conditions in terms of some external property of events, that is, some property pertaining to the relationships between events and something else or between some events and other events. They are not stated in terms of the internal structure of events. Since, generally speaking, identity conditions are to express conceptually significant properties of ontological kinds, the force of either (D3.2) or (D) is that the internal structure of an event is not one of its significant properties. Both these proposals for identity conditions leave it open whether events have a uniform internal structure: indeed they leave it open whether events have an internal structure at all.

In proposing (D), Davidson is claiming that the conceptually significant property of events is that they are the sole participants in the causal nexus of the world. If causation is the cement that holds the universe together, as Hume thought, then events are those things joined. Identity conditions (D) also draw attention to the role that events play in law-governed phenomena. Since many—but not all—laws of nature are universal statements of causation, the predicate terms in these laws pick out sorts of events.

However, despite this attractive rationale for (D), it is not unproblematic. Some authors have objected to (D) on the grounds that it is viciously circular. Tye, whose view is representative, says: "[T]he criterion should not have a definiens which requires quantification over events. For if we permit this quantification, we escape circularity only if we supply another independent criterion for the events over which we quantify. This point . . . spells disaster for Davidson's causal account" (1979, p. 82). (Also see Wilson, 1974.) However, as already pointed out, identity conditions are not required as prerequisites for quantification: only Leibniz's Law is needed in the case of particulars. Since Davidson can avail himself of Leibniz's Law, quantification over events in (D) does not yield vicious circularity.

But there may be a related problem for (D). Davidson (1967b) has argued that all causes and all effects are events. If that is correct, circularity again threatens. For the range of the variables in (D) must be restricted to events, and that presupposes an independent criterion for events. However, this problem is not defeating. One reply is to point out that an independent criterion need provide only identifying conditions, not identity conditions, and thus would not yield circularity. Another and better reply is to restate (D) so that no commitment is made to the claim that all causes and all effects are events; namely,

(D') For any e and any f, if e and f are events, then $e = f$ iff $(x)(xCe \equiv xCf)$ & $(y)(eCy \equiv fCy)$.

Although the claim that all causes and effects are events is highly plausible, it is not uncontroversial. Some philosophers hold that states, dispositions, and processes can be causes or effects (cf. Vendler, 1967); some hold that states of affairs can be causally related; and some hold that substances, including human agents, can be causes (e.g., Chisholm, 1976). This reformulation captures Davidson's thesis that identity conditions are in terms of sameness of causes and effects without commitment to the claim that all causes and all effects are events.

A more serious problem for Davidson's proposal stems from the possibility of ineffectual events. Let an ineffectual event be an event that has neither causes nor effects. Thus according to (D'), all ineffectual events are identical; or equivalently, there is at most one ineffectual event. But it would seem that there can be indefinitely many such events. A related problem is this. Suppose that, first, a physical object does not interact with any other object during a temporal interval and that, second, it undergoes fission and its resulting parts fuse during that interval. There are two events occurring. One event consists of the history of the original object, the motion of one part of the split object and the fused particle. The other event consists of the history of the original object, the motion of the other part of the split object and the fused physical object. These are distinct events because, at some times, they involve distinct objects.

One response, and one that Davidson once suggested, is to say that universal causal determinism is necessarily true.[11] In that case there cannot be ineffectual events; and there are no physical objects that do not interact with some others at every moment. However, this response is inadequate. It is controversial whether universal causal determinism is in fact true. But more importantly, it is extremely implausible that it is necessarily true: it would be very difficult to argue successfully that there *cannot* be ineffectual events. Moreover, even if there are no physical objects that behave in the manner cited in the actual world, there could be physical objects that so behave. It is simply a mistake to rest identity conditions for events on the unlikely thesis that universal causal determinism is *necessarily* true.

Kim (1970, 1973, 1976) holds that events have a uniform internal structure (also see Goldman, 1970). That structure of events consists in physical objects exemplifying properties during times. It is natural then that identity conditions for events be in terms of identity of internal structure. In this regard Kim fundamentally disagrees with both the necessary spatiotemporal coincidence and causal accounts.

The heart of Kim's view can be reformulated as follows:

(K1) For any e, if e is an event, then there is a physical object x, a property F, and a duration t, such that $e = [x,F,t]$;

(K2) For any $[x,F,t]$ and $[y,G,t']$, if $[x,F,t]$ and $[y,G,t']$ are events, then $[x,F,t] = [y,G,t']$ iff $x = y$ & $F = G$ & $t = t'$.

That is, according to (K1), events are structured particulars, consisting of physical objects, properties, and times; and according to (K2), sameness of constituent physical objects, properties, and times is sufficient for event identity. (Actually, (K1) and (K2) concern only 'monadic' events, that is, events consisting of one physical object and one property. Kim (1973) has extended this view to 'n-adic' events; but since this more general formulation introduces complications without substantive change, I shall discuss only the restricted version given by (K1) and (K2).)

There are several difficulties for these identity conditions. First, it is not clear what significance the brackets, '[...],' have. If they are a notational variant of '⟨...⟩,' then they stand for ordered triples. If so, events are sets, and hence abstract particulars, not concrete ones. It sometimes seems that Kim would not object to viewing events as abstract particulars (e.g., 1976, pp. 160–162). But events are things in the world, that is, concrete. On the whole Kim favors this latter viewpoint. The brackets, then, should be interpreted as merely abbreviatory, and without ontological significance. An event occurs just in case a physical object exemplifies a property during a time: "[T]he theory states that just in case a substance x has property P at t, there is an event whose constitutive object is x, whose constitutive property is P, and whose time of occurrence is t" (1976, p. 161).

Second, Kim's identity conditions for events (K2) presupposes identity conditions for physical objects, properties, and durations. Of these, identity conditions for properties are extremely difficult to formulate correctly (see Achinstein, 1974). However, this difficulty is not telling. It is really too much to require that Kim provide adequate identity conditions for properties. Rather it suffices to point out that solutions to a number of key philosophical problems—for example, the relationship between mental and physical states, scientific theory reduction, and meaning change—depend on an adequate account of property identity. By partially assimilating identity conditions for events to identity conditions for properties, some progress has been made.

Third, on Kim's view all events involve physical objects (or "substances"). However, some events do not involve physical objects: for instance, there are lightning flashes, changes in the strengths of fields, odor changes, and so on. This difficulty is somewhat more serious than the previous two. In order to countenance these events, the theory must be amended. The best suggestion is to replace (K1) and (K2) with the following:

(K1') For any e, if e is an event, then there is a spatiotemporal region r and a property F such that $e = [r,F]$;

(K2') For any $[r_1,F]$ and $[r_2,G]$, if $[r_1,F]$ and $[r_2,G]$ are events, then $[r_1,F] = [r_2,G]$ iff $r_1 = r_2$ & $F = G$.

An event occurs just in case a property is exemplified within a spatiotemporal region; event identity consists in sameness of spatiotemporal regions and properties. When a physical object is involved in an event, then the spatiotemporal region of the event is the region occupied by the physical object. According to (K1') and (K2') then, there can be events not involving physical objects.

This amendment significantly alters the ontological picture. On Kim's original version, events and physical objects are particulars; but physical objects are ontologically more fundamental than events, since events could not exist if physical objects did not. On the amended version, events and physical objects are particulars, though neither one is more fundamental than the other: events could exist even if physical objects did not, and conversely. The amended version is closer to the informal picture presented earlier than is Kim's original proposal.[12]

There is another objection to the property exemplification account, and one that defeats it. Kim does not provide a criterion for which properties can be constitutive of events; that is, he does not specify the range of F in (K1), or (K1'). Clearly some properties will not do: for example, being self-identical, being a nonevent, being equal to $\sqrt{2}$, being identical with Socrates. These properties surely are not constituents of events. In other cases it is not clear whether the properties are constituents of events; for instance, being red, being a fast running, being identical with that table. Kim holds that being red is an event constituent because he thinks that there is no significant difference between states of physical objects and events involving change. Kim also holds that being a fast running is not constitutive of events. Rather being a running is constitutive and being fast is a property of events. He does not comment on properties like being identical with that table, though presumably he would hold that they are not constitutive of any event. Now what is *the underlying principle* for making these divisions between properties constitutive of events and those that are not event-making properties? Kim does not provide one. Sometimes he uses low-level generalizations to draw special cases of this distinction: for example, there is, he claims, no significant difference between states of physical objects and events involving change. But what is the underlying rationale for the adoption of these low-level generalizations? The point of these questions is this: in order to specify the underlying principle for being constitutive of events, a conceptually significant property of events must be delineated; and that is tantamount to providing identity conditions for events in terms other than their structure.

To put the criticism again, Kim gives identity conditions for events in terms of their internal structure. The internal structure of a (monadic) event is a physical object's having a property during a time. But (K1) must be supplemented by a principle specifying the range of event-making properties. That principle depends on the external relations into which events enter, not their structure alone. And it is that principle that would specify the conceptually significant property of events. Statement (K2), or (K2'), might be true, but it does not provide adequate identity conditions for events.

At one point Kim suggests—though without full endorsement—a principle for specifying the range of event-making properties. He says that these properties

> may be best picked out relative to a scientific theory, whether the theory is a commonsense theory of the behavior of middle-sized objects or a highly sophisticated physical theory. They are among the important properties, relative to the theory, in terms of which lawful regularities can be discovered, described, and explained. (1976, p. 162)

This view is reminiscent of Davidson's. The conceptually significant property of events is that they are covered by natural laws. The low-level generalization that states and events are the same follows from this view, since no distinction between them is made in scientific theory. However, this view is problematic. It is not clear whether every event is covered by natural law. It seems doubtful that there will be covering-law theories for casual conversation, grocery shopping, artistic innovation, or so on. Perhaps the thought is that some science, maybe physics, will eventually explain all events. At best that is an unrealized future possibility. Most likely it is simply false. Moreover Kim's view is not adequate to the claim that events *could* occur in nonlawful situations. Expressed another way, there are possible worlds in which there are events but which lack nomologi-

cal regularities governing these events. Being covered by a nomo-
logical regularity is an accidental feature of events, not one that
specifies a conceptually significant property.

4. The Semantical Interpretation of Identity Conditions for Events

The identity conditions for events have been stated in terms of necessary spatiotemporal coincidence, that is, repeating,

(D3.2) $(e)(f)$[if e and f are events, then $e = f$ iff $\Box(r)(e0r \equiv f0r)$].

This statement meets the constraints (C1)–(C5) on identity conditions, and is not subject to the objections confronting Davidson's or
Kim's proposals. But (D3.2) leaves unresolved something important:
it is, as it stands, a schema. It does not say what can be substituted
for the variables e and f, and thus does not by itself yield a criterion
for true event-identity sentences. Statement (D3.2) must be supplemented with a semantical principle for applying these conditions.

   The semantical criterion for true event-identity sentences is best
stated using metavariables ranging over standardized event-desig-
nating singular terms. Let a *complete canonical event description* be a
singular term of the form

(15) x's Fing occupies r,

or some tensed or colloquial variant of it, where 'x' is replaced by a
name or definite description of a physical object (including a person), 'r' by a name or other referring expression of a spatiotemporal
region, and where 'F' is a predicate expression. An instance of (15) is
'Nixon's resigning on January 20, 1973 in the oval office.' A *canonical
event description* has the form (15), except that the component referring to the spatiotemporal region, "occupies r," can be suppressed.

   The form (15) is not fully general, and thus the resultant semantical
criterion will not be applicable to all event-identity sentences. Descriptions of the form (15) are 'monadic.' A more general form can be
used, in which n ⩾ 1 physical objects are named and in which 'F' is
replaced by an n-adic predicate. But for the present purposes, the
gain in generality is outweighed by the increase in complexity.
Similarly the form 'r's Fing' might be used in place of (15): that form
would have the advantage of accommodating event descriptions not
involving physical objects. However, though covering a wider range
of cases, the form 'r's Fing' can produce unnatural English instances.
For our current purposes we can ignore event descriptions not making reference to physical objects.

   There remains one important point to make about the canonical
form (15). It does *not* follow from the claim that events are canonically

described by (15) that the nature of an event is a physical object's exemplifying a property during a time. It is one project to describe events in a uniform way; but it is quite another project to specify the nature of events. The form of description is not necessarily tied to its ontological status.

Now a first metalinguistic rendering of (D3.2) is:

(D3.3) For any two canonical event descriptions α and β, $\ulcorner \alpha = \beta \urcorner$ is true iff $\ulcorner \Box(r)(\alpha 0 r \equiv \beta 0 r) \urcorner$ is true.

Consider the following event-identity sentence:[13]

(16) Mark Twain's dying = Samuel Clemens's dying.

Given (D3.3), (16) is equivalent to

(17) Necessarily, for every spatiotemporal region r, Mark Twain's dying occupies r iff Samuel Clemens's dying occupies r.

Since (17) is true, (16) is true. So far, so good.

But consider

(18) Nixon's resigning = the 37th President's resigning.

Sentence (18) is true. On the basis of (D3.3), (18) is true just in case the following is true:

(19) Necessarily, for every spatiotemporal region r, Nixon's resigning occupies r iff the 37th President's resigning occupies r.

But (19) is false. There is a world in which Nixon resigns but the person who is the thirty-seventh President does not; and conversely there is a world in which the thirty-seventh President resigns but the person who is Nixon does not. As Tye (1979) has pointed out, a similar problem arises for the predicate component of a canonical event description. To use his example, suppose that 'Agnes' names Adam's car. Then,

(20) Adam's painting Agnes red = Adam's painting Agnes the color of most fire engines

is true; but

(21) Necessarily, for every spatiotemporal region r, Adam's painting Agnes red occupies r iff Adam's painting Agnes the color of most fire engines occupies r

is false. It is false because there are possible worlds in which most fire engines are, say, green; and thus it is possible that Adam paint his car red without painting it the color of most fire engines.

The problem presented by both of these examples is the same. The event-identity sentences (18) and (20) contain definite descriptions referring to objects in the actual world. For the sentences (19) and (21) to be true, these same objects must be picked out in every world. But they are not. In order to deal with this problem, (D3.3) must be amended.

Kripke (1972) calls a singular term *rigid* just in case it picks out the same individual in every possible world—in every counterfactual situation—in which it names anything at all. Given Kripke's treatment of singular terms, 'Nixon' is rigid, but 'the 37th President' is not. To account for the previous examples, then, we should rigidify the contained singular terms occurring in event-identity sentences. One way to achieve this result is to adapt a device of David Kaplan's (1979): let $Dthat\ (\alpha) = \alpha^+$ be a function that rigidifies contained singular terms. More carefully, let α be a complex singular term containing one or more descriptions or names, and let α^+ be the result of applying $Dthat$ to all the names and descriptions contained in α. Then, if all the descriptions and names contained in α are rigid, α is α^+; if some or all of the descriptions and names contained in α are not rigid, then α^+ is exactly like α except where α contains nonrigid descriptions or names, α^+ contains rigid descriptions picking out the objects designated in the actual world by the names or descriptions contained in α.

Using this function, the semantic criterion can be reformulated as follows:

(D3.3') For any two canonical event descriptions α and β, if α^+ and β^+ are rigid, then $\ulcorner\alpha = \beta\urcorner$ is true iff $\ulcorner\Box(r)(\alpha^+0r \equiv \beta^+0r\urcorner$ is true.

(See Horgan, 1980.) This reformulated criterion gives the correct results for the above cases. According to it, (18) is true just in case

(22) Necessarily, for every spatiotemporal region r, (Nixon's resigning)$^+$ occupies r iff (the 37th President's resigning)$^+$ occupies r

is true; and (22) is true. Similarly, (20) is true just in case

(23) Necessarily, for every spatiotemporal region r, (Adam's painting Agnes red)$^+$ occupies r iff (Adam's painting Agnes the color of most fire engines)$^+$ occupies r

is true; and (23) is true. The *Dthat* function rigidifies all contained singular terms, including those occurring in the predicate part of the expression.

It is worth emphasizing that *Dthat* rigidifies the *contained* singular terms, not the entire canonical event designator (see Brand, 1979). If *Dthat* froze the reference of the entire canonical event designator to the actual world, there would be unfortunate consequences. Suppose that it were claimed that '$\alpha = \beta$' is true for some canonical event designators α and β. It would not help, in that case, to consider other worlds—or counterfactual situations—in order to determine the truth of '$\alpha = \beta$.' By rigidifying the entire event designators, it is not possible that α^+ and β^+ be coreferential in the actual world but not in all possible worlds. Thus whatever difficulties there are in ascertaining the truth of '$\alpha = \beta$' in the actual world would be transferred to other possible worlds. A semantical criterion constructed on the assumption that the entire event designating term be rigidified, then, would be useless in determining the truth-value of many event-identity sentences (cf. Tye, 1979 and Feldman and Wierenga, 1981).[14]

Some *Dthat*ed event designators are not rigid. Consider

(24) Frank's running the mile as fast as Bill,

which *Dthat*ed yields

(24+) (Frank's running the mile as fast as Bill)+.

All the contained names and descriptions in (24+) are rigid. Yet (24+) is not itself rigid. Since Bill might run a 3:59 mile in one world, a 4:00 mile in another, and so on, this event designator picks out different events in different worlds. Compare (24) with

(25) Frank's running a 4:00 mile,

which *Dthat*ed is,

(25+) (Frank's running a 4:00 mile)+.

All the contained names and descriptions in (25+) are rigid; and in this case (25+) itself is rigid. One way to see the difference between (24) and (25) is that whether (25) refers depends only on Frank's abilities and opportunities, whereas whether (24) refers depends not only on Frank's abilities and opportunities but also on Bill's abilities and opportunities.

Predicates are not names and thus, properly speaking, are neither rigid nor nonrigid. But something analogous to being rigid obtains in the case of predicates. Some predicates are, I shall say, *semantically world-independent*, such as 'running a 4:00 mile'; others are semantically world-dependent, such as 'running as fast as Bill.' In every counterfactual situation, the predicate 'running a 4:00 mile' expresses the same property. But the predicate 'running as fast as Bill' does not express the same property in every counterfactual situation: the property expressed depends on how fast Bill ran in that counterfactual situation; in one situation it expresses the property of running a 3:59 mile, and in another it expresses the property of running a 4:00 mile and so on. More formally, the intension of the monadic predicate 'running a 4:00 mile' can be taken as a function from possible worlds into sets of individuals; but the intension of the monadic predicate 'running as fast as Bill' should be taken as a function from possible worlds into an ordered pair consisting of sets of individuals and an individual (or an individual concept). In detail,

(SD) For any monadic predicate ϕ, ϕ is semantically world-dependent *iff* there is a predicate ψ such that $\ulcorner \Box(x)(r)[x\text{'s } \phi\text{ing}$ occupying r occurs $\supset (\exists y)(\exists r')(x \neq y$ & $y\text{'s } \psi\text{ing occupying } r'$ occurs)]$\urcorner$ is true,

where 'x' and 'y' are replaced by names or descriptions of objects and 'r' and 'r''' by names or descriptions of spatiotemporal regions. A monadic predicate is semantically world-independent just in case it is not semantically world-dependent. Thus, for example, 'running as fast as Bill' is semantically world-dependent because Frank's running as fast as Bill occurs only if Bill's running occurs.

Let us say that a canonical event description is rigid just in case its contained names and descriptions are rigid *and* its contained predicate expressions are semantically world-independent. Thus not all canonical event descriptions are rigid; and the antecedent of (D3.3') is not trivially satisfied. But as a consequence, definition (D3.3') has limited applicability; it provides truth conditions only for event-identity sentences containing rigid canonical event descriptions. As I mentioned, this semantical criterion is limited in scope.

Consider now the following event-identity sentence:

(26) Stravinsky's lowering his arm = Stravinsky's signaling to the cellos.

As Horgan (1980) correctly observes, the truth or falsity of (26) has important ramifications for the theory of events. This sentence identifies a person's physical activity—his lowering his arm—with his doing something that is governed by convention—his signaling. If (26) and its ilk are true, then a course-grained theory results; but if (26) and its ilk are false, then a fine-grained theory results. A fine-grained theory countenances more events than a course-grained one.

According to (D3.3'), (26) is false. 'Lowering his arm' and 'signaling to the cellos' are semantically world-independent predicates; thus (26) is true if and only if

(27) Necessarily, for every spatiotemporal region r, (Stravinsky's lowering his arm)$^+$ occupies r iff (Stravinsky's signaling to the cellos)$^+$ occupies r.

But (27) is false. There are possible worlds in which Stravinsky lowers his arm and does not signal to the cellos, for there are worlds in which the convention of signaling by lowering one's arm does not obtain. Similarly there are possible worlds in which Stravinsky signals to the cellos without lowering his arm, for there are worlds in which there are conventions for signaling that do not include lowering one's arm.

Although a fine-grained account does not identify Stravinsky's lowering his arm with his signaling to the cellos, a reasonable version of such a theory will take these events to be related. Goldman (1970), for instance, holds a fine-grained theory for human actions in which he recognizes several generation relations, three synchronic and one diachronic (causal); and Kim (1974), whose view closely resembles Goldman's, suggests that in the case of nonactional events, additional generational relations may be needed. Toumela (1977), in contrast, holds that two relations, a causal one and a conceptual one, are sufficient. A complete fine-grained theory of events would have to provide a detailed account of these generational relations. I shall not attempt to do so.

This much should be said, however. A fine-grained account must hold that there is at least one synchronic relation among events, whereas a course-grained account appears able to do without such a relation. One candidate for this relation, as I mentioned in an earlier chapter, is conventional generation, broadly understood. Event e conventionally generates event f just in case e is distinct from f and the occurrence of e in circumstances C (possibly null) together with conventional rules R is sufficient for the occurrence of f. Thus, for example, Stravinsky's lowering his arm conventionally generates his signaling to the cellos, since there is a rule saying that conductors signal to cello players *by* lowering their arms. Note that conventional generation is an asymmetrical relation in virtue of the rules R: conventional rules are formulated using a by-locution.

Finally, let me consider one objection to this account. The event-designator

(28) (Stravinsky's signaling to the cellos)$^+$,

Horgan contends (1980), is a nonrigid description of Stravinsky's baton-lowering. It designates the baton-lowering in the actual world, but not in every possible world. "[L]ike other nonrigid designators, it refers to an entity (the [arm]-lowering) by citing an *accidental* feature of that entity: the feature of being a cello-signaling" (p. 347). (Cf. Tye, 1979, and Feldman and Wierenga, 1981.) If it is correct that (28) is nonrigid, then (D3.3') is not applicable; and thus even if (28) is nonrigid, it would not follow on the proposed semantical criterion that (27) is false.

The reply is simply that (28) is rigid. The contained singular terms 'Stravinsky' and 'the cello' are rigid—the latter because of the *Dthat*-ing operation. And the contained predicate expression 'signaling to the cellos' is semantically world-independent. There is some temptation to think that this predicate expression is semantically world-dependent because there appears to be another event, the cellos being signaled to, which is necessary for the occurrence of Stravinsky's signaling to the cellos. But someone can signal without being successful. I have often signaled to taxi drivers and waiters in vain; and similarly Stravinsky could signal to the cellos without their being signaled.

It might be retorted that, even if all the contained singular terms are rigid and even if the predicate expression is semantically world-independent, the canonical event designator can be nonrigid; and in particular, (28) is nonrigid. But this response begs the question. It must be shown that (28) nonrigidly designates Stravinsky's lowering his arm; and that has not been done—indeed, if I am right, it *cannot* be done.

5. Mental Events

I take it that there are mental events. As I mentioned, this claim is neither entirely uncontroversial nor necessary to generate an action theory. Radical behaviorists in psychology, such as Watson and Skinner, hold that there are no mental events: all behavior can be explained by complexes of stimulus-response connections. The philosophical counterpart to radical behaviorism is eliminative materialism, on one version of which talk of mental events is meaningless. However, without argument, I assume that these radical theories are false. There are, I take it, mental events and these events play a role in the production of behavior.

One important consequence of the event theory detailed here is that it provides identity conditions for mental events. These identity conditions are independent of a theory about the relationship between the mental and the physical. Moreover the semantical criterion for event-identity sentences is applicable to mental events. Consider the following event-identity sentences.

(29) Lincoln's now desiring to attend the play this evening = Lincoln's now believing that he will attend the play this evening.

(30) Lincoln's now believing that he will attend the play this evening = Lincoln's now believing that he will be shot this evening.

(31) Lincoln's now believing that he will be shot this evening = Lincoln's now believing that the sixteenth President will be shot this evening.

(32) Lincoln's now believing that Cicero was a Roman orator = Lincoln's now believing that Tully was a Roman orator.

These event-identity sentences are all false. Desiring to do something is basically favoring or preferring to do it, while believing that one will do something is predicting that one will do it. Although Lincoln simultaneously desires to attend the theater and believes that he will, two distinct events are occurring. Similarly Lincoln's belief that he will attend the theater and his belief that he will be shot, though simultaneous, are distinct. Moreover his belief that he will be shot is distinct from his belief that the sixteenth President will be shot; and his belief that Cicero was a Roman orator is distinct from his belief that Tully was a Roman orator.

The event designators 'Lincoln's now desiring to attend the theater this evening,' 'Lincoln's now believing that he will attend the theater this evening,' 'Lincoln's now believing that he will be shot this evening,' and so on, are rigid, since the contained descriptions are rigid and the predicate expressions are semantically world-independent. It follows from (D3.3'), then, that (29) to (32) are false just in case the corresponding necessity statements are false. Consider the first and third of these statements.

(33) Necessarily, for every spatiotemporal region r, (Lincoln's now desiring to attend the theater this evening)$^+$ occupies r iff (Lincoln's now believing that he will attend the theater this evening)$^+$ occupies r.

(34) Necessarily, for every spatiotemporal region r, (Lincoln's now believing that he will be shot this evening)$^+$ occupies r iff (Lincoln's now believing that the 16th President will be shot this evening)$^+$ occupies r.

There are possible worlds in which Lincoln desires to attend the theater but does not believe that he will, and conversely. Similarly there are possible worlds in which Lincoln believes that he will be shot this evening but not that the sixteenth President will be shot, and conversely; for there are some worlds in which he fails to think that *he* is the sixteenth President. Likewise the corresponding necessity statement for (32) is false; for there are possible worlds in which Lincoln fails to realize that Cicero is Tully.

These results are welcome, since they accord with common intuition. There is a problem, however, that requires attention. Truth values can be assigned to (33) and (34) and similar statements, only if sense can be made of locating mental events spatiotemporally. With regard to the temporal parameters, it is not more problematic to determine temporal location for mental events than it is for physical events. That is, there are no *special* problems about the temporal location of mental events. The central issue in applying (D3.3′) to mental events concerns spatial location.

Although persons are likely not the only things in which mental events occur, let us, for simplicity, restrict attention to them. There are in that case four significant hypotheses about the spatial location of mental events, not all of which are mutually exclusive.

(H1) Mental events do not have spatial locations.

(H2) For any person S, the spatial location of a mental event of S is identical with the spatial location of some brain event of S.

(H3) For any person S, the spatial location of a mental event of S is identical with the spatial location of S's body.

(H4) For any person S, the spatial location of a mental event of S is identical with the spatial location of S.

Hypothesis (H1) would be defended by Cartesians and other dualists. Dualist theories take physical events, but not mental events, to be spatially locatable. Thus the spatial location of all mental events is, trivially, the same. And hence, a mental event-identity sentence is true just in case the event designators refer to cotemporal events in every possible world. If hypothesis (H1) is true, then (33) and (34) are false. There are, for instance, possible worlds in which Lincoln's now desiring to attend the play occurs but his believing that he will attend does not, and hence, trivially, the times of these events are distinct. The key point is that the truth of (H1) is compatible with applying (D3.3′) to mental events.

Hypothesis (H1), however, presents some difficulties. Mental events are not abstract entities; they are not like numbers or sets. Mental events like physical events are things in the world. It is difficult to conceive of something being in the world, and yet not occupying some spatial region. Hypothesis (H1) in short makes mental events into something mysterious: they are not abstract objects, yet they are not spatially locatable. This issue has always confronted dualists. (Notice that this problem is not alleviated even if events were construed as states of affairs or propositions. Although mental events would be abstract on that view, their occurrences nevertheless would be things in the world. Hypothesis (H1) would then be reconstrued as saying that particular occurrences of mental events do not have spatial location, and *that* hypothesis is implausible.)

The token-token Identity Theory, stated baldly, says that every mental event is identical with some physical event. If these physical events are brain events, then the location of a mental event is identical with the location of a brain event; that is, (H2) obtains. Observe that if (H2) obtains, (33) and (34) are false. There are, for instance, possible worlds in which the brain event that is Lincoln's desiring to attend the play occupies a spatiotemporal region not occupied by the brain event that is Lincoln's believing that he will attend. In fact (33) and (34) appear to be false in the actual world, given hypothesis (H2). The neurological event that is Lincoln's desiring to attend the theater, it would seem, does not involve the identical spatial region as the neurological event that is Lincoln's believing that he will attend.

One difficulty for (H2) is that it locates mental events too restrictively. Lincoln's desiring to attend the play is something that happens in space; but it is odd to think that that spatial location is within a minute part of Lincoln's skull. Rather the location of Lincoln's desiring to attend the theater seems not to be entirely localized; indeed it is not implausible to think that it involves some of the space occupied by the central nervous system, and perhaps his limbs, facial features, and so on. This consideration suggests hypothesis (H3). Note that (H3) is also consistent with the token-token Identity Theory, since the physical events with which mental events are identical need not be restricted to occurrences within the brain.

But Hypothesis (H3) might not provide the right 'fit.' On the one hand, it seems too permissive. In some cases it will include parts of a person's body that are irrelevant to his mental state. For instance, the minute regulatory changes in Lincoln's spleen might well be unconnected with his desiring to attend the theater. And on the other hand, (H3) seems too restrictive. Some physical objects, not strictly part of a person's body, might be so intimately connected with him that they are involved with his mental events. It is not entirely implausible, for example, that if Lincoln were to have had lengths of filament substituted for some central nerves, these physical objects would be, somehow, involved with his mental events.

Hypothesis (H4) provides a better fit. It might be thought that a person is identical with his body: in that case (H4) reduces to (H3). But that is implausible. Some physical objects might be part of that person; and conversely, some bodily parts, such as an unknown and ineffectual birthmark on the roof of one's mouth, are not part of the person. Or it might be thought that a person is identical with his mental events: in that case (H4) is not helpful for spatially locating mental events. But that too is implausible. A person, as Strawson (1959) forcefully argued, has physical attributes. It might be that a person occupies the same space as his brain, central nervous system, and vital organs. Admittedly a deep analysis of personhood is required to determine the force of (H4). But even without that analysis—on the basis only of preanalytic intuition—hypothesis (H4) is the most attractive.

Although (H4) is attractive, more so than (H2) or (H3), it is not necessary to decide among them. On each, (33) and (34) are false. Each provides a basis for applying (D3.3') to mental events. In summary, the main points are that all events, including mental ones, are spatiotemporal, that identity conditions for events are to be given in terms of necessary spatiotemporal coincidence, and (D3.3') provides truth conditions for many event-identity sentences, including some that contain descriptions referring to mental events.

4

The Objects of Mental Attitudes

I take a mental attitude to be a mental event that has an object. Thus, for example, believing and hoping are mental attitudes, but being in pain and feeling anxious are not. This stipulation does not correspond to some definitions put forward by philosophers and psychologists; but it does yield a general designation for an important class of mental phenomena.[1]

In this chapter I shall focus on believing, desiring, and intending. I assume now, but attempt to justify later, that these attitudes are irreducibly distinct. Though believing, desiring, and intending are not the only mental attitudes, they are the most important ones from the perspective of clarifying the nature of human action. Many other attitudes are analyzable in terms of these and I shall make brief suggestions for some analyses in the next chapter. It is unclear, however, whether all mental attitudes are so analyzable: certain weak cognitive attitudes, for example, assuming, entertaining, and considering, seem not to be.

One focal issue of this chapter is the ontological status of the objects of attitudes. This issue has ramifications for another focal one: marking the differences between the attitudes. My point of departure is the work of Hector-Neri Castañeda (especially 1975). My final view, however, is substantially different from Castañeda's, and owes much to Lewis (1979) and Chisholm (1979, 1981). In the first section I contrast Castañeda's approach to the traditional one. The traditional approach takes intending, desiring, and believing to be different attitudes toward propositions. The second section deals with Castañeda's primary objections to the traditional view. In the third section I take exception to Castañeda's constructive view; and in the next three sections I defend an alternative. The objects of mental attitudes, I will argue, are properties. That is, all attitudes, including attitudes about oneself, physical objects, other persons, and abstract objects, can be analyzed in terms of attitudes that take properties as objects.

1. Object-Assimilationism versus Attitude-Assimilationism

Two general approaches can be distinguished for characterizing the differences between believing, intending, and desiring. The first— which I label *object-assimilationism* — is that all attitudes have the same objects but are different types of attitudes toward these objects. The second general approach—which I label *attitude-assimilationism* — is that believing, intending, and desiring have different objects but are the same type of attitude toward these objects. Put again, suppose that the general form of an attitude and its object is expressed by 'ψ (x).' Then object-assimilationism distinguishes between believing, intending, and desiring by altering the values for 'ψ' while holding 'x' constant; and attitude-assimilationism distinguishes between believing, intending, and desiring by altering the values for 'x' while holding 'ψ' constant.

Object-assimilationism has enjoyed great popularity. The objects are usually taken to be propositions, or their kin. Indeed these attitudes are often called 'propositional attitudes.' It is to be noted, however, that this general approach is not committed to the common objects being propositions; they may be objects of some other ontological category.

Propositional object-assimilationism until recently has been part of the philosophical lore. Consider

(1) Richard believes that Lincoln was the sixteenth President.

According to this view, that-clauses name propositions. Thus the object of Richard's belief is the proposition that Lincoln was the sixteenth President. Statements of intending and desiring might also be expressed using that-clauses. For instance:

(2) Richard intends that there be turkey for Thanksgiving dinner.

(3) Richard desires that there will be peace on earth.

Surface grammar points to the objects being propositions in (2) and (3). Sometimes, however, the surface grammar suggests otherwise. For example:

(4) Richard intends to vote in the next election.

(5) Richard wants Pat to vote in the next election.

The propositional object-assimilationist claims, however, that (4) and (5) can be paraphrased as:

(4a) Richard intends that he vote in the next election.

(5a) Richard desires that Pat vote in the next election.

Under these paraphrases the objects of Richard's intention and desire are the proposition that Richard vote in the next election and the proposition that Pat vote in the next election.

Although it is not clear exactly what propositions are, there is general agreement about their main features. These features are:

(i) propositions are abstract (that is, nonspatiotemporal);

(ii) propositions are structured in some way that corresponds to or matches declarative sentences;

(iii) propositions are the bearers of truth and falsity;

(iv) propositions are person-independent and context-independent.

Of course not everyone holds that there are propositions; and some who hold that there are propositions will not agree that they have all these features. Those who identify propositions with sets of possible worlds, for instance, do not hold that the structure of a proposition corresponds to that of an indicative sentence. But generally speaking, there is a tradition, which includes Frege as a prominent member, which takes it that there are propositions and that they have these features. This is the 'orthodox view' of propositions.

Since it postulates uniformity of objects, object-assimilationism permits straightforward understanding of sentences such as:

(6) Richard intended what Pat predicted.

(7) Pat did not want what Richard intended.

According to the propositional version of this approach, (6) says that there is a proposition such that Richard intended to make it true and such that Pat believed that it will be true; and (7) says that there is a proposition such that Pat did not want it to be true and such that Richard intended to make it true. I take it that this capacity to make straightforward sense of claims about sameness or difference of attitudes is the most compelling reason for an object-assimilationism.

Castañeda has argued for attitude-assimilationism (see especially 1975, 1976, 1980).[2] He holds that the objects of believing and intending belong to different ontological categories. The objects of desiring are the same type as those of intending, since both desiring and intending are essentially practical attitudes. A complete attitude-assimilationism would assign different types of objects to desiring and intending, since, as I will argue later, desiring and intending are irreducibly distinct.

According to Castañeda, the psychological attitude common to intending, desiring, and believing is full endorsement of the object of that attitude. He holds that other attitudes are generated when there is less than full endorsement. For instance, considering is like believing in having the same kind of object, but differs from it in being only partial endorsement; similarly aiming to is like intending in having the same kind of object, but differs from it in being partial endorsement. It may be that some cognitive attitudes are not cases of endorsement, even partial endorsement, for instance assuming (in the process of a *reductio* argument) and merely entertaining (for the sake of illustration). Let us, however, restrict ourselves to believing, desiring, and intending, where Castañeda's view is most plausible.

The objects of belief are orthodox propositions. The objects of intending and desiring are not propositions but rather *practitions*. A practition seems to have the same ontological status as a proposition; but it differs from a proposition in two important respects: its structure and its semantical values. Propositional structure mirrors declarative sentences; the subject is often connected to the predicate by a copula, a form of the verb 'to be.' Practitional structure mirrors sentences in which the subject is connected to the predicate in a different way. For example, in 'Rose Mary, shut off the recorder,' Rose Mary is to bring about what is expressed by the verb phrase, 'shut off the recorder.' This structure is also illustrated by the sentences 'It is obligatory for Pat to vote' and 'I want Richard to apologize.' In these cases the result of deleting the deontic and affective terms yields 'Pat to vote' and 'Richard to apologize,' which indicate that the agents are to bring about the action types named by the verb phrases. Castañeda expresses this point by saying that there is a practitional copula, different from the ordinary copula, that connects the subject term with the verb phrase. Linguists do not recognize more than one type of copula, and thus Castañeda's mode of explanation is misleading. But bracketing that, his primary point remains: there are constructions in English that connect a subject with an action type to be brought about. These constructions are the linguistic counterparts to practitions. Turning to semantical values, practitions are neither true nor false. Rather they are, in Castañeda's terms, legitimate or illegitimate. A practition is legitimate, roughly, when it is required in the context of the agent's hierarchy of ends and the ends of other persons he considers important. In short, practitions and propositions share the features of being abstract and context-independent, but differ with respect to the features of internal structure and semantical values.

There are first-person, second-person and third-person practitions. The object of an intention, Castañeda maintains, is a first-person practition, which he calls 'an intended' (1980). He claims that first-person practitions are not reducible to second- or third-person ones. Second- and third-person practitions are prescriptions. Unlike the objects of intending, the objects of desiring can be either first-, second-, or third-person practitions. Thus I can want to go to the polls, in which the object is 'I to go to the polls'; or I can want Pat to go to the polls, in which the object is the third-person practition 'Pat to go to the polls.'

Underlying Castañeda's theory is the claim that features of mental attitudes—what's happening in the head, as it were—can be derived from features of ascriptions of mental attitudes. For example, features of belief can be garnered from belief-ascribing sentences. This view is the consequence of a more general one, which I label *the Fregean Presumption*: natural language and thought are structurally similar. A great deal of recent work in the philosophy of language and mind is based on the Fregean Presumption. It is, moreover, highly plausible. The expressive power of thought must be at least that of natural language: we are able to think all that we say. One natural explanation is that the relevant structural features of language are isomorphic to thought. Of course the representational system of thought might differ considerably—and no doubt does—from that of natural language. Thus the structural similarities might appear, say, only at the deep level of logical form. But at whatever level these similarities appear, it is plausible to think that thought and natural language are isomorphic with respect to primary structural features.

The Fregean Presumption has a way of taking hold. As a result there is easy movement—and sometimes, confusion—between the structures of natural language and thought. For instance, existential generalization and substitutivity of identicals are often taken to be tests for sentence transparency. From 'Richard believes that John is a friend,' it cannot be deduced that John exists, nor, with the addition of 'John = the least loyal person,' can it be deduced that Richard believes that the least loyal person is a friend. Although some belief sentences are opaque, it is a mistake to say then that some *beliefs*, which are mental events, are opaque. Rather the Fregean Presumption warrants only the claim that beliefs are isomorphic in some way to ascriptions of belief, not that they have precisely the same properties. There are two types of beliefs, corresponding to the distinction

between transparent and opaque belief sentences; but beliefs themselves do not exhibit the logical features of belief ascriptions.[3]

2. The Problem of Self-Referentiality

One way to object to propositional object-assimilationism is to argue
that propositions do not exist, at least under the orthodox construal.
For my part I have not found convincing arguments to sustain this
objection. But this is not the place to pursue that issue. Rather I shall
focus on a different objection to propositional object-assimilationism. This objection, first raised by Castañeda, concerns the self-
referentiality of certain attitudes. (See Castañeda, 1966, 1967, 1968,
1969, 1975, especially chapter 6; also see Perry, 1977, 1979, Lewis,
1979, and Chisholm, 1979, 1980, 1981.)

Consider the following:

(8) Richard believes that he is married to Pat.

According to propositional object-assimilationism, the object of
Richard's belief is a proposition. But is it? 'That he is married to Pat'
does not name a proposition. One feature of a proposition is that its
truth value is context-independent; but the truth value of 'that he is
married to Pat' is not context-independent. 'That he is married to Pat'
seems to name a propositional function in which 'he' functions as an
unbound variable.

It might be thought that (8) can be paraphrased so that the object of
Richard's belief is a proposition. A first attempt might be:

(9) Richard believes that Richard is married to Pat.

But (8) can be true while (9) is false if for some reason Richard does
not realize that he is Richard. For instance, circumstances might be
such that he thinks that Richard has certain distinctive features such
as highly unique behavioral traits, and at the same time thinks that
he himself lacks these distinctive features. Similar considerations
also show that (8) cannot be paraphrased without loss of meaning by
replacing 'he' with a definite description. For the resulting statement
can be false while (8) is true if Richard does not realize that that description is true of him. Furthermore, the use of demonstratives will
not yield the requisite parsing of (8). Suppose that Richard looks into
a mirror and points, thinking that the person he sees is married to
Pat. Thus it is true

(10) Richard believes that *that* person is married to Pat;

but (8) is false, if Richard is sufficiently confused. Richard might have forgotten that he is married to Pat, mistakenly think that some-one else is married to Pat and *that* man's image is reflected in the mirror. Moreover, parsing (8) in terms of demonstratives raises the additional problem that a proposition is not named as the object. 'That *that* person is married to Pat,' like 'that *he* is married to Pat,' is not context-independent and names a propositional function, if it names anything at all.

This problem for propositional object-assimilationism is nicely il-lustrated by an example of John Perry's:

> I once followed a trail of sugar on a supermarket floor, pushing my cart down the aisle on one side of the tall counter and back the aisle on the other, seeking the shopper with the torn sack to tell him he was making a mess. With each trip around the counter, the trail became thicker. But I seemed unable to catch up. Finally it dawned on me. I was the shopper I was trying to catch. (1979, p. 3)

Prior to his moment of enlightenment,

(11) Perry believed that the shopper with the torn sack is mak-ing a mess.

is true but

(12) Perry believed that he himself is making the mess.

is false. Thus (12) is not equivalent in meaning to (11). Moreover (11) cannot be rephrased to make it equivalent in meaning to (12) by substituting a different description, name, or demonstrative for 'the shopper with the torn sack,' since Perry might not realize that that description or name is true of him or that he is pointing to himself.

This problem is not restricted to believing. Consider

(13) Richard desires that he retire early;

and consider the earlier (alleged) paraphrase of (4)

(4a) Richard intends that he vote in the next election.

These formulations are intended to reflect the view that propositions are the objects of all attitudes. But 'that he retire early' and 'that he vote in the next election' do not name propositions. They name, if anything at all, propositional functions. As in the case of (8) and (12) there is no way in which 'he' can be replaced in (13) and (4a) without changing the meaning of these sentences. The problem is especially acute in the case of intending, since, as I shall argue, all intendings are self-referential.

A propositional object-assimilationist might try to defend his position by relaxing the requirement that propositions are independent of context and person (cf. Perry, 1979). Some propositions, namely, those whose natural language counterparts contain a reflexive pronoun or indexical, must be relativized to person, place, and time. It is clearly possible to construct a formal theory that takes propositions to be context-dependent. However, that theory will have unattractive features. The new abstract objects would not be familiar and would not be uniform. They would not be familiar because they would be dependent on spatiotemporal situations and persons, a feature not normally thought to be true of abstract objects. They would not be uniform because some objects, such as mathematical truths and specific, dated truths, would be nonrelativistic, while others would be relativistic. Uniformity can be preserved by allowing some truths to name something trivially relativized, say to all contexts or to the null context. But this suggestion is merely a sleight of hand. An important ontological distinction would remain unexplained: namely between those propositional-like objects that are trivially relativistic and those that are substantially relativistic.

From our perspective the most unattractive feature of taking propositions to be context-dependent is that it fails to solve the problem of self-referentiality. The context-dependent proposition named by the self-referential belief sentence (8) is, let us say, 'that he$_{(Richard)}$ is married to Pat.' But Richard can believe this indexed proposition and not believe that he himself is married to Pat, if he does not believe that the index picks him out. Richard must not only believe that he$_{(Richard)}$ is married to Pat, but he must also believe that *he himself* is the person picked out by the index 'he$_{(Richard)}$'. But in that case, the element of self-reference reappears.

However, the propositional object-assimilationist might be able to avail himself of a different solution to the problem of self-referentiality. Consider this sentence:

(14) Richard believes that he himself is married.

Castañeda would rewrite (14) as

(14*) Richard believes that he* is married,

where the force of the asterisk is to treat 'Richard' as a special quantifier binding 'he.' The element of self-referentiality in (14), then, is captured by 'Richard' picking up the reference of the variable *in* the belief context. Richard's belief that he himself is married is analyzed, in short, by means of a special sort of quantification. This purported solution to the problem of self-referentiality, attributable to Castañeda (especially 1975; cf. Chisholm, 1979), is initially attractive.

Castañeda (1975, chapter 6) suggests that this solution generates an argument for attitude-assimilationism, since the contents of the attitudes behave differently. But not so. The objects of belief are propositions. The problem of self-referentiality is to be resolved by introducing a new type of quantification to analyze belief sentences such as (14). This solution does not require alteration of the view that the objects of beliefs are propositions. The problem of self-referentiality also arises in the cases of desire sentences and intention sentences such as (13) and (4a). The same solution is available in these cases. Sentences (13) and (4a) can be rewritten as:

(13*) Richard desires that he* retire early;

(4a*) Richard intends that he* vote in the next election.

In these rewritten sentences 'Richard' again acts as a quantifier binding the reflexive pronoun, marked by an asterisk. If the problem of self-referentiality can be solved for belief sentences without giving up the claim that the objects of believing are propositions, then, given the parallelism of treatment, the problem of self-referentiality can be solved for desire sentences and intention sentences without giving up the claim that the objects of desiring and intending are propositions. In short, given this solution, the problem of self-referentiality does *not* constitute a reason for preferring attitude-assimilationism to propositional object-assimilationism.

More important, the proposed solution is problematic. Suppose that, for the sake of the argument, we think of propositions as ordered pairs, consisting of an object and a property,[4] and that we think of belief as a relation between a person and a proposition. Then (14*), Castañeda's rendering of (14), can be expressed as

(15) (Richard x) B (x,⟨x,λy(y is married)⟩).

The problem now is to make sense of (15). Although linguists sometimes talk about proper names as quantifiers, their concern is with syntax. The only account known to me of truth conditions for this type of quantification is given by Fodor, who says: "Suppose . . . that 'a' names the individual a. Then the corresponding quantifier '(ax)' is the formula such that '$(ax)[Fx]$' is true iff all the members of the class whose single member is a are F" (1975, p. 139). Thus, for instance, '(Richard x)Fx' is true just in case '$(\exists x)(x = $ Richard $\&$ Fx)' is true. Extrapolating this account to (15) yields

(16) $(\exists x)(\text{Richard} = x \;\&\; B \;(x,\langle x,\lambda y(y \text{ is married})\rangle))$.

But (16) does not capture the meaning of the self-referential (14*). Sentence (16) uses ordinary quantification, which disallows substitution into belief contexts; but (14*) on Castañeda's construal was noteworthy for quantifying *into* a belief context. It might be thought that (16) is a special case and that it has a reading permitting quantification into the belief context. Then (16) is equivalent to

(17) $B \;(\text{Richard},\langle\text{Richard},\lambda y(y \text{ is married})\rangle)$.

That is, Richard believes that Richard is married. But this rendering is also unacceptable. The self-referential (14*) can be true and (17) false if Richard fails to realize that he himself is Richard. Thus Fodor's translation of this special quantification into first-order quantification will not preserve the self-referentiality of sentences like (14*).

There may be another interpretation of '(Richard x)' that treats it like a first-order quantifier and preserves the self-referentiality of (14*) (and of (13*) and (4a*)), though I cannot think of one. Or alternatively '(Richard x)' might be given some nonstandard semantical development, perhaps treating it like a second-order quantifier, or in terms of some binding device other than quantification. No doubt the appropriate formal machinery can be devised. But clearly it would be better to resolve the problem of self-referentiality without introducing nonstandard quantification. A purely formal solution would add little to our understanding of self-referential sentences and the attitudes they express. A substantive solution is required. However, before attempting to provide that solution, I want to discuss the related issue of Castañeda's answer to our fundamental question in action theory.

3. Action Initiation

Our fundamental problem for philosophical action theory is to explain the initiation of action. More specifically it is the problem of becoming clear about the properties of the mental event proximately causing action. Some mental events, such as believing, do not directly initiate action. A person might believe that he will jump up and touch the ceiling; but no matter the strength of his belief, this attitude by itself will not result in his jumping and touching the ceiling. A person must be moved to do so. I labeled the proximate mental antecedent to action 'immediate intention,' and pointed out that it has cognitive and conative properties. But that merely labels the problem: it does not solve it. We require an account of these cognitive and conative features of immediate intention.

Castañeda's solution to this fundamental problem is intimately tied to his attitude-assimilationism. Since the difference between intending and believing rests on a difference in objects, it is in virtue of its objects that intending initiates action. Suppose that Richard intends to kiss Pat. He thus fully endorses the first-person practition 'I myself to kiss Pat' and the event of his fully endorsing that practition results in his kissing Pat. If Richard had, alternatively, fully endorsed the first-person proposition 'I myself will kiss Pat,' he would be merely predicting what he will do, not initiating that activity. Fully endorsing a first-person practition is, under propitious circumstances, sufficient for action; fully endorsing a first-person proposition is not sufficient for action. The conative feature of action initiation, in short, is having an attitude of fully endorsing toward a special type of object.

Unfortunately this solution is not successful. Compare again:

(18) Richard's fully endorsing 'I myself to kiss Pat.'

(19) Richard's fully endorsing 'I myself will kiss Pat.'

In both cases the same type of mental event, fully endorsing, is occurring in Richard's head, as it were. Both of these episodes lead to the action of Richard's kissing Pat, or neither does. The particular episodes (18) and (19) are of course distinct. Castañeda makes this point by saying that each episode is a complex set of dispositions, and that these sets of dispositions are distinct (1975, chapter 10). Although these episodes are distinct, the difference between them is not the type that would result in one episode initiating action but not the other. Consider the additional episode,

(20) Richard's fully endorsing 'Pat wants me myself to kiss her.'

This episode is not sufficient to initiate action. But (20) differs from (19) in the same way that (18) differs from (19): the attitudes are the same, full endorsings; the person and the action are the same; and the contents are different. Since a difference in contents in (19) and (20) does not make a difference in action initiation, a difference in contents in (18) and (19) also does not make a difference in action initiation.

Stripped of the details, the criticism is this. Like causes produce like effects. This principle warrants: if F_1 and F_2 are species of F and F_1 does not cause G, then F_2 does not cause G. Believing and intending are species of fully endorsing. Believing does not cause action.

Thus, intending does not cause action. *But* in fact intending does cause action. Therefore, it is not the case that believing and intending are species of fully endorsing.[5] This argument can be generalized to a criticism of all versions of attitude-assimilationism; it does not depend on Castañeda's view that the common attitude is fully endorsing. The following claims cannot be consistently maintained: (i) believing does not initiate action; (ii) intending does initiate action; (iii) intending and believing are species of a single kind of attitude.

The following response might be made. When the agent fully endorses a first-person practition, he thinks of himself as realizing its object; he does not think of himself in this way when fully endorsing a proposition. The agent's special relationship to a first-person practition is represented linguistically by the so-called practitional copula. Although 'fully endorsing' occurs in (18) and (19), it picks out different types of episodes in each case, different networks of dispositions. It is this difference that accounts for (18) being an action initiator but not (19). The attitudes of intending and believing are distinct.

Castañeda (1982, 1983b) in fact has made this response, though he puts the matter slightly differently. Intending and believing are species of full endorsing. A species might be defined in terms of the genera to which it belongs plus specific differences. But this type of definition does not universally obtain. In particular, Castañeda claims, genera are sometimes disjunctions of distinct species. Color is a prime case. There is no common property shared by red, green, blue, and so on; rather they are distinct, and disjointly constitute being a color. Similarly believing and intending are full endorsings, but share no common property. They are distinct attitudes. I take it, however, to be controversial whether there can be genera whose species have no common, essential properties. Red, green, and so on, do share common properties, such as being constituted of electromagnetic waves whose frequency is in the visual range. This property (or some similar one) is what makes red, blue, etc., colors; without it they would not be colors. And similarly, believing and intending, if they are species of fully endorsing, as Castañeda says, must share some essential properties. But this is not the time to argue about Aristotelianism. Let us allow that intending and believing are distinct attitudes, as Castañeda's response requires, and leave suppressed the issue of whether they are species of a single genus.

This response, however it is to be justified, foregoes attitude-assimilationism. The difference between (18) and (19) is now a difference in *both* object and attitude. The attitudes of intending and believing are distinct and the objects of these attitudes are distinct.

Indeed the position is nonassimilationist, as Castañeda himself recognizes. This new position is, then, less parsimonious than either attitude-assimilationism or object-assimilationism. All else being equal a parsimonious theory should be adopted: this dictum applies to philosophical theories as well as scientific ones. Of course it must be shown that all else is equal. Attitude-assimilationism, I argued, cannot account for action initiation. I will next argue that a version of object-assimilationism can account for action initiation, as well as other issues facing an ontological theory of attitudes.

4. Property Object-Assimilationism and Self-Referentiality

It is plausible to think that the objects of intending and desiring are properties. Suppose that Richard intends to eat lunch. What is his goal? He does not set out to eat at a specific time, taking specific bits of food in a specific order, raising his fork with a specific velocity with each bite. Rather he sets out to perform some action or other of the kind eating lunch. The object of his intention is not a particular spatiotemporal action, but rather a kind of action. Similarly, suppose that Richard desires to go to Washington next week. He does not desire to take a plane that leaves at a specific time, carrying specific passengers with certain luggage, and arriving at a specific spatiotemporal point on the runway. If persons' desires were so detailed, it is unlikely that any of them would be satisfied. Rather Richard wants to perform some actions that would have the result of his being in Washington next week. He does not think about most of the details of his trip, and certainly they are not part of his desire. As in the case of intention, the object of his desire is a kind of action.

The surface grammar of belief sentences does not immediately suggest that the objects of beliefs are properties; rather it suggests that the objects are propositions. If the objects are propositions, then the problem of self-referentiality arises. But consider again:

(14) Richard believes that he is married.

Taking my lead from Lewis and Chisholm, I recommend that (14) be rewritten as

(21) Richard self-ascribes the property of being married.

From the viewpoint of conceptual analysis, self-ascribing a property is primitive. Analysis must begin somewhere and this a good place. Of course designating a notion primitive does not mean that nothing further can be said about it. Conceptually it can be explicated by means of its relationships to other notions.

The problem of self-referentiality for belief is resolved by construing (14) as (21). When a person ascribes a property to himself, he fixes on its being he who has the property. In terms of Perry's example, when the careless shopper realizes it is his bag that is torn, he ascribes to himself the property of making a mess. Prior to his enlightenment he does not ascribe to himself this property. *Basically, this resolution of the problem consists in taking self-referentiality to be in the attitude itself.* Previous attempts to deal with the problem concerned ways to build the element of self-reference into the objects of belief. As we saw, these attempts are problematic. This solution retains the context-independence of the objects but reconstrues belief to be an attitude that essentially involves reference to oneself. If belief is an attitude in one's head, then self-referentiality too is in the head, not in the abstract objects of belief.

An exactly similar approach to the problem of self-referentiality for intending and desiring is available. The sentence

(22) Richard intends to eat dinner.

is to be rewritten as

(23) Richard sets himself to acquire the property of eating dinner.

And the sentence

(24) Richard wants to run for office.

is to be rewritten as

(25) Richard self-favors acquiring the property of running for office.

The self-referential aspects of first-person intending and desiring are also made part of the attitudes, not the objects. As in the case of self-ascription, setting oneself to acquire a property and self-favoring acquiring a property are conceptually primitive. But also as in the case of self-ascription, these attitudes can be further explained by means of their conceptual roles.

Sometimes there is multiple self-reference. For example, consider 'Richard believes that he loves himself.' This sentence is to be rewritten: 'Richard self-ascribes the property of loving oneself.' Sometimes, moreover, there are reiterated attitudes of self-reference. 'Richard wants himself to believe that he is healthy' goes into 'Richard self-favors acquiring the property of self-ascribing the property of being healthy.' Richard wants himself to have the property of believing himself so-and-so; when he gains this property, then he will have the attitude of believing himself so-and-so. More complicated cases of multiple self-reference, reiterated self-reference, and mixed multiple and reiterated self-reference are to be dealt with along similar lines.

The account so far deals only with self-referential believing, intending, and desiring, that is, as Lewis (1979) has labeled them, *de se* attitudes. The account needs to be extended to include attitudes toward other persons and things and toward propositions, that is, to *de re* and *de dicto* attitudes. This extension concerns the issue of *other-referentiality*. However, before developing that extension, I want to point out an important difference between intending on the one hand and desiring and believing on the other.

Consider

(26) Pat intends Richard to raise his arm.[6]

This sentence might be interpreted as expressing that Pat *wants* Richard to raise his arm. That interpretation presents no special problem—that is, no problem in addition to other-referentiality. It consists in treating Pat's attitude as not being a case of intending. But (26) can also be interpreted as a genuine intending. In that case there are two readings of (26), a 'multiactional' one and a 'uniactional' one. According to the multiactional reading it says, nonliterally, that Pat intends to do something or other such that her action brings about Richard's action of raising his arm. Pat might intend to cajole or command Richard to raise his hand. There are two actions in the offing, one performed by Pat and another by Richard. This situation is clearly possible. On the Causal Theory I am defending, there would be two immediate intentions, Pat's immediately intending to do something and Richard's immediately intending to raise his arm. Pat's intending is self-directed; she intends herself to do something. This reading of (26), then, involves only cases of persons setting themselves to acquire properties; in particular, Pat sets herself to acquire some property such that a result of her having this property is Richard's setting himself to acquire the property of raising one's arm.

On the uniactional reading of (26) Pat literally intends Richard to raise his arm. She intends *for Richard* to do something, not that she herself perform some action. There is exactly one immediate intention and one action; Pat's intending, which is an event in her head, directly results in Richard's raising his arm. Read in this way (26) is impossible in a logical or conceptual sense. The actual world is not such that Pat's head is directly wired to Richard's body. But physically it could be so. Suppose that it is. Even then, Pat could not directly intend for Richard to perform *an action*. Rather she could only directly move Richard's body. That situation would be like one in which a mad physiologist stimulates Richard's brain so that his limbs move. Richard would not be performing an action; rather something would be happening to him. *If* it were the case that events in Pat's head directly cause Richard to perform an action, without filtering through Richard's intentions, there would be a single person involved, not two: 'Pat' and 'Richard' would in that case be names for parts of a single person.

Generally put, sentences of the form 'S intends for S* to A,' where S ≠ S*, are not literally true; indeed they are arguably necessarily false. Sentences of this form are true on a multiactional reading in which S intends to do something that will result in S*'s Aing. But there can be no true uniactional reading. Immediate intention is exclusively first person. It is something one must do for oneself. This conclusion is reminiscent of Castañeda's (1975) view that only first-person practitions (intendeds) are the objects of intending.

5. Property Object-Assimilationism and Other-Referentiality I

One way for property object-assimilationism to account for other-referentiality is to take other-referential attitudes as primary and treat self-referentiality as a special case. That is, take *de se* attitudes to be reducible to *de re* attitudes.[7] In particular, *de se* attitudes are *de re* attitudes about oneself. Steven Böer and William Lycan explicitly hold this view: they say ". . . attitudes *de se* are simply attitudes *de their owners*" (1980, p. 432). Böer and Lycan are primarily concerned with the plausibility of this view, and not its development. Let me present an account, *prima facie* attractive, that develops a rationale for reducing *de se* attitudes to *de re* ones.[8]

There is a distinction between the mental state of the agent and the object of the agent's attitudes, between what happens in the agent's head, as it were, and what he believes, desires, or intends. Suppose that Richard wants to eat lunch and so does Pat. There are, then, the mental states of Richard and Pat and there are the abstract objects of Richard's and Pat's attitudes. Take these abstract objects to be ordered pairs consisting of persons (or physical objects) and properties, namely ⟨Richard,λx(x is eating lunch)⟩, ⟨Pat,λx(x is eating lunch)⟩ and take the mental states to be represented as functions from the subjects to the ordered pairs. Thus Richard's mental state is represented as a function that assigns to Richard the pair ⟨Richard,λx(x is eating lunch)⟩, and Pat's mental state is represented as a function that assigns to Pat the pair ⟨Pat,λx(x is eating lunch)⟩.

This scheme accommodates *de re* attitudes straightforwardly. Suppose that Richard believes of the recorder that it is turned off. Then there is an ordered pair, ⟨the recorder,λx(x is turned off)⟩, and a function f such that f assigns to Richard this pair. A *de se* attitude is one in which the first object in the ordered pair is the subject and the function assigns to the subject that ordered pair. If Richard believes that he will be re-elected, then there is an ordered pair, ⟨Richard, λx(x is re-elected)⟩, and a function f such that f assigns to Richard the pair ⟨Richard,λx(x is re-elected)⟩. Differences in types of attitudes would be reflected in differences in functions mapping persons onto ordered pairs. For instance, the difference between Pat's wanting to eat lunch and Pat's believing that she will eat lunch is reflected in a difference of functions, say f and g, that assigns to Pat the common ordered pair ⟨Pat,λx(x is eating lunch)⟩.

This account, however, is problematical. Consider the following.

(27) Richard believes of himself that he is in danger.

(28) Richard believes of Richard that he is in danger.

According to this reductive account these sentences receive the same rewriting:

(29) There is an ordered pair ⟨Richard,λx(x is in danger)⟩ and a function f such that f assigns to Richard the pair ⟨Richard,λx(x is in danger)⟩.

But (27) and (28) are not equivalent, and hence cannot receive a single rewriting. Sentence (28) can be true and (27) false. Suppose that Richard looks across the room and sees a man. But for some reason he fails to realize that he is looking into a mirror and that the person he sees is himself. Suppose also that he thinks he sees Richard, and that, being confused, he forgets that he is Richard. Now someone else, Alex, says to Richard while he is looking toward the mirror: "They are wise to you. You are in danger." Richard then believes of Richard that he is in danger; but since he does not believe that he himself is Richard, he does not believe of himself that he is in danger.

The difference between (27) and (28) is that the former has epistemic import lacking in the latter. In the first case Richard is cognizant that his belief is about him himself. In (27), 'of himself' does double-duty: it indicates that the agent has a self-directed attitude and that he is aware that his attitude is self-directed. In (28), 'of Richard' indicates that the subject has a self-directed attitude; but it does not indicate that the agent is aware that his attitude is self-directed. The main point is that (27) entails that Richard has a thought (the mentalese equivalent of) 'I myself am in danger,' whereas (28) can be true and Richard not have this thought.

Various responses might be made. It might be suggested that looking into mirrors, or so on, does not yield *de re* belief. So that, although (27) is false, (28) is also false, and thus the nonequivalence of (27) and (28) has not been demonstrated. But this response construes *de re* attitudes too restrictively. Suppose that I have a *de re* belief about part of my throat: say, I believe of my throat that it is marked. This is a perfectly reasonable *de re* belief, but being normal, my view of my throat will be indirect, by means of mirrors, video screens, or so on. In general a *de re* attitude toward an object does not require direct perception of that object. Richard's indirect perception by means of a mirror does not preclude his having a *de re* belief toward that which is reflected.

Related responses are that (28) is false because Richard does not know all the properties, or all the essential properties, or the property of being named 'Richard,' of the object he sees in the mirror. But clearly these replies are inadequate. There are many objects about which I obviously have *de re* attitudes, for instance, my wife and my automobile, without knowing all their properties, or all their essential properties. And there are many objects about which I have *de re* attitudes without knowing their names, for instance, my neighbor's dog and the traffic officer who gave me a ticket. There are, furthermore, objects about which I have *de re* attitudes that do not have names.

Another response is that Richard cannot fail to realize that he is Richard. Of course Richard might forget that his name is 'Richard.' But the example requires something more than that: something of which Richard cannot fail to be aware. However, though not ordinarily the case, Richard can fail to realize that he is Richard. Consider the third-person case. Richard can fail to realize that Pat is Pat. Of course this is not to say that Richard fails to know an instance of a tautology; rather he fails to recognize or identify Pat. Although he is well-acquainted with Pat, he might see her under conditions in which he does not realize that the person he sees is Pat. Third-person cases of this sort are not rare. Pat, for instance, might appear to Richard under lighting conditions such that he is not aware that he sees Pat. By analogy, Richard might see himself under conditions in which he does not realize that the person he sees is himself. The lighting or angle of reflection from the mirror might mislead him. It is this kind of case that shows the nonequivalence of (27) and (28).

Richard is *de re* related to Richard through indirect perception, but he does not realize that it is he himself to whom he is related.[9]

Still another response is to deny that (27) and (28) have distinct entailments, and that the difference between them is pragmatic or conventional (Böer and Lycan, 1980). Sentence (27), in normal contexts, presupposes that Richard is aware that the one in danger is he himself, whereas (28) does not have this presupposition. However, these sentences differ in truth conditions, and not merely in situational constraints on appropriateness. It is not possible that Richard believe of himself that he is in danger and not have the thought 'I myself am in danger.' Of course Richard's actions cannot be infallibly predicted on the basis of this thought: although he can be expected to act in some way to avoid the danger, he might not do so, for any number of reasons. To say that (27) entails that Richard has the thought 'I myself am in danger' is not to be committed to logical behaviorism.

It is clear, in short, that there is a difference between the ordinary case in which Richard believes of himself that he is in danger and the type of case in which Richard thinks of someone who is in danger, not realizing that it is he who is that person. True, ordinary language does not dictate the precise forms in which this difference should be marked. Sentences (27) and (28) are somewhat contrived; but they can be construed as reflecting this difference. These sentences differ in their truth conditions, since they describe different situations. Thus the problem of other-referentiality cannot be solved by this reduction of *de se* attitudes to *de re* ones. Generally speaking, other attempts to reduce *de se* attitudes to *de re* ones will differ in detail, but they too will be subject to the same objection. Given only the resources of Fregean semantics, there appears to be no way to mark the uniqueness of first-person cases in which there is self-awareness.[10]

The solution to the problem of other-referentiality depends on taking *de se* attitudes as primary and elucidating *de re* attitudes in terms of them. There are two cases to consider: other-directed believing and other-directed desiring. There is no other-directed intending, since a person can only intend for himself. In the cases of believing and desiring, attributing properties to other persons and things can be understood by means of self-ascription and self-favoring. The basic idea is that a person attributes a property to something else when he attributes to himself the complex property of standing in a unique relation to that person or thing which has the property (Lewis, 1979 and Chisholm, 1980). For instance, I attribute to Richard the property of having resigned if there is a unique relation, say, being the man observed by me to be holding his dog Checkers, and I self-ascribe the complex property of having observed the man holding his dog Checkers who resigned. Or, I favor Pat's acquiring the property of being divorced if I stand in a unique relation to Pat, say, being the person known by me to be married to Richard in 1983, and I self-favor acquiring the property of knowing the person married to Richard in 1983 becoming divorced. More exactly:

> (D4.1) S ascribes to x the property F just in case there is a relation R^* such that S bears R^* to x and S self-ascribes the property of bearing R^* to something that is F.

> (D4.2) S favors x acquiring the property F just in case there is a relation R^* such that S bears R^* to x and S self-favors acquiring the property of bearing R^* to something that is F.

Some observations are in order. First, the property S self-ascribes or self-favors acquiring is not R^* itself, but rather the complex property of bearing R^* to something that is F. Second, the relational property R^* is such that there is exactly one thing that S bears R^* to. The relation R^*, to use Chisholm's term, is an identifying relation; it is a relation by which the subject singles out that to which his belief or desire is ascribed.[11] Third, S falsely ascribes a property to a person or external object when, and only when, S bears the relation R^* to that person or object, S self-ascribes the property of bearing R^* to something that is F, but that person or thing does not have F. In order to falsely ascribe a property to a person or thing, one must first be in a position to ascribe a property by standing in an identifying relation to it. Miscues in cases of other-directed desires are less straightforward. A subject might want another person or external object to acquire a property it already has, or acquire a property that is incompatible with a property it has or will have. But as in the case of other-directed belief, the subject must first stand in an identifying relation to that person or object.

It might be thought that there are many things to which we ascribe properties or favor their acquiring properties but to which we do not stand in any special relation. But this objection overlooks the ease with which identifying relations can be generated. All that is required is that the subject know a unique way to pick out the object or person. For example, I can ascribe properties, including ascribing them falsely, to Xanthippe in virtue of her being known by me as the wife of Socrates at his death. I ascribe to Xanthippe the property of having black hair if I self-ascribe the property of knowing the person who was the wife of Socrates when he died and who has black hair. Indeed to have other-directed attitudes toward persons it is sufficient to know only their names. If I know only Pope John III's name and nothing else about him, I can ascribe properties to him in virtue of the identifying relation being the thing named 'Pope John III.' Of course in this kind of situation, my truly ascribing properties to John will be a matter of luck.

Another objection is that too much is required of the subject to ascribe properties to others or to favor their acquiring properties. The subject must be aware of standing in an identifying relation to that thing, since self-ascription and self-favoring imply awareness. But persons are not ordinarily aware of standing in these identifying relations. Furthermore, given that these definitions are to be used to elucidate *de re* belief and desire in terms of *de se* attitudes, the resulting definitions of *de re* belief and desire will be too intellectual, since they require that the subject know at least one way to uniquely pick out the object of his attitude. We can have *de re* beliefs and desires without conceptualizing the objects in any way (cf. Bach, 1982).

In reply it should be observed that definitions (D4.1) and (D4.2) require only that the subject stand in a unique relation to the thing to which he is attributing a property and he self-ascribe standing in this relation to that thing. It is *not* required that the subject have conscious awareness, awareness that is introspectively available, that he is standing in this unique relation. The subject might be only dispositionally aware that he stands in this relation. Richard, for instance, may attribute many properties to Pat throughout the day, but not have before his mind an identifying description or image of Pat. But when queried about to whom he is attributing properties, he can readily produce an identifying description, such as 'my only wife.' Further, given that these definitions will be used to define *de re* belief and desire, the resulting definitions will be somewhat intellectual in that the subject conceptualizes standing in a relation to something, even if he does not do so with awareness. But contrary to the objection, this degree of conceptualization does not preclude *de re* belief and desire. Some degree of conceptualization appears necessary for *de re* belief and desire. There are other relations to external objects in which persons stand that are devoid of conceptualization, such as purely causal relations; but in cases of *de re* belief and desire the external objects must at least be categorized, or otherwise represented within one scheme of things.

Armed with the notions of ascribing and favoring, *de re* attitudes can be specified. One suggestion, which has simplicity on its side, equates *de re* belief and desire with ascribing and favoring. That is:

(D4.3) *S* believes of *x* that it is *F* just in case *S* ascribes to *x* the property *F*.

(D4.4) *S* desires of *x* that it is *F* just in case *S* favors *x*'s acquiring the property *F*.

There is no *de re* attitude of intending. Ordinary English does not have a standard form for expressing *de re* attitudes. Sometimes the 'believes of' and 'desires of' locutions are used; but sometimes 'believes that' and 'desires that' locutions express *de re* attitudes. I adopt the convention of using 'believes of' and 'desires of' for *de re* attitudes and reserve 'believes that' and 'desires that' for *de dicto* attitudes.

These definitions, however, appear to be too liberal. According to (D4.3) I have a *de re* belief about Xanthippe, despite my only relation to her being that of being known by me as the wife of Socrates at his death. I must rather be more 'intimately' related to an external object to have a *de re* attitude toward it. I have *de re* attitudes toward my wife, my colleagues, and my neighbor I occasionally see. It is controversial whether I have *de re* attitudes toward Nixon, whom I never saw in person; it is doubtful, though not entirely implausible, that I have *de re* attitudes about Plato, of whom I have read a great deal; but it is far-fetched that I have *de re* attitudes toward Xanthippe, about whom I know practically nothing.

In defense of these definitions it should be said that intuition is of little help in demarcating the class of things about which we have *de re* attitudes. Quine (1956) called our attention to the distinction between 'Ralph believes that someone is a spy' and 'Someone is such that Ralph believes that he is a spy.' If Ralph is like most of us, the first sentence is true and the second false. Few of us believe of some particular person that he is a spy. This distinction *is* reflected by these liberal definitions. In the second case but not the first, Ralph believes of someone in particular that he is a spy. Intuition clearly sanctions Quine's distinction: but it is far from clear whether it also sanctions a distinction yielding a narrower class than that demarcated by (D4.3) and (D4.4); and if so, by what principles. My guess is that a less liberal account of *de re* attitudes is not generated by ordinary intuition, but rather by intuition tainted by theory. As a result there are a number of competing ways to generate less liberal accounts of *de re* attitudes, with no clear procedure for deciding among them. Each account is satisfactory only if it marks the distinction Quine noted; beyond that, they reflect certain theoretical commitments.

There is an underlying issue here, one that is also at the root of the earlier objection to (D4.1) and (D4.2). To what extent must definitions (analyses) of *de re* attitudes respect psychological reality? The answer, I suggest, is that such definitions must be compatible with statements of psychologically real processes. But they are not themselves summary descriptions of these processes. An analysis of *de re* attitudes subserves conceptual development. Such an analysis must not hypothesize psychologically impossible processes; but beyond that, theoretical considerations dominate, not empirical ones. Given that there are alternative theoretical frameworks, there is no one correct analysis of *de re* attitudes. Some authors give a different answer, according to which an account of *de re* attitudes is a summary description of the relevant psychological processes (Bach, 1982). When we perceive an array of external objects, that information is encoded and our perceptual beliefs become fixed. These beliefs are *about* external objects. *De re* belief *is* belief generated by normal perceptual processes. *De re* desires are to be explained in a similar fashion. But this answer is misleading for two reasons. First, it overlooks the fact that there is no natural concept of *de re* attitude. '*De re* attitude' is a term of art. In this respect the concept of *de re* attitude differs from, say, the concept of knowledge. Though there are serious disagreements among philosophers about the correct analysis of knowledge, it is reasonably clear that there is a natural, unitary concept. In the case of *de re* attitudes that is simply false. Second, this answer fails to assign to the analysis the appropriate level of abstraction. That there are *de re* attitudes and that they have certain properties are not claims within psychology, nor, strictly speaking, psychological claims at all. Rather they are conceptual claims that underlie psychological theory. In short, the only factual constraint of an analysis of *de re* attitudes is that it be compatible with psychological reality.

One legitimate conceptual concern is the development of a parsimonious account of the various types of attitudes. There is *some* connection between *de re, de dicto,* and *de se* attitudes, between attitudes about things, attitudes that so-and-so is the case, and attitudes about oneself. In the next section I will sketch an account of *de re* attitudes that yields a conceptually unified picture. That picture is compatible with psychological reality, but is not dictated by it. The key idea will be that a subject's *de re* attitudes are both causal and actional.

6. Property Object-Assimilationism and Other-Referentiality II

Persons have *de re* attitudes toward other persons, toward physical objects, events, and abstract entities. Someone might have a *de re* attitude toward his dog, his pet rock, or his typewriter. Similarly someone might believe of the 1981 Super Bowl that it was exciting, or believe of Ford's pardoning Nixon that it was irresponsible. A person can have a *de re* attitude only toward that which exists. No one, for instance, can have a *de re* belief or desire about phlogiston. With regard to abstract entities, someone might believe of the number two that it is prime, or desire of the property happiness that it be exemplified.

The common core of all these cases of *de re* attitudes is that they are generated by *selective consideration*. Selective consideration is a type of mental action. It is the active directing of attention. But it is a 'thin' action, not preceded by deliberation nor performed *by* doing something else. As a rule, it is not intentional. Rather selective consideration resembles, in many respects, reflex actions.

Some understanding of selective consideration can be gained by placing it in the context of recent discussions of attention in the psychological literature. The textbook example of attention is the cocktail party case. Imagine that a person is at a cocktail party in which there are a number of conversations occurring simultaneously, that the volume of the conversations are equal, and that no one of them involves any special distinguishing feature. In this circumstance the subject is able to focus on one conversation and not attend to the others. Broadbent (1958), in an influential account, proposed a filter model in which unattended information is blocked out. The filter selects a class of stimuli for processing on the basis of physical characteristics, such as location or tonal quality; irrelevant stimuli are simply not processed for semantical content. However, shadowing experiments have shown that, while much of the unattended stimuli are not processed, at least some are. In a typical dichotic shadowing experiment the subject wears a headphone in which different tapes are presented to each ear. He is asked to attend to one source, and repeat or write it immediately, that is, shadow it. The task is made sufficiently difficult so that the subject must concentrate on the shadowed material. The extent to which information is processed that is not the focus of attention is determined by querying the subject about the unattended source. A person can tell, for instance, whether his name was mentioned in the unattended message and he can disambiguate one conversation using information provided by the unattended conversation. Broadbent's model might be saved by modifying the filter so that it attenuates some information on the basis of physical characteristics but does not wholly block it (Treisman, 1964, 1969). An alternative view, which seems better supported by the experimental evidence, is that all inputs are processed to some degree, though only a portion of what is processed is stored in long-term memory. That view, advocated by Norman (1968, 1969) and Deutsch and Deutsch (1963), differs from Broadbent's filter model basically in claiming that selection of inputs occurs at a late stage.

Common to all these accounts of attention, independently of whether the input is said to be processed early or late, is the assumption that the subject is passive. Information impinges on him. In contrast, Neisser (1976) and Hochberg (1970) hold that attending is an active process. Attending, according to Neisser, is similar to other human activities. "Organisms are active: they do some things and leave others undone. To pick one apple from a tree you need not filter out all the others; you just don't pick them. A theory of apple picking would have much to explain (How do you decide which one you want? Guide your hand to it? Grasp it?) but it would not have to specify a mechanism to keep unwanted apples out of your mouth" (Neisser, 1976, pp. 84–85). Similarly a theory of attention should explain why and how one message is attended to, but not why and how other messages are ignored. Neisser holds that attention is an extended process of anticipation, exploration, and information pickup. This process involves matching inputs to existing perceptual schemata. Hochberg holds a similar view: stimuli are matched to sets of expectations stored in memory; unmatched stimuli are normally rapidly forgotten. This active perspective corresponds more closely to the ordinary notion of attending than the passive one. In selecting a conversation to follow at a cocktail party, a person is actively engaged in anticipating the discussion and connecting it with his past experience. Something must be *done* to change the focus of attention to another conversation, barring a loud noise or some such jolting stimulus.

The point of this digression is to suggest that selective consideration can be understood as the early stage of focusing attention on the active psychological model. It is not the listening to a conversation, but rather putting oneself in the position to listen. Selective consideration is directing oneself toward an input, not storing the input or reacting to it. Directing oneself toward an input can involve overt behavior such as turning one's head or refocusing one's eyes: but it need not; it may only involve the rearrangements of one's covert set of expectations, or as Neisser might put it, the accessing of alternative schemata.

The primary kind of selective consideration is directing one's perception. Basically, to perceive is to be caused to be appeared to in a certain way by physical objects and events. Let us say that person S *directed his perception to x's* being F if: (i) S set himself to acquire the property of being in a position to perceive x's being F and (ii) S's having set himself to acquire the property of being in a position to perceive x's being F caused his having perceived x and F. For instance, Richard directed his perception to Alex's being pale if he intended to place himself in a position to see Alex being pale, say, by turning toward him, or by anticipating his demeanor, or some such, and as a result, he perceived Alex's being pale. Note that, ordinarily, Richard does not believe of Alex that he is pale prior to directing his perception to Alex's being pale. Perceiving something does not presuppose a prior *de re* attitude toward that object. Some cognitive psychologists might say that this explanation of perception is too passive: stimuli, by themselves, do not cause us to perceive, but rather do so only when an appropriate set of expectations is brought to bear. For them perception always involves direction. This issue is controversial, and not one I shall attempt to resolve. I put forward the distinction between perception and directing one's perception tentatively: if all perception involves direction, none the worse for this account of *de re* attitudes.

A second type of selective consideration is directed recall. Like perceiving, remembering results from a causal process. To remember is, basically, to have a mental representation as a result of a causal process starting from some stimulus event to processing and storage of information and finally, to accessing the information. Person S *recalled x's being F*, in the sense required here, if S had a memory of x such that: (i) S set himself to acquire the property of being in a position to remember x's being F and (ii) S's having set himself to acquire the property of being in a position to remember x's being F caused his having remembered x's being F. For instance, I recalled Nixon's first Presidential victory if I intended to arrange having had this memory, say, by freely associating about twentieth century politics, and as a causal result, did remember that event. Of course more needs to be said about remembering if this account of directed recall is to be tenable. In particular the account must be supplemented, on the conceptual side, by a way of dealing with deviant causal chains between the stimulus event and the memory event and, on the empirical side, by a psychological theory of memory processing and structure. A similar comment also applies to the account of directing one's perception (cf. Peacocke, 1979b).

There is at least one additional case to consider. Persons have *de re* attitudes toward abstract entities, such as mathematical objects—at least according to this proposed notion of *de re* attitudes. One approach is to say that a person can directly think of abstract entities. Then, approximately, a person has a *de re* attitude toward an abstract entity when he sets himself to be in a position to conceive of it and his so doing in fact causes him to conceive of it. The main assumption of this approach is that we can directly conceive of abstract entities. There is a long-standing tradition in philosophy that supports this assumption. Plato held that persons can think of the Forms; and in this century Frege and Russell (at one time) held that we are directly related to universals and abstract entities. However, despite that tradition the nature of this direct relation remains mysterious. How is it that a person is *directly* related to nonspatiotemporal objects? Chisholm (1981), who follows in the tradition, takes 'x conceives y,' where x is a person and y a property, to be primitive. While it is interesting to see how much philosophical theory can be generated using this primitive locution, I for one do not feel completely enlightened about direct conception of abstract entities. For those not plagued with these doubts, an account of *de re* attitudes toward abstract entities along the above lines can be generated. But for those who are skeptical about there being direct conception of abstract entities, a somewhat different account is needed.

Persons have concepts. I take this to be a well-confirmed psychological claim that has been incorporated into recent cognitive theory (see Smith and Medin, 1981). There is, of course, controversy about the nature of concepts, including the way in which we represent them to ourselves and the roles they play in processing and storage. But it appears indisputable that there are mental concepts. Some concepts are about classes or categories of concrete objects, such as Richard's concepts of chair and table. Other concepts are about abstract entities. There can be concepts of individual abstract entities, such as Richard's concept of the number two and his concept of happiness; and there can be concepts of classes or categories of abstract entities, such as Richard's concept of prime number.

Selective consideration of an abstract entity is indirect. In particular it is mediated by a person's concepts under which that entity falls. Let us say that S *focused on x's being F*, where x is an abstract entity, if: (i) S set himself to acquire the property of being in a position to access the concept of x's being F and (ii) S's having set himself to acquire the property of being in a position to access the concept of x's being F caused his accessing the concept of x's being F. (Assume again that there are appropriate qualifications on this causal chain.) Thus for example, Richard actively attends to, focuses on, the concept of prime number when he puts himself in a position to access this concept and, as a causal consequence, does so.

Notice that focusing on abstract entities is similar to perceiving physical objects in that the object itself is not selectively considered but rather the object's having a property. A person does not, literally, see a ball; rather he sees it being red or round or so on. Similarly a person does not, literally, focus on a concept. Rather one accesses it within a structure, and by so doing attributes to it properties in virtue of its place in that structure. If someone focuses on the concept of prime number, then he attributes to it the property of being mathematical, being rational, and so on. True, we ordinarily speak of seeing the ball or thinking of being prime. But this ordinary talk is elliptical. The context or situation makes it reasonably clear which property (or properties) of the object or concept are elided.

Matters unfortunately are still more complicated. There are two types of *de re* attitudes, stable ones and unstable ones. This distinction is tied to the ability to reidentify objects. Let us say that, for any person S, any property F, and any x, S *identifies* x as F just in case there is at least one occasion on which S selectively considers x's being F. Likewise, S *reidentifies* x as F just in case there are at least two occasions on which S selectively considers x's being F. And furthermore S is *able to reidentify* x as F just in case there are at least two occasions on which S has the ability and opportunity to selectively consider x as F. Then:

(D4.5) S stably ascribes of x that it is F just in case:
(i) S identifies x as F and S is able to reidentify x as F, and
(ii) S other-ascribes to x the property F.

(D4.6) S unstably ascribes of x that it is F just in case:
(i) S identifies x as F, and
(ii) S other-ascribes to x the property F.

(D4.7) S stably favors of x that it is F just in case:
(i) S identifies x as F and S is able to reidentify x as F, and
(ii) S other-favors acquiring the property F.

(D4.8) S unstably favors of x that it is F just in case:
(i) S identifies x as F, and
(ii) S other-favors acquiring the property F.

The second clauses of these definitions refer back to definitions (D4.1) and (D4.2). These clauses, or at least those of (D4.5) and (D4.6), are redundant, given the above explication of selectively considering. In sum, definitions (D4.5) to (D4.8) provide an actional and causal account of *de re* attitudes. Selective consideration is an action by which a person becomes related to an object through the mediation of mental events. In the case of physical objects and events, both past and present, this relation is solely causal. But *de re* attitudes toward abstract entities cannot be explained by causal laws alone. Persons actively attend to mental representations of abstract entities; but the connection between these abstract entities and the mental representations is not purely causal.

Two further comments. Notice, first, that this account is not viciously circular. The action of selective attention is necessary for *de re* attitudes; and selective attention involves intending: but there is no *de re* intending. The root notion in this account of *de re* attitudes is intending (setting oneself). Second, the subject *S* must stand in an identifying relation to that about which he has a *de re* attitude, he must be related to the object of his attitude in some unique way. This requirement is reasonable in cases of physical objects and events. It is also reasonable for *de re* attitudes about abstract entities (cf. Chisholm, 1981, pp. 37–38). For generally there will always be an identifying relation between a subject and an abstract entity when the subject has a concept of that entity. Suppose that Richard believes of the number two that it is prime. There is then a unique relation in which he stands to the number two such that he ascribes being prime to that which he stands in this relation. In general that relation is being the referent of the concept he is now accessing (or had accessed at such-and-such time). That is, approximately, Richard ascribes to the number two that it is prime if he focuses on the number two's being prime and there is a unique relation he bears to the number two, say, being the referent of the concept which he is now accessing, such that he self-ascribes the complex property of having this relation to that which is prime. Richard might also stand in other identifying relations to the number two, for instance, it might be his favorite number; but in any case there will always be at least one unique relation in virtue of his having a concept of that abstract entity. Recall, incidentally, that standing in an identifying relation to something does not require awareness by the subject; there need not be any occurrent mental event in addition to the *de re* attitude itself.

The examples of *de re* attitudes previously cited are accommodated by these definitions. When I believe of my neighbor that he has brown hair, I have a stable *de re* belief. When someone believes of Ford's pardoning Nixon that it was irresponsible, he has an unstable *de re* belief, since he cannot reidentify that event. And when someone desires of the property happiness that it be exemplified, he has a stable *de re* desire. Another kind of case easily accommodated is one that concerns momentary exposure. Suppose that I am being charged by a mad bull. I have *de re* attitudes toward that bull, but it is doubtful that I can reidentify that particular bull. Here my beliefs and desires about the bull are unstable. The stability of a *de re* attitude depends not only on the kind of object to which the attitude is directed, but also the situation in which the subject interacts with it.

This analysis is also adequate to the earlier distinction between

(27) Richard believes of himself that he is in danger.

and

(28) Richard believes of Richard that he is in danger.

This distinction is between a *de se* belief and a *de re* belief about oneself. Sentence (27) would be rewritten as 'Richard self-ascribes the property of being in danger.' Assuming the background context of Richard looking at himself in the mirror but not realizing that he sees himself, (28) would be rewritten as 'Richard unstably ascribes of Richard that he is in danger,' which could be further rewritten using (D4.6). Self-ascribing a property involves an awareness on the part of the agent that it is he himself who has the property; but *de re* attitudes, even about one's own person, do not involve this awareness.

This approach to *de re* attitudes threads a path among cases, without ruling on the more controversial ones. A feature of a good theory on this topic is to account for the clear cases and, rather than rule on the controversial ones, indicate why they are controversial and what additional theory is necessary to make a decision about them. A person can have *de re* beliefs and desires about objects seen by means of mirrors, or the like, since it is not necessary to have direct perception of an object in order to selectively consider it. But to what extent can the perception and memory be indirect? I have never seen Nixon in person, but only by means of television and other photographs. Is that kind of perception and memory too indirect to generate *de re* attitudes? The answers to these questions depend on a theory of indirect perception and memory. Presumably I do not have *de re* attitudes about Plato, despite having read what he has written and much about him. I am not able to selectively consider him, since the causal chain from Plato to myself would surely be too indirect to count as a perception or memory of him.

One more step remains: *de dicto* attitudes have to be analyzed in terms of *de re* attitudes. The basic idea is that *de dicto* attitudes are *de re* attitudes in which the property of being true is attributed to propositions. In particular,

> (D4.9) *S* believes that *p* just in case *S* stably ascribes of *p* that it is true.

> (D4.10) *S* desires that *p* just in case *S* stably favors of *p* that it is true.

Quine's distinction between 'Ralph believes that someone is a spy' and 'Someone is such that Ralph believes that he is a spy' is captured by the difference between (D4.9) and (D4.5). *De dicto* belief is common, playing roles, for example, in scientific and mathematical reasoning. *De dicto* desire is not as common as *de re* or *de se* desire, but there are instances of it. 'Pat desires that there will be peace on earth,' we can suppose, is true. [12]

Definitions (D4.9) and (D4.10) require that persons selectively consider propositions. As before, one approach is to claim that there is a direct relation between these abstract entities and the persons who attend to them. Persons *conceive of* propositions. This relation is noncausal, since propositions are not concrete events. Chisholm (1980, 1981) explicitly takes this approach; indeed except for some nominalistically inclined philosophers such as Carnap, this approach has been the favored one. However, the alleged direct relationship persons bear to propositions is no less mysterious, no less in need of explanation, than the relationship that persons are said to bear to other abstract entities. For those who see no problems for direct attention to propositions, (D4.9) and (D4.10) are adequate as they stand. But for those like myself who are skeptical about there being a noncausal process of attending, a mediate relationship between persons and propositions must be found. And as before I suggest that a person actively attends to some mental events, and that these events mediate the process of ascribing properties to the abstract entities.

One highly plausible candidate for these psychological intermediaries is sentences in the language of thought. Fodor (1975, 1978) has argued that there is an internal, representational language, or code, in which persons think. This internal code is not some particular natural language, say English, since persons who do not know English can nonetheless think. Moreover it is unlikely that the internal code differs among persons according to their natural language; for young children and members of some nonhuman species think without knowledge of a natural language. The internal code, rather, is the processing language common to all normal persons, and perhaps some other species as well. It is reasonable to hold that all persons have this internal language innately; that is, to use the computer metaphor, it is hardwired into us. The picture then is this. There is an internal representational language. Persons actively attend to sentences in this mental language. The occurrence of a sentence in one's head, as it were, is an event; so attending remains a causal process. Sentences in the internal code are related to propositions. We ascribe properties to these abstract entities in virtue of our relationship to the mental representations that express them.

It might be objected that this picture is overly complicated. We actively attend to events in our head, to mental representations. Why not simply say that *these* are the objects to which we ascribe properties? Propositions are excess ontological baggage: let's lighten the load! The reply is that a semantics for the internal representational language requires that linguistic constituents express propositions. Indeed any language, public or private, with the expressive resources of natural language requires that there be propositions. Suppose that Lyndon was born on August 27, 1908. Thus it is true that Lyndon was born on August 27, 1908. But *what* is true? If truth is a property of sentences in the language of thought, then if no one is now thinking that Lyndon was born on August 27, 1908, there is nothing to be true. Similarly if truth is ascribed to sentences in a public language, then if no one is now asserting that Lyndon was born on August 27, 1908, there is nothing to be true. Perhaps all that is required is that the sentence 'Lyndon was born on August 27, 1908' be written somewhere and *that* is what is true. However, even if all these written sentences were destroyed, it would nevertheless remain true that Lyndon was born on August 27, 1908. Rather what is true must be independent of the contingencies of persons' thinking, speaking, and writing. What is true, then, must be nonspatiotemporal. Propositions are the bearers of truth (and falsity), and sentences in private and public languages *express* propositions. Of course the relation of expressing that a sentence bears to a proposition remains to be articulated. But it does not have the mystery about it that the purported relation of directly attending to a proposition has. Attending is a causal process, and thus its relata are events. But expressing is a semantical relation, and thus there is no compelling *a priori* reason to take its relata to be events.

It might also be objected that this account of *de dicto* attitudes is circular. Pat, for instance, believes that Richard is honest only if she attends to a mental representation of the sentence 'Richard is honest.' But to attend to a mental representation of 'Richard is honest' is already to believe that Richard is honest. The reply is that, while attending to a mental representation of 'Richard is honest' is necessary for believing that Richard is honest, it is not, as the objection presupposes, sufficient for that belief. A person can attend to his mental representation of 'Richard is honest' without believing that Richard is honest if he merely entertains that Richard is honest. Someone has a *de dicto* belief only if he attributes the semantical value of truth to the propositional object of that belief. But a person can focus on a mental representation that expresses a proposition without attributing the semantical value of truth to that proposition, indeed without attributing any truth value to that proposition.

One more objection. The *objects* of attitudes are sentences in the language of thought, even if these sentences express propositions (see Fodor, 1978). The objects of attitudes are not themselves propositions. I take this objection to be partly verbal. It does not matter whether we label the sentences in the language of thought or the propositions the sentences express 'the objects of attitudes,' provided that the overall picture remains the same. There is some reason, however, to call the expressed propositions the objects. Suppose that two persons, Richard and Pat, have different attitudes toward the same possible event. Suppose also that Richard wishes that it will not happen while Pat predicts that it will. What is *it* about which they both have attitudes? It is implausible to think that it is a sentence in either Richard's or Pat's private languages of thought, since each has access to only his or her own mental sentences. Rather it makes more sense to talk about the objects of attitudes being publicly accessible. These objects, however, cannot be events because the attitudes can be directed toward something that has not yet happened, indeed might never actually happen. It is best, then, to take the objects of *de dicto* attitudes to be the propositions expressed by mental (or public) sentences.[13]

The discussion in this chapter has been complicated. Its main features can be summarized by the following schematic argument.

(i) Natural language and thought are structurally similar. [The Fregean Presumption]

(ii) Belief sentences (ascription of belief) and beliefs (what occurs in the head) are structurally similar. (from (i))

(iii) Some belief sentences are irreducibly first person. [Castañeda's Thesis]

(iv) Some beliefs are irreducibly self-referential. (from (ii) and (iii))

(v) All belief sentences can be translated into first-person ones.

(vi) All beliefs can be analyzed in terms of self-referential ones. (from (ii) and (v)).

Premise (i) is highly plausible, and has been assumed without argument. The nature of the resemblance between public language and thought, beyond that of structural similarity, has been left open. Premise (iii) has been justified by showing that there is no way to eliminate first person reference from sentences like 'Richard believes that he himself is married' without changing its meaning. I defended premise (v) by adapting a strategy used by Lewis and Chisholm. Irreducible self-referential belief is taken as primitive, and belief about objects other than oneself (*de re* belief), including belief about propositions (*de dicto* belief), are to be understood in terms of it. *De re* belief is, essentially, ascribing a property to an object that is selectively considered (that is, actively attended to). *De dicto* belief is a special case of *de re* belief: it is ascribing a property to a proposition, through the intermediate step of selectively considering a sentence in one's representational language that expresses the proposition. A parallel argument to (i)–(vi) can be constructed for desire—but not for intention, since all intention sentences are irreducibly first person.

Part III

THE FOLK PSYCHOLOGY OF INTENDING, DESIRING, AND BELIEVING

5
Desiring

The primary concern of this chapter is to delineate the folk psychological, or commonsensical, concept of desiring. In the first two sections I argue that desiring is distinct from intending. My central constructive thesis is that desiring is a species of preferring and that its role in action is to form or generate intentions. The third through fifth sections articulate this thesis. Attention is paid both to the causal role of desire in action and to the 'logic' of desire. In the final section some other folk psychological attitudes, such as wishing and hoping, are analyzed.

1. Desiring Is Not a Necessary Condition for Intending

It has often been held that there are two primary psychological attitudes, desiring and believing, and that other attitudes, including intending, can be reduced to them. Beardsley (1978) and Audi (1973), for instance, have explicitly defended the reduction of intention to desire plus belief. The core of this analysis can be formulated as follows:

> (DB) S at t_i intends to A at t_j iff: (i) S at t_i desires to A at t_j; and (ii) S at t_i believes that he will A at t_j,

where t_i and t_j are temporal durations of moments, and where, as usual, S ranges over persons and A over action types. Beardsley distinguishes between prospective and concurrent intention. A person prospectively intends to do something if he intends to do it at some later time, that is, in terms of (DB), t_j is later than t_i. Concurrent intention is, in our terminology, immediate intention: that is, referring again to (DB), $t_j = t_i$. There are no true instances of 'S at t_i intends to A at t_j' where t_j is earlier than t_i.

The reductive analysis (DB) is not without plausibility. Suppose that Richard intends to take a plane from New York to San Francisco tomorrow. He wants to take a plane tomorrow, and he believes that he will take one. If something happens that causes him to form a new intention, say, illness in the family, he no longer wants to take a plane to San Francisco tomorrow and he no longer believes that he will do so.

However, this analysis is problematical. I will postpone discussion of the claim that believing one will succeed is necessary for intending—clause (ii)—until the next chapter. There I will argue that this claim importantly oversimplifies the cognitive component of intending. Here the focus is the claim that desiring is necessary for intending—clause (i).

An initial difficulty for clause (i) is that it does not take into account conflicting desires. Suppose that John is entrusted with some secret of Richard's. Suppose also that he has conflicting desires about making this secret public. His loyalty to Richard leads him to want to keep the secret; but his conscience leads him, more strongly, to make it public. To round out the case, imagine also that John is not a good judge of his own character and that he predicts that his loyalty will result in his keeping the secret. *In fact* his strongest desire generates an intention to make his knowledge public, and he acts on that intention. Thus the definiens of (DB) is satisfied: John wants to keep the secret and he believes that he will. But the definiendum is not satisfied: he never forms the intention to keep the secret.

The following revision of clause (i) appears adequate to this and related cases of conflicting desires.

> (i') S at t_i desires to A at t_j and there is no B such that: (a) S at t_i desires to B at t_j; (b) S's desire at t_i to B at t_j is stronger than S's desire at t_i to A at t_j; and (c) S's Bing at t_j is incompatible with S's Aing at t_j.

A subject's Bing is incompatible with his Aing if it is physically impossible that he perform both actions at the same time. On this amended version of (DB), in short, a person intends to do something only if his strongest desire is to do it. John does not intend to keep Richard's secret because it is not his strongest desire to keep it.[1]

There is another, far more serious difficulty for (DB). A person might intend to do something without his strongest desire being to do it, indeed without his desiring to do it at all. One type of case is a person's intending to act on the basis of duty alone. Suppose that Pat intends to visit the Veterans Hospital in the morning and that she intends to do so only because she takes it to be her duty to cheer up the patients. In fact she most strongly desires not to visit the hospital because crippled men depress her. Thus Pat intends to do something without her strongest desire being to do it. It might be replied that Pat *is* acting on her strongest desire, contrary to appearances: she desires to do her duty and that desire is identical to her desiring to visit the hospital. But this response does not save (DB). Recall the discussion of event identity. For any events e and f, e is identical to f just in case e and f are necessarily spatiotemporally coincidental. This criterion obtains for mental as well as physical events. Thus Pat's desiring to do her duty is distinct from her desiring to visit the hospital. It is not necessary that these mental events are spatiotemporally coincident. Pat could, for instance, desire to visit the hospital and not desire to do her duty if she had failed to perceive that she had a duty to visit the hospital.

Another type of case that makes the same point concerns coercion to act. Suppose that Richard intends to resign from office tomorrow. He does not want to do so; in fact he most strongly desires to remain in office. But he must resign in order to avoid severe penalties. He is forced to resign by the current circumstances. Thus Richard intends to do something without desiring to do it. As in the previous case, it will not do to dismiss this example by claiming that Richard's wanting to resign and his wanting to avoid the penalties are identical and hence he *really* wants to resign. These mental events, though simultaneous, are not identical. It is not necessary that Richard's wanting to resign and his wanting to avoid the penalties are spatiotemporally coincidental, since he could have wanted to resign and not wanted to avoid the penalties, and conversely.

There are other cases that make the point. A person might intend to do something without desiring to do it, if he does it because of a psychological or physiological compulsion that he wants not to be effective. Reluctant cleptomaniacs and pyromaniacs fall into this category. Note that it will not do to say that these persons do not intend to steal or set fires. They may well make elaborate plans, wait for the right moment, and perform their acts fully aware of what they are doing. Similarly a drug or alcohol addict might be reluctant and desire not to have another fix or another drink. Yet he intends to do so; he makes plans about how to obtain the drug or alcohol, and he knowingly acts on these plans. Being compelled to do something is consistent with intending while not desiring to do it.

2. Desiring Is Not a Species of Intending

Although not explicitly endorsing (DB), some philosophers hold a thesis similar to it. Desiring, they claim, is a species of intending. For instance, Sellars says "desires are relatively long-term dispositional intentions" (1966, p. 117). Castañeda (1975) distinguishes between blind inclinations and nonblind wants. Blind inclinations do not involve conceptualization; they are common to both humans and other species. Nonblind wants are what we labeled 'desires.' About these, Castañeda echoes Sellars and says: "[N]onblind *wants* . . . are inclinations to intend, some of which can be inclinations merely to have the core propensities of the acts the agent can perform at will, but others are inclinations to intend plans of different complexity and breadth" (1975, p. 286). Unlike Sellars, Castañeda recognizes short-term desires, and correctly so. A person might have a desire to sky dive, though only briefly and only once.

Sellars supports his contention that desiring is a species of intending by claiming that the semantical values of the objects of intending and desiring are the same. "Desires clearly resemble intentions in the sense that they are capable of being realized. Realization in this sense is a concept akin to truth. Intentions . . . are realized if and only if the state of affairs intended comes to exist. Similarly, a desire is realized if and only if the state of affairs desired comes to exist" (1966, pp. 118–119). Castañeda echoes Sellars here too. As discussed in the previous chapter, Castañeda holds that the objects of desires are practitions. The semantical values of practitions are legitimacy and illegitimacy. A practition is legitimate when, basically, it is in accord with the subject's hierarchy of ends, adjusted if necessary to the ends of other persons considered important by the subject (1975, especially pp. 143–145).

Although the objects of desiring and intending are the same (namely properties according to our earlier arguments), it is not obvious that the semantical values of these objects are identical. It is plausible to think that desires are satisfied (or unsatisfied), and intentions are fulfilled (or unfulfilled). The difference between satisfaction and fulfillment is that satisfaction obtains provided only that the end-state is achieved, whereas fulfillment obtains only if the end-state is achieved through the agent's efforts. A desire can be satisfied by luck or through the efforts of other persons, as well as through one's own efforts. But an intention is fulfilled only if the agent contributes in some essential way to the end-state.

It is important to see, however, that even if Sellars and Castañeda are correct in claiming that the objects of intending and desiring have the same semantical values, it does not follow that desiring is a species of intending. Many attitudes have objects that share semantical values without being related in this way. For instance, believing and merely entertaining have propositional objects which are true or false, yet believing is not a species of merely entertaining, nor conversely. Similarly, knowing and doubting have objects with identical semantical values, but doubting is not a species of knowing, nor conversely. Sellars and Castañeda cannot establish their thesis that desiring is a species of intending by means of the identity of the semantical values for objects of these attitudes.

More important, there are differences between desiring and intending that militate against the thesis that desiring is a species of intending, whether a long-term dispositional intending or some other purported species of intending. Indeed these differences also militate against the converse possibility that intending is a species of desiring.

First, the strength of a desire can change over time, but not so for an intention. An intention, especially a complex one, can become more articulated; that is, the means or plan for achieving the end-result can become more detailed over time. Also an intention can be replaced by another intention if, for example, the subject's goal changes. And an intention can be dropped or put aside, when the subject is interrupted or becomes preoccupied with another task. But an intention cannot become weaker or stronger: a person either intends to do something or he does not.

Second, and related to the first difference, desiring can be scaled in strength, but not intending. One problem in scaling desires is to establish an intersubjective common mark. A reasonable suggestion is to scale on viscerogenic deprivations. For instance, deprive a person of food for a specified period, taking into account his metabolism, prior consumed foods, eating habits, and so on. A person's desire to do some arbitrary act A could be ascertained by asking him to assign a magnitude to his desire to A by thinking of it in comparison with the strength of his desire to eat after the standard deprivation. An assumption of this procedure is that desire strengths can be compared independently of the objects of the desires. Without this assumption, magnitude estimation scaling can be accomplished, but with some difficulty. In any case scaling of desires is possible.[2] But scaling of intentions is not. Intentions differ among themselves, but not in matters of strength.

A third difference is that it is possible for a normal person to have incompatible desires but it is not possible for him to have incompatible intentions. There is no difficulty in imagining, say, someone who both wants to eat a second piece of pie and at the same time wants to refrain from eating it. The strongest desire issues in an intending, provided that the environment and background psychological conditions are friendly. When competing desires are equal in strength, there is a conflict situation. That situation is resolved by the incursion of additional desires or additional beliefs about the probabilities of satisfying these desires, or by an appeal to high-level principles. Life would be far more harmonious if no one had incompatible desires. But having incompatible desires is not abnormal. Nor is it irrational—though being unable to order one's desires might be. There is serious difficulty, however, in imagining a normal person who has conflicting intentions. What would it be like to be in a mental state such that one, say, *both* intends to eat a second piece of pie and at the same time intends to refrain from doing so? That person is not merely in a state of conflict: rather he lacks coherence among his mental states to a degree that inhibits action.

A fourth difference between desiring and intending is this. If a person intends to do something, say B, and if he realizes that Aing is the means to Bing, then he intends to A. If I intend to go to town and realize that going to town includes driving Interstate 10, then I intend to drive Interstate 10. But it could happen that a person desire to B and realize that Aing is the means to Bing, and not desire to A. I might desire to be rid of my toothache and realize that in order to be rid of it, I must visit the dentist; but at the same time I might well not want to visit the dentist. Indeed it is far from extraordinary when someone desires to achieve some end but does not desire to do what is necessary to achieve it.[3]

There is a fifth difference, which has already been mentioned. A person can desire to do something himself or he can desire that someone else do something. Richard can desire that he himself vote, and he can desire that Pat vote. But a person can only intend to do something himself. Richard cannot intend that Pat vote. Of course Richard can intend to do something, say, cajole or threaten Pat, such that as a causal consequence of his action, Pat votes. But it cannot be the case that Richard intends to do something such that as a direct causal result *Pat* performs an action. To say it another way, there is a true uniactional reading of 'Richard desires that Pat vote,' that is, a literal reading in which this sentence is true and there is exactly one action in the offing. But there is no true uniactional reading of 'Richard intends that Pat vote'; read literally, this sentence is true only if there are two actions in the offing, one performed by Richard and one by Pat. This last difference between desiring and intending suggests that intending is more 'intimately' or 'closely' connected with action than desiring.

Taken together, these differences strongly point toward distinguishing between the folk psychological attitudes of intending and desiring. The differences between these attitudes cannot be explained by the claim that intending is a complex attitude consisting of desiring plus believing. The first two differences between intending and desiring concern the fact that intending is not a graded attitude, whereas desiring is. This difference is not eliminated if believing is added to desiring. Believing too is graded; and a non-graded attitude is not generated by conjoining two graded ones, as it were. The third difference is, basically, this: a sentence of the form 'S Vs to A and S Vs to refrain from Aing' is trivially false if 'V' is 'intend' but may be true if 'V' is 'desire.' Adding belief to desire does not yield an attitude such that a sentence of this form is trivially false. It is not inconceivable—indeed, it sometimes happens—that persons have contradictory beliefs about what they will do. The fourth difference is that means are always intended, though not always desired. An undesirable means does not become desired if the subject believes that he will in fact perform that action. The fifth difference is that intending, but not desiring, is always self-directed. Since beliefs about future actions are not restricted to one's own actions, adding belief to desire does not yield an attitude that is always self-directed.

There are certain essential distinctions to be made among the mental events antecedent to action. One of these distinctions is between those events that directly initiate and guide action and those that set background preferences leading to a course of action. My main quarrel with the thesis that desiring is a species of intending, as well as the reductive thesis (DB), is that it suppresses this distinction. The folk psychological attitudes of intending and desiring reflect the distinction between initiating and guiding action, on the one hand, and setting preferences, on the other. Or at least they reflect this distinction as well as folk psychology reflects any sharp, analytical distinction. This distinction can be seen more clearly in the context of a reconstructed folk psychological picture of the act-sequence.

3. A Reconstructed Folk Psychological Model of the Act-Sequence

Basically, desiring is an intention-former, that is, a partial cause of intention. In combination with background beliefs, and moderated by physiological needs, emotional demands, and environmental conditions, desire brings about intention, which then yields overt action. This folk psychological model is depicted by figure 5.1.

The arrows between boxes represent causality and the boxes represent events (or more exactly, sequences of events). This diagram depicts deliberate, intentional action involving perceptual feedback. In some ways the diagram is overly complicated, and in some ways it is overly simple. Not all action is deliberate and intentional; and not all action involves feedback. Strictly speaking, the only element common to all action is immediate intention. This model is sim-

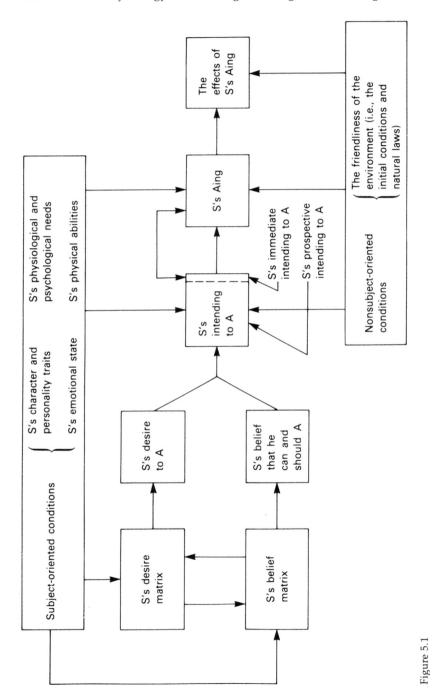

Figure 5.1
The simplified, folk psychological model of the act-sequence.

plified in that background conditions are assumed constant throughout the sequence. That assumption is especially noteworthy in the
case of the subject's emotional states. A person's affective states can
short-circuit planned activity and can affect the manner in which an
action is performed. Here, however, I assume that affective states
remain constant and relatively ineffectual throughout the act sequence. A complete account of the act sequence would detail the role
of the emotions in action.

A subject's desire matrix includes his preferences about Aing, as
well as his preferences about alternatives to Aing. Similarly a subject's belief matrix includes his beliefs about his opportunity and his
ability to A, as well as beliefs about alternatives to his Aing. These
two sets of psychological attitudes interact, resulting in the formation
of a desire to A and a belief that he is able to A and that A is valuable.
The subject's beliefs concern not only what he is able to do, but also
what it is *valuable* for him to do. The value attributed to Aing can
result from matters of interest as well as deontic considerations, such
as duties and obligations. Desire concerns only the subject's preferences; belief concerns his prediction of success and what he should
do (but cf. Davidson, 1978).

Subject-oriented conditions are causally relevant prior to the formation of the desire and belief to A, remain relevant through the
performance of A but cease to be affective after the subject has Aed,
though they normally continue to obtain after this time and affect
other actions. Nonsubject-oriented conditions, in the single-agent
case depicted here, involve only the environment. These events become causally relevant when the subject intends to A, and they remain relevant through the production of the action's effects.

Practical reasoning is not explicitly depicted in this simplified
model. It is, basically, the process by which intentions are formed
from beliefs and desires. Aristotle is often interpreted as claiming
that the conclusion of a practical syllogism is an action. But this claim
confuses the psychological events leading to action with their representation. The spirit of Aristotle's claim, I think, can be captured
by taking the belief and desire to be psychological events represented by the premises of a practical syllogism and the intention to
be an event represented by the conclusion of the syllogism. The intention causes the action, provided that the environment is friendly
and the subject's emotions, personality, needs, physiological condition, and so on, do not prevent the intention from being effective. If
the prospective action is complex, the intention involves a plan to
accomplish it. This plan can be represented as a practical sorites, that
is, a chain of practical syllogisms. Under this interpretation Aris-

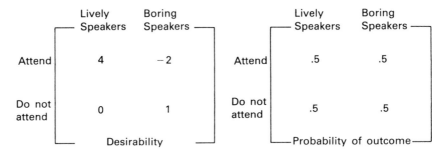

Figure 5.2
Desirability and probability schemata for attending the conference.

totle's view of practical reasoning corresponds to the folk psychological model. Of course not all action is preceded by practical
reasoning. A desire can lead directly to an intention, for example, in
impetuous action, and an intention can be formed despite desires to
the contrary, for example in dutiful, unpleasant action.

Deliberation is the first stage of practical reasoning; it is the interaction of the desire and belief matrices—the weighing of alternatives, as it were. It is an interesting psychological question how, and
the extent to which, people actually form beliefs and desires as a
result of deliberation. A different, equally interesting conceptual
question concerns the rationality of deliberation. One plausible answer to the latter is that the rationality of deliberation is a measure of
similarity to the deliberations of an ideally rational subject. Many
decision theorists assume that an ideally rational subject would fit
the Bayesian model, in which an action type is selected on the basis
of expected utility (desirability) and probability for success (beliefs
about oneself and the environment). For instance, suppose that our
ideally rational subject is deliberating about accepting a conference
invitation. He does not know who the speakers are, and he fears that
he will be bored. We can imagine him setting up the desirability and
probability schemata shown in figure 5.2.

The first square in this figure indicates the values attached to each
possible outcome, and the second indicates the subjective probability assigned to the likelihood of each outcome. Multiplying these together, we obtain the schemata in figure 5.3. Now adding across, the
desirability of attending the conference is 1 and the desirability of
not attending is .5. Thus this framework yields that the ideally rational subject will take steps to attend. I leave the details and complications of the Bayesian model of decision making to others (see

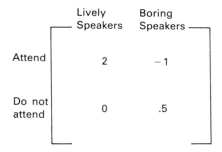

	Lively Speakers	Boring Speakers
Attend	2	− 1
Do not attend	0	.5

Figure 5.3
Combined schemata for attending the conference.

especially Jeffrey, 1965). I also leave to others the issue of the discrepancy between this ideal and actual decision making (cf., e.g., Grether, 1980).

4. Some Preliminary Remarks about Desiring

The previous section dealt with the causal role of desiring. But folk psychology is not limited to issues of causal status: it also concerns conceptual structure. In this and the next sections I discuss the 'logic' of desire.

The primary form of desire sentences is:

(1) S desires to A,

where S ranges over subjects (typically, persons) and A over action types. This sentence form is to be rewritten as 'S self-favors acquiring the property of Aing,' though here I shall use the conversational form (1). It was argued in the previous chapter that *de re* desires are to be understood in terms of self-referential desires; that is, sentences of the following forms are definable in terms of (1):

(2) S desires S' to F (or, S desires of S' that he F),

(3) S desires x to F (or, S desires of x that it F),

where F need not be an action type. Instances of (2) are 'Richard desires John to take out the trash' and 'Pat desires of Richard that he resign.' Instances of (3) are 'Jerry desires his car to start' and 'Ronny desires of the country that it become conservative.' The range of x in (3) includes spatiotemporal objects, such as physical objects and events, as well as abstract and constructed entities. *De dicto* desires are also to be understood in terms of self-referential desires. *De dicto* desires are reported by sentences of the form

(4) *S* desires that *p*.

An instance of (4) is 'John Paul desires that there be peace on earth.'

There is another form that a desire sentence can take:

(5) *S* desires *x*.

Here again *x* ranges over spatiotemporal objects as well as abstract and constructed entities. Instances of (5) are 'Pat desires that dress' and 'Richard desires happiness.' I take it that (5) is a version of (1) with a suppressed action-type variable. Sentences of this form can be made nonelliptical by adding a verb phrase in which '*x*' occurs as a direct object. Of course the verb phrase cannot always be determined from a sentence of the form (5) alone; a context is usually required. 'Pat desires that dress' most likely would come to 'Pat desires to own that dress'; but depending on the context, it might be a circumlocution for 'Pat desires to fondle that dress,' or some such. Usually when *x* is an abstract entity, the missing verb is 'to exemplify' or some synonym. For instance, 'Richard desires happiness' becomes 'Richard desires to exemplify (the property) happiness,' or in better English, 'Richard desires to be happy.' To repeat, (5) is an abridged form of (1), where the verb for the action type in (1) takes a direct object; the particular verb is context-dependent, and generally cannot be determined by a sentence of the form (5) alone.

Forms (1) to (5) contain 'desire.' Some instances of these forms are more natural when 'want' is substituted for 'desire.' For example, 'Pat desires that dress' and 'Richard desires John to take out the trash' seem stilted and might be better expressed as 'Pat wants that dress' and 'Richard wants John to take out the trash.' There are a number of contrasts that ordinary usage of 'desire' and 'want' probably reflect. 'Desire' is often used when the action type involves the 'lower' appetites, especially sexual appetites, or when the action type involves some sort of impulsive activity. 'Want' is often used when there is forethought. For simplicity, however, I shall not introduce machinery to reflect these contrasts and shall use 'desire' and 'want' interchangeably.

Goldman makes a distinction between standing and occurrent desires (or wants). "An occurrent want is a mental event or mental process; it is a 'going on' or 'happening' in consciousness. A standing want . . . is a disposition or propensity to have an occurrent want, a disposition that lasts with the agent for a reasonable length of time" (1970, p. 86). (See also Alston, 1967.) This is a useful distinction. Suppose that every time I have the opportunity to have french-vanilla ice cream for dessert, I take it. It is then true of me that I want to have french-vanilla ice cream for dessert. But I do not want french-vanilla ice cream every moment of every waking day. When engaged in many activities, the thought of having this dessert does not occur to me. At those times, I want french-vanilla ice cream for dessert, but not in an ongoing, occurrent way. I want it in the sense that, if I am in the appropriate circumstances and there are no interfering conditions, there will be an occurrent mental event of wanting going on in me.

There is an interesting potential problem lurking here. It is highly reasonable to maintain that occurrent desires play a role in causing action—presumably, that specified by the folk psychological causal model. But this reasonable claim appears contrary to an intuitively acceptable principle about causation: namely, if one event causes another, then there cannot be a temporal gap between these events. Hume stated this principle more carefully as follows: " 'Tis an established maxim both in natural and moral philosophy, that an object, which exists for any time in its full perfection without producing another, is not its sole cause . . ." (Treatise 1.3.2). That is, for any events e and f and time interval t, if e occurs during t and e does not genuinely change during t and e is the cause of f, then f occurs during t. (An example of a genuine event change is a magnetic field's increasing in strength. Genuine changes are to be contrasted with so-called Cambridge changes, in which an event gains or loses a relational property; for instance, the event of Socrates' drinking hemlock changes, in a Cambridge way, when it gains the relational property of being admired by me.) It follows from Hume's maxim that it is impossible for an occurrent desire to cause an intention, since the occurrent desire would exist for duration t and only at the terminal point of t would it bring about the intention. If desire causes intention, it must do so immediately, and not after an interval of time. In his version of the Causal Theory Davidson (1963) says that it is the onslaught, or coming into existence, of a dispositional desire (plus belief) that is causally efficacious. Occurrent desires themselves, strictly speaking, are not efficacious. Davidson has been widely followed on this point (see, e.g., Vermazen, 1980). It might well be that he was led to the view that only the onslaught of mental events are causally efficacious by reflections similar to those that led Hume to his maxim.

This objection to occurrent desires being causes can be raised against many other cases of causation (see Brand, 1980). Suppose that the failure of the traffic signal caused the automobile accident. Imagine also that the signal failed at noon, but the accident did not occur until a few minutes past noon. According to Hume's maxim, this situation is impossible. The cause, the failure of the traffic light, persisted for some time before the effect, the accident, came into existence. In short there is a dilemma. Hume's maxim is intuitively plausible but some of the situations it appears to rule impossible in fact occur. The answer to the dilemma consists in splitting the horns. Hume's maxim does not preclude actual causal situations. There are two kinds of cases to consider. An event might cause another event in virtue of being a necessary part of some complex event, or an event might cause another event in virtue of reaching a threshold, given background conditions. An example of the first kind is the failure of the traffic signal causing the automobile accident. The failure of the traffic light did not, by itself, cause the accident. Rather there is a complex event, consisting of the two automobiles traveling toward the intersection, such that these events in conjunction with the failure of the traffic light cause the accident. In this example the traffic light's failure is a necessary part of a causally sufficient condition for the accident (see Mackie, 1974). A case of the second kind is the lowering of temperature of a quantity of water causing the water to freeze. Here the event of the temperature being lowered must reach a certain threshold in order for the water to freeze, given background conditions concerning the purity of the water, atmospheric pressure, and so on. Both kinds of cases satisfy Hume's maxim. In the first example when the total cause consisting of the traffic signal's failure, the automobiles' momenta, and so on, obtains, the effect occurs. In the second example the cause is not, strictly speaking, the lowering of the temperature, but rather the temperature's reaching a threshold; and the effect occurs as soon as that threshold is reached.

Occurrent desires can be efficacious in bringing about other mental events in either of these ways. An occurrent desire, when combined with other mental events, usually beliefs, causes an intention. I take it that desires are typically linked to intentions in this way. But it might well be that there are also situations in which a background psychological state causes an intention when an occurrent desire reaches some threshold strength. Thus Davidson's claim that only the onslaught of a dispositional desire is causally efficacious is unwarranted. Occurrent desires themselves are efficacious.

5. A Preference Theory of Desire

To desire to do something is to favor doing it. That is,

(D5.1) S at t_i desires to A at t_j *iff:* (i) it is not the case that S at t_i believes that t_i is later than t_j and (ii) S at t_i favors Aing at t_j.

Consider, first, the temporal condition. Desires are often future-directed, though they need not be. Clause (i) permits concurrent desiring. Suppose that I am now eating my favorite dessert. I desire to continue eating it in the future, but I also desire to do just what I am now doing. Or suppose that Richard desires to win the race. He has this desire from sometime before the race and continues to have it until he wins or loses. Once the race is completed, he no longer desires to win, though he might well have some other, related attitude toward the race.

Persons cannot knowingly desire to change the past. They might, however, be mistaken about which events are past, and thus unknowingly desire to act in the past. For instance, on Wednesday, Richard might think that it is Monday and desire to buy a new tape recorder on Tuesday. Of course he cannot buy a new recorder on Tuesday, since it is already Wednesday; but he can, nevertheless, desire to do so because he thinks that it is not yet Tuesday. If Richard realized that Tuesday is past, then he could *wish* he had bought the recorder, but he cannot *desire* to have bought the recorder.

The key clause of (D5.1) is, of course, (ii). Favoring is a type of preference. Favorings are pro-attitudes, usually of moderate duration. Typically they are not lifelong inclinations or prejudices, such as unwillingness to take financial risks or hatred of cold weather, nor are they momentary impulses or urges, such as a sudden and short-lived impulse to smile at a passing stranger. There are, however, no hard-and-fast rules about the duration of favorings; some can be relatively long-term and stable, while others can be relatively short-term and unstable.

'Favor' is not closed under implication. Let us say that kind F entails kind G just in case it is necessary that everything that is F also is G. Thus it is false that:

(6) If S favors Aing and Aing entails Bing, then S favors Bing.

Suppose that Richard favors reading a story by Mark Twain. Reading a story by Mark Twain entails reading a story by Samuel Clemens. But Richard might not favor reading a story by Samuel Clemens; he might mistakenly think that Samuel Clemens and Mark Twain are distinct persons, and that Clemens, unlike Twain, is the quintessential dull writer.

An interesting question is whether a doxastically restricted version of (6) is true, say:

(7) If S favors Aing and Aing entails Bing and S believes that Aing entails Bing, then S favors Bing.

Clearly the counterexample to (6) is not in conflict with (7). Since Richard does not believe that reading a story by Mark Twain entails reading a story by Samuel Clemens, the antecedent of (7) is false.

It seems reasonable to require (7) as a constraint on rationality. Being rational involves more than having a consistent set of beliefs. At the very least, it also involves having a consistent pattern of desires. Of course not all human agents have consistent patterns of desires; and thus as a matter of fact, (7) is false. Persons are rational some of the time, perhaps most of the time, but not all the time. This principle would be true only if the range of S were restricted to ideally rational agents.

Consider the following principle:

(8) If S favors Aing and S favors Bing, then S favors Aing and Bing.

One problem for (8) is that an agent might never put together his desires, as it were.[4] The consequent of (8) seems to require S to form a new attitude, one which has as its object a conjunctive action; but the antecedent of (8) does not require S to form any attitude having a conjunctive object. There are, moreover, counterexamples to (8). Sometimes persons have equally strong, competing desires. Suppose that I favor eating bananas for a midday snack and that I also favor eating pickles for that snack. But I do not favor eating both bananas and pickles. It might be thought that my initial attitudes are disjunctive, in that I favor eating bananas *or* I favor eating pickles. But not so. I want to eat the bananas and I want to eat the pickles, but not both at once.

Let us turn from the critical to the constructive. 'Favor,' like other mental attitude predicates, can be either internally or externally negative. That is,

(9) S favors not-Aing

is to be distinguished from

(10) It is not the case that S favors Aing.

There is some difficulty in interpreting (9). 'Not' cannot be given a sentence-operator interpretation, since it prefixes a singular term. The most natural reading is that (9) says *S* favors refraining from *A*ing. An alternative interpretation is that *S* favors being indifferent with respect to *A*. There are cases in which we desire to be neutral about some future course of action, though these cases are not common. Under both interpretations of (9), the following four locutions form a square of opposition: *S* favors *A*ing, *S* favors not-*A*ing, it is not the case that *S* favors not-*A*ing, it is not the case that *S* favors *A*ing. '*S* favors *A*ing' and 'it is not the case that *S* favors *A*ing' are contradictories; and '*S* favors not-*A*ing' and 'it is not the case that *S* favors not-*A*ing' are contradictories.

Favoring is definable in terms of preferring one action to another. Preferring one action to another is comparative, while favoring to do something is noncomparative. The general strategy for explicating a noncomparative notion in terms of a comparative one is, first, to define a notion of indifference and then to define the noncomparative notion as surpassing what is indifferent.

One initially attractive suggestion for defining preferential indifference is the following (cf. Chisholm and Sosa, 1966):

(11) *S* is indifferent with respect to *A*ing *iff:* (i) it is not the case that *S* prefers *A*ing to refraining from *A*ing; and (ii) it is not the case that *S* prefers refraining from *A*ing to *A*ing.

But this is a very weak notion of indifference. Being indifferent in this sense is compatible with the subject having no preferences at all with respect to *A*ing. A subject is indifferent, according to (11), to infinitely many actions, toward most of which he has no attitudes or beliefs. Another way to make the point is to observe that the definiens of (11) is satisfied if the subject is dead, since it does not require that he have any attitudes at all. But clearly, the subject is not indifferent if he is dead, at least not in any interesting sense of 'indifferent' that concerns the subject's desires. Rather, indifference is to be explicated relative to a subject's actual preferences.

Let us say that a person has a *normal preference matrix* if he has at least a moderate number of preferences and these preferences are broadly distributed in strength and direction. Subjects who have no preferences or who prefer performing very limited kinds of actions or doing everything to the same degree do not have normal preference matrices. The requisite notion of indifference is now definable:

(D5.2) If S has a normal preference matrix, then S is indifferent
with respect to Aing *iff:*
(i) it is not the case that S prefers Aing to refraining from Aing
and it is not the case that S prefers refraining from Aing to Aing;
and
(ii) there is some action type B such that S prefers Aing to Bing
and there is some action type C such that S prefers Cing to Aing.

Clause (ii) guarantees that S has preferences with regard to Aing and
that Aing is not some action type foreign to S's attitudes and beliefs.
I assume that normal subjects are indifferent in this sense to some
actions.

Defining 'favoring' in terms of 'comparative preferring,' now,

(D5.3) S favors Aing *iff:* for any action type B, if S is indifferent
with respect to Bing, then S prefers Aing to Bing.

For example, Pat favors drinking wine just in case, for every type of
action toward which she is indifferent, say, kissing Richard good-
night this evening, she prefers drinking wine to it. Disfavoring is
similarly definable.

(D5.4) S opposes Aing *iff:* for any action type B, if S is indifferent with respect to Bing, then S prefers Bing to Aing.

We are also in a position to explicate totally or fully favoring and
totally or fully opposing doing something.

(D5.5) S fully favors Aing *iff:* (i) S favors Aing and (ii) there is no
action type B such that S prefers Bing to Aing.

(D5.6) S fully opposes Aing *iff:* (i) S opposes Aing and (ii) there
is no action type B such that S prefers Aing to Bing.

An ardent conscientious objector, for instance, fully opposes bearing
arms in battle: he opposes it, and there is no action type such that he
prefers bearing arms to it. Granting that 'prefers' is asymmetrical, the
second clause of (D5.6) is equivalent in this case to saying that every
action type is such that it is preferred to bearing arms. Notice that a
subject may fully favor or fully oppose many actions simultaneously,
since he might favor or oppose them with equal strength and favor or
oppose no action more than these.[5]

One consequence of these definitions is that it explains why de-
sirings can be ordered in strength and scaled, while intendings
cannot. Desiring is defined in terms of favoring, and favoring is unpacked by means of comparative preferring. Since preferences can be
compared, and thus ranked, desires too can be ranked, or graded.

But intending is not definable in terms of a comparative notion, as we shall see. Unlike desire, then, it does not admit of degrees.

The distinction between favoring and comparative preferring is orthogonal to the distinction between intrinsic and extrinsic preference. With regard to action, the latter divides favoring doing something for its own sake, as an end in itself, from favoring doing something as a means; and it divides comparatively preferring doing something for its own sake from comparatively preferring doing something as a means. That is, there are four categories of preference in action: intrinsic favoring, extrinsic favoring, intrinsic comparative preferring, and extrinsic comparative preferring. Pat might favor looking at a certain painting for its own sake, and not in comparison with other paintings; or she might favor looking at that painting as a means to something else, say, as a potential investment, without, however, comparing it to other possible investments. Richard might prefer one wine to others intrinsically, for its own sake; or he might prefer that wine to others for some extrinsic reason, say, because of its prestige value.

Comparative preference is primitive in these analyses. But that does not mean that nothing further can be said about it. There are indeed two complementary methods for gaining an understanding of comparative preference. One is descriptive. The goal of this method is to give an account of the properties of preference exhibited by actual subjects. An account of this type is generated by psychological testing and measurement. There is recent work in cognitive psychology that bears on such an account, though caution is required in extrapolation. For example, Kahneman and Tversky have produced interesting results about actual decision making (see especially Kahneman, Slovic, and Tversky, 1982). However, the vast majority of this work concerns subjects' reasoning under conditions of uncertainty; but preference, as understood here, is not a process of reasoning at all.

The second is normative. This method consists, basically, in providing an account of the properties of preference exhibited by ideally rational subjects. Such an account is conveniently summarized by an axiom system. Some results from microeconomics bear on the normative theory of preference, though here too caution is required in extrapolation. For example, there is some temptation to identify preference and expected utility, as that notion is developed by von Neumann and Morgenstern. However, expected utility concerns the value of a course of action assigned, partially, in virtue of the subjective probabilities the subject attaches to present and future states of nature. That is, expected utility is, partially, a function of the subject's beliefs. But preference, as understood here, is independent of the subject's beliefs: it is subjects' raw pro-attitudes. (For an introduction to this normative approach, see Sen, 1970.)

From the normative perspective, preference seems to be transitive, asymmetrical, and irreflexive (cf. Körner, 1976, chapter 4). But it is highly controversial whether actual preferences exhibit these properties. Transitivity, in particular, does not appear to reflect actual orderings. In fact the following principle of weak transitivity appears to be descriptively inaccurate (from Chisholm and Sosa, 1966):

(12) If it is not the case that S prefers Aing to Bing and it is not the case that S prefers Bing to Cing, then it is not the case that S prefers Aing to Cing.

Suppose that S does not prefer Aing to Bing, but almost does. The reason why he does not prefer Aing to Bing is that the difference between them is not greater than his threshold for preference. Suppose also that S does not prefer Bing to Cing, but almost does. In this case the subject might well prefer Aing to Cing. When the differences between the two pairs of actions are added, it is greater than the minimal threshold for preference. This case resembles that of perceptual relations. Relations such as 'is louder than,' 'is brighter than,' and 'is more salty than' do not obey analogues of (12). The subject might not be able to distinguish between the loudness of sounds a and b; though the decibel reading of b is greater than a, it is not sufficient to be noticed by the subject. The subject also cannot distinguish between the loudness of b and c, since b is not louder than c by an amount greater than the subject's threshold of discrimination. But the added differences between a and c are greater than the subject's threshold, and thus he can discriminate them.

From our vantage point, a descriptive account of comparative preferring is more valuable than a normative one. Our objective is to explain the folk psychological attitudes leading to action. One of these attitudes is desiring; but desiring, in turn, is to be analyzed in terms of comparative preference. Thus the focus of attention should be primarily the properties of comparative preference exhibited by normal persons. The descriptive theory of comparative preference is fertile ground for future investigation.

6. Some Other Attitudes

Intending, desiring, and believing are distinct kinds of attitudes. A number of other folk psychological attitudes can be defined in terms of these, though it is doubtful that all attitudes can be so defined.

Prior to offering such definitions, let me reissue a warning. The following definitions do not purport to capture the totality of pre-analytic intuitions. Those intuitions, more than likely, do not form a consistent, unified whole. These definitions are partially stipulative: they are refinements of ordinary intuitions made to reflect important conceptual distinctions.

A person wishes to do something when he wants to do it but thinks that doing it is impossible. That is,

(D5.7) S at t_i wishes to A at t_j iff: (i) S at t_i desires to A at t_j; and (ii) S at t_i believes that it is impossible for him to A at t_j.

The impossibility mentioned in clause (ii) is typically physical. Suppose that a middle-aged, overweight jogger, wishes to run a four-minute mile. Thus he wants to run a four-minute mile, but he believes that, given the initial conditions, it is physically impossible for him to do so. Or suppose that a paraplegic wishes to walk across the room. He wants to walk, but believes that, given the state of his body, it is physically impossible for him to do so. The subject's belief can be either occurrent or standing. It is physically impossible for S to A at t if there is no world w identical to the actual world with respect to the laws of nature and the conditions at $t-\Delta t$ such that S A's at t in w. The impossibility mentioned in clause (ii) might be logical, where it is logically impossible for S to A at t if there is no world w such that S A's at t in w.[6] Thus Richard's wish to be at two places at once amounts to Richard's wanting to be at two places at once but believing that that is (logically) impossible. Given normal presumptions about knowledge, past-directed preferences are wishes. If Jimmy knows that he lost the race, he cannot want to have won, only wish to have won. He believes, rightly, that it is now (logically) impossible for him to bring it about that he won earlier (cf. Chisholm and Taylor, 1960).

Ascriptions of wishing do not always have the form 'S wishes to A.' They can also have the form 'S wishes that p' or 'S wishes for x,' where p ranges over propositions and x over physical objects. These forms can be understood in terms of 'S wishes to A.' S wishes for x just in case there is some A such that S wishes to A x. For instance, Richard wishes for jewels if Richard wishes to own jewels, to obtain jewels, or some such. Further, S wishes that p just in case S wishes to contribute to p's being the case. John Paul wishes that there would be peace on earth if he wishes to contribute to there being peace on earth. Richard wishes that he had not made the recordings if he wishes to contribute to the recordings not having been made.

An attitude that bears some similarity to wishing is hoping. But hoping is more closely connected with action than wishing. When someone hopes to do something, he has set himself to do it, but thinks that there are potential obstacles to his doing it. More exactly,

(D5.8) S at t_i hopes to A at t_i iff: (i) S at t_i intends to A at t_i; (ii) S at t_i believes that there are conditions K such that there is a reasonable probability P that K will occur and K's occurring will prevent him from Aing.

Ted hopes to win the race if he intends to win it, though he believes that there is a reasonable chance that someone else will win. Here too the subject's belief can be either occurrent or standing.

Conditions K are not normally within the subject's control to bring about or to prevent from occurring. A person hopes to do something when he suspects that the environment or other persons are not friendly to his action. But conditions K could be within S's control, in which case hoping sometimes includes an additional intending. Suppose that I hope to fly to New York. To do so, let us also suppose, I must make a reservation. However, I am forgetful and sometimes neglect to make airplane reservations. Thus I intend to fly to New York, but I believe that there is a non-negligible chance that I will forget to make reservations. In this kind of case I could be expected to intend to make the reservations. I have two distinct but related intentions: I intend to fly to New York and I also intend to do what is necessary to put myself in a position to carry out my intention to fly to New York.

Judith Jarvis Thomson claims that 'hopes' is compatible with 'knows.' " 'Hope,' " she says, "suggests uncertainty. But I am inclined to think that this is a mere suggestion (as opposed to an entailment)" (1977, p. 260). According to (D5.8), 'hopes' does suggest uncertainty, in that clause (ii) says that the subject believes that there is a reasonable chance of failure. But hoping, contrary to Thomson's claim, is incompatible with knowing. Presumably a person knows that p only if he justifiably believes that p. Justifiable belief is not the same as certainty; nevertheless, it would seem that a person cannot justifiably believe that p, while also believing that there is some chance, perhaps a good chance, that p is not the case. Notice that this conclusion has not been reached by means of the premises that hoped-for actions are future events and that we cannot know anything about the future. We can, I would contend, know some propositions about the future. As in other cases of knowledge, it depends on the evidence.

Thomson (1977, pp. 255 ff.) also claims that hoping is necessary for doing something intentionally. This claim too is mistaken—unless some technical sense of 'hopes' is introduced. Sometimes we intentionally do something while having full confidence in our doing it, without having the slightest doubt that we will succeed. Simple actions, such as winking, can be intentionally performed under these conditions. Observe that the converse of the claim is also false: hoping is not sufficient for acting intentionally. Hoping consists, in part, of intending. But as I argued in the first chapter, intending is not itself sufficient for acting intentionally. To act intentionally is to act according to plan; but not everything we do is according to plan.

A somewhat different kind of attitude is needing. Needing is connected with lacking: a person needs to do something if he lacks something and desires not to lack it. Lacking, in turn, can be thought of as a deficiency or deprivation. For the moment let us restrict consideration to physiological deprivations. So, for example, Pat needs to drink water if her body lacks water and she desires that it not do so. Her body lacks water if it is deficient in water, as measured on an appropriate physiological basis. These considerations suggest the following:

(D5.9) S at t'_i needs to A at t_j *iff:* S is in a state of physiological homeostatic imbalance I such that (i) S's Aing at t_j will cause I to cease to exist or to decrease and (ii) S at t_i desires to A at t_j.

There is an implicit *ceteris paribus* qualification to clause (i).

Definition (D5.9) explicates a restricted sense of 'need'; it concerns only the need to act. An organism might have a deficiency for, say, vitamin A, without needing to act; for the subject might not desire to do something to alleviate the problem. Or similarly an unconscious patient might need glucose, but not desire it because, being unconscious, he has no desires. The needs most likely associated with a desire to act are those for air, water, food, sexual activity, safety, environmental stimulation, affiliation, and so on.

Persons have intellectual as well as physiological needs. There are needs to solve nonpractical problems, for instance, in mathematics and chess; there are needs for fantasy and suppression of guilt; there are needs for understanding one's environment. Such needs do not seem to result from physiological homeostatic imbalances—or rather they do not seem to have direct physiological causes in the way that thirst and hunger do. The most plausible approach for dealing with these needs is to say that the subject is in a state of mental conflict such that performing some action will cause his conflict state to subside and he desires to perform that type of action. For instance, 'Bertrand needs to prove the theorem' means that Bertrand is in a state of mental conflict such that his proving the theorem will cause his conflict to subside and he wants to prove the theorem. The notion of a conflict state plays the same role as physiological homeostatic imbalance. It is, however, far from clear what a mental conflict state is. It might best be understood in terms of anxiety (cf. Weiner, 1972). However, it may be that anxiety is a symptom of mental conflict, not a defining characteristic, and that conflict can be understood only by invoking some conceptual apparatus that divides the mind into parts.

There is another attitude, caring, on which some light can also be shed. We care about animate as well as inanimate objects. People care about their favorite hats, their new automobiles, their potted palms, their pet cats, their friends and children. Someone can care only about what he believes exists. No one at all world-wise cares about unicorns or gremlins. It might be said that someone can care about abstract entities, such as the ideal of freedom from oppression. In these cases to care about something is to desire to perform actions that contribute toward making the world more like that ideal than it is presently.

To care about a person or physical object is to desire to take steps to prevent that person or object from being harmed or destroyed and to desire to take steps to nurture and improve that person or object, given certain beliefs about the environment. For instance, Richard cares about his dog; and thus he wants to prevent it from being harmed, if the occasion should arise, and he wants to nurture it and improve its well-being, by feeding it nutritious food, giving it exercise, and so on. In another less passive sense, to care about a person or object involves not only desiring to prevent harm and to nurture and improve the person or object, given certain beliefs, but also to intend to take steps in these directions. Richard *actively cares* for his dog, then, only if he intends to act on his desires about its well-being.

We can go further. Armed with the notion of caring, the nonaffective part of loving can be defined. A person S loves something x if he cares about x and there is no other thing he cares more about than it. He cares more about x than, say, y, if he cares about both and his desires about the well-being of x are stronger than his desires about the well-being of y. It is thus possible to love more than one thing, since persons can care equally strongly for a number of objects. Ordinarily the objects of love are persons. But they need not be: a cowboy might love his horse, a spinster her cat, or a miser his money.

One consequence of this definition of 'loving' is that, for all the objects we love, we love them equally. But, it might be said, a father can love his two daughters, though love one more than the other. This objection shows the difficulty of separating the affective and nonaffective part of loving. If the father loves both daughters, he cares for them equally: he is equally concerned about their well-being and protection. Nevertheless the father might *feel* differently toward each daughter. He might feel more affectionate or proud of one. With regard to the nonaffective features of loving, that is, with regard to caring, his attitude toward both daughters is the same; but that is compatible with his having different emotional responses to each daughter.

These definitions can be made more precise, but I will not do so here. The point to stress is that seemingly diverse attitudes are plausibly taken to be an admixture of desiring, intending, and believing. One point, however, should be emphasized. In the case of highly complex attitudes folk psychology sometimes fails to sanction any one definition. This difficulty occurs in the case of loving, for instance, even if attention is restricted to the nonaffective component. Sometimes love is associated with restricted types of desires. Medieval courtly love permits the desire to show deep respect, but forbids the desire to make one's love known. 'Platonic' love permits the desire to share intellectual excitement and friendship, but excludes the desire to have sexual intercourse. Sometimes other sorts of constraints are placed on loving. It is sometimes held that loving must endure for an extended time period, or that only subjects that achieve emotional stability can love. I shall, however, leave a discussion of the varieties of loving to the sociologists and poets.[7]

6

Intending and Believing

In the previous chapter I discussed the conceptual foundations for the folk psychology of desiring. Intending was not the primary target, although that discussion did serve to distinguish intending from desiring. In this chapter and in the remaining ones, the primary target will be intending.

Intending has both conative and cognitive properties. That is, it has motivational properties and properties concerned with the representation of future activity and the environment. Intention is both initiatory and representational. In this chapter I will focus on the folk psychological characterization of the cognitive aspect of intention.

A highly plausible view, and one that has been adopted by many philosophers of mind, is that believing is the cognitive component of intending. The purported reduction of intending to desiring plus believing, discussed in the previous chapter, rests on that view. In sections 1 and 2 I argue that that view is mistaken. There are compelling objections to every formulation of it; and moreover, for all versions, there is the serious problem that identifying the cognitive component of intention with a belief significantly oversimplifies the content of the intention. An adequate account of intending, I will contend, must be based on a conceptual framework richer than that of folk psychology. That framework is scientific psychology, broadly understood.

Sections 3 and 4 are a brief methodological interlude: there I discuss the relationship between folk and scientific psychology. That discussion is intended to ground the critique of the first sections and to provide a rationale for the ensuing account of intention in scientific psychological terms. The issue of the relationship between folk and scientific psychology obviously has ramifications beyond that of specifying the nature of intention—however, I will not follow the argument in that direction.

1. Intending and Believing

As I mentioned, it is often held that believing is the cognitive component of intending. A first version of this folk psychological view is:

(F1) S intends to A only if S believes that S will A.

Accordingly, Gordon intends to shoot Jack only if Gordon believes that Gordon will shoot Jack.

Two immediate modifications are required to make (F1) plausible, both of which refer to earlier discussions. First, (F1) fails to reflect the self-referential nature of the subject's belief. Suppose that Gordon does not believe that he is Gordon: he believes that he is, say, James Bond. Imagine further that he believes that the person who is Gordon is a staunch pacifist. Hence Gordon does not believe that *Gordon* will shoot Jack, though *he* intends to shoot Jack. In chapter 4, I proposed a general solution to these types of problems: the objects of attitudes are properties; and attitudes such as believing are self-referential on the primitive level. Thus the consequent of (F1) should read '*S* self-ascribes the property of being someone who will *A*.' In colloquial English the self-referential feature of the consequent would be emphasized by formulating it in terms of a reflexive pronoun, namely, '*S* believes that he himself will *A*.' Let us use this colloquial mode of expression, but understand it in terms of the subject self-ascribing a property.

Second, (F1) fails to reflect the double temporal indexes of intention reports. The time at which someone is intending can be different from the time at which he intends to do something. For instance, Gordon may *now* be intending to shoot Jack *tomorrow*. The general form of an intention report is

(1) S at t_i intends to A at t_j,

where t_i and t_j are temporal durations, and where, as usual, S ranges over persons and A over action types. Following our previous terminology, let us call cases in which (1) reports an intention where t_j is later than t_i 'prospective intention,' and cases in which (1) reports an intention where $t_j = t_i$ 'immediate intention.' It is an important fact about intention that there are no true instances of (1) in which t_j is earlier than t_i; that is, there is no retrospective intention. Immediate intendings are best reported by the simplified form '*S* intends to *A* now.' In colloquial English the first temporal index, especially in first-person reports, is expressed by the present tense.

Taking these two modifications into account, (F1) can be formulated as:

(F1') S at t_i intends to A at t_j only if S at t_i believes that he himself will A at t_j, where t_j is not earlier than t_i.

Notice that believing is also doubly temporally indexed. Thus if Gordon (now) intends to shoot Jack in the morning, Gordon (now) believes that he himself will shoot Jack in the morning.

Though initially plausible, (F1') is false. The main problem is that (F1') necessarily associates predicting that one will succeed in doing something with intending to do it; but a person can intend without thinking that he will succeed. Several types of cases serve to make this point. Sometimes we intend to do something though we know that we lack the ability for invariable success. Suppose that Hilary has gotten himself into a precarious situation while climbing, the only way to safety being to leap across a wide chasm. He might have serious doubts about his ability to leap the distance successfully, but he nonetheless intends to jump it. Another type of situation involves cases of *akrasia* in which a person knows that he will not be able to abide by his own strong resolve. Suppose that Richard now intends to jog every day next week. But, based on observations of his own past behavior, he believes that he will not jog every day.

The thesis that believing is necessary for intending might, as a result, be weakened to the following:

(F2) S at t_i intends to A at t_j only if S at t_i believes that there is probability P that he himself will A at t_j, where t_j is not earlier than t_i.

Probability P is non-negligible and relative to the agent's view of the chances for success given the type of action and the circumstances. Surely Hilary believes that there is a non-negligible probability that he will complete the leap. He is not confident that he will be successful; indeed he might even be pessimistic about jumping the distance. But he thinks, it would seem, that there is some chance of success. Similarly, though Richard thinks it highly unlikely that he will in fact jog every day next week, he holds that there is some chance that his resolve will remain intact and that, contrary to his expectations, he will jog.

Nevertheless there are counterexamples. Imagine this case. Richard is absolutely convinced that, no matter the strength of his current resolve, he will succumb to weakness and not exercise. He has coolly and carefully collected data on his own behavior and has observed that whenever he intends to undertake a program of exercise, he changes his mind before he can complete the program. He is as confident about the continuation of this pattern as he is about any behavior pattern of anyone. Thus, although he now intends to jog every day next week, he does not believe that he will do so. The advocate of (F2) might reply that Richard must believe that there is some chance he will not change his mind; for without this belief, he would be wishing to jog, not intending to do so. But this response is unconvincing. Richard now has the resolve to jog; he is now fully committed to jogging. But he knows on the basis of overwhelming evidence that this resolve will dissipate prior to the week's end. At the present time he *does* intend to jog every day next week; but he does *not* believe that there is a chance that he will keep his resolve. He does not believe that it is physically impossible for him to jog every day next week; rather, he thinks that he will change his mind.

At this point another version of the thesis that believing is necessary for intending will doubtless be proposed:

> (F3) S at t_i intends to A at t_j only if S at t_i believes that he himself will try to A at t_j.

Believing that one will try to do something is consistent with believing that one will fail. Although Richard thinks that he will be unable to keep his resolve to jog, it would appear that he is confident he will at least try to do so. Similarly, although Hilary has serious doubts that he will succeed in leaping the chasm, it would seem that he does believe he will at least try to complete the jump. Hampshire and Hart, to name some proponents, essentially hold (F3): they say ". . . the minimum force of 'I intend to do x' is 'I believe that I will try to do x'" (1958, p. 11; cf. Meiland, 1970, pp. 112–115).

There are, however, problems for this version of the thesis. One problem not shared with previous versions is that it has untoward systematic consequences. Consider what it is to try to do something. Richard Taylor (1966) has argued that trying is performing one action in order to perform another (also see Chisholm, 1966). Suppose that I try to clear the highbar. I set myself and run to the bar in order to jump it. It can be objected that Taylor's view does not capture the commonsense notion of trying. Suppose that my run to the bar was slow and lackadaisical. In that case it would be judged that I did not try. The point is that, for a certain class of actions, a person tries to do something only if he makes a genuine effort. The notion of making an effort is extremely difficult to explicate: in particular, it resists analysis in purely causal terms. But even if it is agreed that Taylor's approach neglects the element of effort for some cases of trying, at least the following principle is true:

> (P1) S tries to A only if there is an action type B, distinct from A, such that S B's in order to A.

Principle (P1) in conjunction with (F3) yields that a Causal Theory in which the antecedent to action is an intention is circular. For (F3) uses the notion of trying; and trying, as (P1) says, is to be analyzed in terms of action. But action is to be understood by means of intention. A defender of (F3) could reject this type of Causal Theory of action; but that is an enormous price to pay for (F3).

A related problem for (F3) arises, given (P1). Since a person tries only if he performs one action in order to perform another, it is impossible to try to perform simple, or basic, actions. But it has been recognized for some time that a normal person *simply* raises his arm or *simply* winks: under ordinary conditions, he does not do something in order to raise his arm or in order to wink (see, e.g., Danto, 1973, especially chapter 4). Suppose now that our subject is apprised of this fact and hence, does not believe that he can try to perform simple or basic actions. It would be absurd, however, to conclude that this subject does not intend to perform these simple actions.

Furthermore, (F3) is too restrictive in the case of some nonbasic actions. Normal persons often intend to perform routinized actions without believing that they will try. Someone might well intend to get dressed in the morning, have a cup of coffee, and drive to work without having the belief, either beforehand or during these activities, that he will *try* to do them. He has been successful so often at these tasks that the thought of trying to do them never enters his mind. He performs them without thinking of trying to be successful.

There is, in addition, another type of problem for (F3), which is more fundamental. Consider Hilary's predicament again. He intends to leap the chasm; but he does not *merely* think of himself as trying to leap it. Imagine yourself in Hilary's place. What, at that moment, are you likely to be thinking about? To say that you are thinking 'I will try to leap the chasm' is to grossly oversimplify. Rather you would probably be thinking about the many details of the leap, where, for instance, to plant your foot, where to begin your approach, where to land, and so on. It is likely, moreover, that you would have a mental representation of completing the leap. The source of this representation is the memory of having completed similar, though lesser, leaps. And all the while you would also be aware that the chance for failure is high. The content of your thought at the time you intend to leap is exceedingly complex. To say that the total content is the belief that you will try to leap the chasm is to significantly, and misleadingly, oversimplify. The case of our intrepid jogger is similar. He represents to himself his jogging each day. Perhaps he imagines the route he will follow, the shower after each run, and the beer at the end of the day; perhaps he imagines his feelings of accomplishment when quite unexpectedly he completes his week of workouts. The content of his thought is complex; it includes many details extrapolated from memory. His thought may be like, as it were, a video tape or film of these workouts. It is a dramatic oversimplification to say that the total content of his cognitive attitude at that time is the belief that he will try to jog each day next week. In short, the problem with (F3) is that it loses information about the content of the subject's attitude.

The last problem is crucial—and general. The folk psychological thesis that believing is necessary for intending, in all its forms, fails to specify the cognitive component of the antecedent to action in an informative way. When a person intends to do something, he has a representation of his doing it, including a representation of the route he will follow to put himself in a position to perform the action. In the case of complex actions he sees himself carrying out a plan under the prevailing conditions. Intending involves more than believing that one will succeed, or believing that one will try to succeed, if it involves that at all.

To reinforce the point, consider an additional version of the folk psychological thesis. Davidson (1978) argues, on one reading, that a person intends to A just in case he takes it to be desirable to A and he believes, all things considered, that the world is friendly toward his Aing in the immediate future. Davidson calls the second, cognitive conjunct 'an all-out judgment.'[1] There are, however, apparent counterexamples to this cognitive condition. Someone might intend to do something despite believing that the world is unfriendly, all things considered, toward that which he takes to be desirable. For instance, Hilary might believe that, given the condition of his muscles, his fatigue, and the distance, he is not able to leap the chasm; yet since that is the only way to safety, he intends to do so. But the major difficulty with Davidson's proposal, like the earlier folk psychological ones, is that it fails to detail the mental representation a person has when initiating an action. Davidson's proposal is an improvement over (F1)–(F3) in that it makes reference to the person's beliefs about the environment, rather than merely his subjective estimate of success. However, it does not take the matter sufficiently far. Davidson formulates his proposal in terms of the folk psychological notion of belief. 'Belief' in common usage is often a dummy variable for a variety of cognitive attitudes. But even so, this folk psychological notion will be stretched beyond its bounds if its content has the necessary complexity for the cognitive component of the cause of action.

2. The Limits of Belief

The argument is this. The cognitive component of intention exhibits a high degree of complexity. Intention is temporally divisible into two: prospective intention and immediate intention. The cognitive function of prospective intention is the representation of a subject's similar past actions, his current situation, and his course of future actions. That is, the cognitive component of prospective intention is a plan. The cognitive function of immediate intention is the monitoring and guidance of ongoing bodily movement. Taken together, these cognitive mechanisms are *highly* complex. The folk psychological notion of belief, however, is an attitude that permits limited complexity of content. Thus the cognitive component of intention is something other than folk psychological belief.

Consider poor Hilary again, stranded on the cliff. He has weighed the alternatives, remaining in this precarious situation or leaping, and has decided that his best chance for survival is to leap. Having made this decision, he begins to plan his jump. He does not want to omit any detail because a minor miscalculation can be disastrous. He recalls past jumps—the foot with which he normally pushes off, the position of his body when he lands. He studies the rock formations on both sides. Finally a plan emerges. The main segments are that he will toss his pack across, kneel in the left corner, use a four-step approach, and so on. The plan is thorough and specific, and he reviews it over and again. This plan is the content of Hilary's prospective intention to leap the chasm. It is a highly complex, integrally connected representation of what he intends to do.

Hilary starts his approach. He focuses on the point of expected departure and begins running. His running, as well as other bodily movements made during the leap, proceed automatically. That means that Hilary does not attend to these movements—*not* that the movements are unmonitored or unguided. Indeed there is a complex process of monitoring and guidance, of perceptual feedback and minute course correction, that occurs. This process also involves a complex pattern of representations, though not ones ordinarily available to consciousness. This changing pattern of representations for the monitoring and guidance of bodily movement is the cognitive content of his immediate intentions.

The cognitive component of intending to perform some large-scale action, as the case of Hilary's leap illustrates, involves two distinct, though complementary representations. One is a prospective representation of the course of action and the other is a detailed pattern of representations for specific bodily movements. The first concerns the agent's plan for action and remains relatively stable throughout the activity; the second is the basis for feedback and correction during the course of the plan, and thus changes as the plan proceeds.[2] Suppose that belief were the cognitive component of intention. Then this highly complex, dual representation would be the content of a belief. But the folk psychological notion of belief is not an attitude that can support contents of this complexity. Thus the cognitive component of intention is something other than belief.

It should be clear that the cognitive component of *immediate intention* is not belief. Beliefs are consciously accessible and relatively stable. But the monitoring and guidance of motor activity is in general neither consciously accessible nor stable. Occurrent belief is at issue, not dispositional belief. In occurrent belief the contents are, as it were, kept before the mind all at once. But the monitoring and guidance of ongoing motor activity is not within consciousness at the time it is occurring. There is good reason for this. Consciousness has limited capacity. If that capacity were occupied with the monitoring and guidance of ongoing motor activity, there would be none left for the high-level prospective thinking necessary for the continued survival of the organism. It would seem that if belief is to be identified with the cognitive component of intention, it is *prospective intention* that is meant. But here too the cognitive aspect of intention is not plausibly taken to be belief. This cognitive attitude is itself too complex to be the content of a belief, construed commonsensically.

It is a feature of the folk psychological attitude of belief that its content is a *relatively simple proposition*. By that I mean the following. The 'focal' cases of belief are those in which the content is an atomic proposition, the negation of an atomic proposition, or a universally or existentially quantified proposition not containing conjunctions or disjunctions or embedded clauses. So, for example, 'Pat believes that Richard is innocent' and 'Richard believes that all lawyers are wise' are focal beliefs. Note that it will not do to say that the class of focal beliefs does include ones having conjunctive and disjunctive forms, since an atomic proposition is logically equivalent to one having a conjunctive or disjunctive form, and similarly for quantified statements. (For instance, $'p'$ and $'p \vee (q \ \& \ {-}q)'$ are logically equivalent, and so are $'(x)Fx'$ and $'Fa \ \& \ Fb \ \& \ ... \ \& \ Fn,'$ for a finite domain $\{a, b, ..., n\}$.) For from the facts that a subject believes that p and that p is logically equivalent to q, it does not follow that he believes that q: if it did, mathematics and logic would be trivial enterprises.

In addition to focal beliefs, there are 'distal' ones. One type of distal belief has an object that contains disjunctions or conjunctions. An example is 'Richard believes that either Rose Mary is a loyal friend or she is forgetful or she should play basketball for the Lakers.' However, the folk psychological notion of belief does not permit propositional contents consisting of indefinitely many conjuncts or disjuncts. It is not clear what is the maximal permitted complexity. In addition to the number of conjuncts and disjuncts, the permitted complexity is also a function of the complexity of the contained conjuncts and disjuncts and the subject's learned association between them. For example, a normal English speaker might conceivably believe that 'a' is the first letter of the alphabet and 'b' is the second letter and so on, in which case that person has a single belief with twenty-six conjuncts. The relationship between the conjuncts in this case are overlearned. However, when there is no significant association among the conjuncts and disjuncts, and each conjunct and disjunct is not itself complex, a single belief for a normal person does not contain many connectives, perhaps as few as three or four.[3]

Another type of distal belief concerns contents with embedded clauses. An example is 'Pat believes that Richard desires that John hopes that Gordon believes that Richard believes that Alex is loyal.' Here too the folk psychological notion of belief does not permit indefinite complexity. But here too the maximal permitted complexity is not a simple quantitative measure. It is a function of the complexity of the embedded clauses and the subject's prior associations between them. Where prior association is irrelevant, the complexity is again limited, perhaps to three or four embedded clauses. The belief attributed to Pat seems to be at the limit of the folk psychological notion—or perhaps beyond it.

It is not clear how to explain this limited permitted complexity. One observation is that the limited permitted complexity of belief is similar to that of hearer comprehension. After a point, comprehension of ordinary speech is hindered by complexity. Utterances with more than three or four connectives or embedded clauses are difficult, at best, to understand. As in the case of belief, prior associations of the hearer and the complexity of the contained sentences affect comprehension. It might be that belief and hearer comprehension are analogous in these respects because there are similar information processing mechanisms that underlie both—or even that there is a single mechanism. But I leave these conjectures to others.

One response to this argument is to agree that beliefs cannot be arbitrarily complex, but *strings* of beliefs can be. Although it is unreasonable to hold that a subject can believe that p_1 & p_2 & ... & p_n, for a large n, it is not unreasonable to hold that he simultaneously believes that p_1 and he believes that p_2 and ... and he believes that p_n. The cognitive attitude associated with intention, then, is an arbitrarily long string of beliefs. However, this response is sophistical. The requisite type of complexity has not been achieved. The subject might have a string of beliefs without connecting the contents of these beliefs. The cognitive attitude associated with intention involves having a complex representation consisting of interconnected parts. This interconnectivity among the parts is not guaranteed by having a string of beliefs. One might claim that the subject also has second-order beliefs, beliefs about the connectivity of his beliefs. But this line is desperate. It threatens to be viciously regressive and, moreover, fails to be psychologically realistic.

Stich (1978) has pointed to a distinction between beliefs and what he calls subdoxastic states. Beliefs are accessible to consciousness and have global inferential connections. A simple belief such as that the cat is on the mat is implicated with the entire network of beliefs about animals, living things, furniture, houses, and so on. Subdoxastic states lack these two properties. Stich cites the processes constituting vision and grammatical speech production as examples of subdoxastic states. In vision there are complex event sequences that take the incoming stimuli into a form of mental representation; and in grammatical speech production there are complex rules that take a mental representation into outgoing phonemes. Persons do not have access to the processes constituting vision or grammatical speech production (though under special circumstances they can gain access to some portions of them). Moreover these states are not an integral part of the web of inferences characteristic of belief. There might be some inferential connections between, say, the states constituting vision; but these connections are local.

The monitoring and guidance of motor activity would be another instance of a subdoxastic state. There are complex rules, or operations, that map patterns of representations onto bodily movements. Persons do not normally have access to those representations. And although there is inferential connection with prior plans, these connections are not global. Representations for monitoring and guiding bodily movements are not implicated with all or most high-level mental states.

Stich's distinction can be extended to a tripartite one. Some mental states are *superdoxastic*. This type of state (or rather event) shares with belief the property of being inferentially connected. The degree to which this connectivity is global depends on the type of superdoxastic state; but generally speaking, superdoxastic states are far more inferentially bound than subdoxastic ones. However, superdoxastic states have two properties that folk psychological beliefs lack. First, these states exhibit significant internal complexity. This complexity is twofold. A mental representation of eating in a fancy French restaurant, for instance, involves a large number of minute steps, clearly more than three or four—probably on the order of three or four dozen. These minute steps, moreover, are ordered either serially or hierarchically in terms of the major segments of the activity. The ordinary notion of belief, as I argued, cannot support this degree of complexity in content. The second, related difference is that superdoxastic states are accessible to consciousness but normally only in parts. Given the enormous complexity of a representation for eating in a fancy French restaurant, it is not possible under ordinary circumstances to access all the parts simultaneously. Generally speaking, persons access plans of this type by means of some abbreviatory device; or they access part of the representation, such as the major segments without the contained minute steps, or only a single segment with its contained minute steps. In contrast, folk psychological beliefs are accessible in full on a single occasion.

Let me fix this last distinction with another example.[4] Suppose that Pat believes that the constitution is true. She knows very little about the constitution, never having read it or listened to others talk about it. The total content of her belief is *that the constitution is true*. That belief is inferentially connected with others, but it itself is a simple, focal belief. Now contrast Pat's belief with Richard's attitude toward the constitution. He has read it many times and knows its underlying principles, its subtleties, and its details. The content of Richard's attitude is far more complex than Pat's. Pat can easily access the content of her attitude, but at any one time Richard cannot keep before consciousness the entire content of his attitude. The content of Richard's attitude exhibits significant internal structure, whereas the content of Pat's attitude is relatively simple. And while Pat's attitude toward the constitution is inferentially connected with other attitudes she has, the lines of connectivity are minuscule in comparison with Richard's. An adequate account of mental states would draw a distinction between these attitudes. Folk psychology makes none, taking them both to be beliefs.

In general, folk psychology has an impoverished taxonomy of cognitive attitudes. A more refined theory is required to explain the differences and similarities between subdoxastic states, medium-level cognitive states (beliefs), and superdoxastic ones. Scientific psychology has long—though not continuously—been concerned with cognitive attitudes. I suggest that an explanation of these attitudes, especially the sub- and superdoxastic ones, is provided by scientific psychology, tempered by folk psychology.

Suppose that this suggestion is right. There is in that case an important consequence for action theory. An action is an event caused by an intention. Since the cognitive component of intention cannot be informatively explained within the framework of folk psychology, neither can intention itself—nor, consequently, action. An informative explanation of cognitive events will be within the context of scientific psychology. Thus explanations of intention and action will be within this context, at least to some significant degree. This is action theory naturalized. An explication of the key concepts of intention and action will be at least partially within a scientific context. Folk psychology alone is not adequate to the task.[5]

There is room for confusion here. It was argued that, in order to explain intention, the folk psychological notion of belief must be replaced by some scientific construct. But then is the purely folk psychological notion of intention being explained? Similarly if actions are events caused by intentions, and intentions are to be explained within a scientific context, is the purely folk psychological notion of action being explained? The answer to both questions is '*no.*' The result of replacing belief with some scientific construct has the effect of *transforming* the folk psychological notions of intention and action into ones that are to be understood, at least partially, within a scientific context.

Let us be clear about the terminology. The reconstructed notion of belief is not to be referred to by 'belief,' but there was no concomitant eschewal of 'intention' and 'action.' We could introduce new terms for the scientifically reconstructed concepts of intention and action, though I shall refrain from doing so. (Actually some technical terminology has been introduced, since 'immediate intention' and 'prospective intention' do not occur in folk psychology.) I shall drop 'belief' where possible, since that term seems to have well-entrenched folk psychological connotations; but not follow suit for 'intention' and 'action.' These terminological fiats are admittedly arbitrary. The key point which is not terminological is that the phenomena in which we are interested are best explained within a scientific context.

In response it might be questioned whether the turn to scientific psychology is really necessary. Even though folk psychology lacks the resources to explain intention and action, can it not be enriched to do so? Consider the cognitive attitude associated with prospective intention. Granted, it is not belief. But cannot a new attitude with the requisite permitted complexity of content be added to folk psychology? Of course such an attitude can be invented and added to folk psychology. Indeed philosophers concerned with action plans (for example, Goldman, 1970 and Toumela, 1977) can be read as attempting to do just this. The discussion in chapter 1, in fact, is consistent with this approach. But while an enriched folk psychological explanation is a useful first step, it will not yield an entirely adequate explanation. An adequate explanation of intention and action must meet the condition of being psychologically realistic. The explanation must be formulated using terms that cut nature at its joints, as it were. An enriched folk psychological explanation might meet this condition; but if it does, it would be happenstance. More important, not being formulated in testable form, it would be unknown whether an enriched folk psychology meets this adequacy condition. The conceptual framework of scientific psychology is better suited than that of folk psychology, even enriched folk psychology, for formulating explanations that are realistic.

Lest it be thought that we should turn our full attention to experimental psychology, there is another condition for an adequate explanation: it must be conceptually coherent. An explanation is conceptually coherent only if the framework in which it is embedded is consistent, parsimonious, ontologically well-grounded, and, let us say, maximally extensive. A framework is maximally extensive if its explanatory capacity is not merely local, if it is capable of explaining a type of phenomenon in all its manifestations. This adequacy condition is familiar to the physical sciences. But it also obtains for the sciences of the mental. Thus, for instance, an explanation of the cognitive attitude associated with prospective intention is embedded within a maximally extensive framework if that framework has the capacity to explain cognition in all its forms, not merely the high-level states of a specific species. There is a qualification. It could be that some psychological phenomena are species-typical, and thus a maximally extensive explanatory framework for them would be local. I will argue later that this is the case for conation. In sum, conceptual considerations of these sorts are outside the province of experimental psychology. Experimental psychology is limited in scope.

There are, then, two constraints on an adequate explanation of intention and action: one empirical and the other conceptual. These constraints can be satisfied when folk psychology is transformed into scientific psychology. The remaining chapters are devoted to discussion of specific proposals for the transformation of the cognitive and conative components of intention. But before turning to these proposals, it is well to make explicit the underlying methodological stance.

3. Folk Psychology and Scientific Psychology

A folk psychology can be modeled by the ordered pair

(2) $\mathcal{F} = \langle K, G \rangle$,

where K is a set of kind terms and G a set of generalizations in which the members of K occur essentially. The set K contains, among others, terms for the sense modalities, the attitudes, other central processes (such as 'remembers,' 'infers'), and physical activities. A scientific psychology has the structure:

(3) $\mathcal{S} = \langle N, L, T \rangle$,

where N is a set of natural kind terms, L a set of law-like generalizations in which the members of N occur essentially, and T a set of theories in which the members of L occur essentially. Folk and scientific psychologies are not unique. There are often competing such psychologies at one time, though typically there is a dominant folk psychology and a dominant scientific psychology. Moreover, folk and scientific psychologies change over time. In these respects folk and scientific psychologies are person- and time-dependent.

Folk psychologies suffer from at least two types of vagueness. First, the members of K have neither well-defined extensions nor intensions. Consider the predicate 'wants.' Its core sense is the same as 'desires.' But at one extreme 'wants' blends into 'wishes,' and at the other extreme 'wants' resembles 'intends.' Typically a folk psychology has no definitive, unambiguous taxonomy. Second, the members of G are often not well-articulated. These generalizations are implicit in ordinary thinking. There is, moreover, nothing to preclude real disagreement about the membership of G, and hence nothing to guarantee that G is consistent. As a result of these two types of vagueness, a definitive formulation of a folk psychology is extremely difficult to produce—if possible at all. Discussions of folk psychology will, then, be skewed. In order to formulate a consistent and coherent theory, some reconstruction is necessary. But no one reconstruction is mandated; the evidence will support alternatives. The present discussion is no exception to that rule. My reconstruction of folk psychology, for instance, is supported, but not uniquely determined, by the evidence.

With these caveats in mind we can, nonetheless, say something useful. Consider G, the set of folk psychological generalizations. The members of G are best labeled 'rules of thumb.' The set G covers a wide range of phenomena, from pathological disorders to personality development, from perceptual illusions to language acquisition, from behavioral reactions to long-term planned activity. For example, we commonly accept rules of thumb such as: 'Social interaction beginning at an early age is necessary for normal personality development'; or 'People automatically compensate for perceptual distortions, such as sticks that appear bent when seen through water'; or 'Second languages are spoken without accent only if learned before adolescence,' and so on. These rules of thumb are first approximations to nomic regularities. They are analogous to commonsense generalizations about physical phenomena. Most people can reasonably well predict the flight of a projectory, such as a baseball, without thinking about Newtonian mechanical laws, much less quantum relativistic formulae. Similarly most people can reasonably well predict water-seeking behavior when an animal has been deprived of water for a considerable length of time, without the benefit of learning curves or other such theoretical apparatus.

Ideally, scientific laws, whether physical or psychological, differ from rules of thumb in that commonsense rules of thumb are neither systematically confirmed nor precisely formulated and codified within a unified structure, whereas nomic generalizations are systematically confirmed, precisely formulated, and part of a unified structure. In fact nomic generalizations often are neither well-confirmed, nor well-formulated, nor placed within a unified structure. And conversely, rules of thumb are sometimes well-confirmed, carefully formulated, and part of a system of generalizations. For the most part, however, nomic generalizations seem to have these features to a greater extent than rules of thumb. But I shall not attempt to provide explicit criteria for distinguishing nomic generalizations from rules of thumb. For one thing, that project involves providing a criterion for being a nomic generalization. The formulation and testing of potential criteria has spawned an enormous literature without, it appears, finding a satisfactory one. Indeed it is not clear that providing a satisfactory criterion of this type is a tractable problem.

However, in passing I want to point to one difference between nomic generalizations and rules of thumb: nomic generalizations have an implicit *ceteris paribus* clause that can be clearly and precisely unpacked, whereas rules of thumb have an implicit *ceteris paribus* clause that cannot be stated in this way. Consider some purported scientific psychological generalization, such as Hull's claim that $E = f(D \times H \times K)$: that is, excitatory potential (motivation) is a multiplicative function of drive, habit, and incentive. This statement has an implicit *ceteris paribus* clause saying that the boundary conditions of the model dictate all the relevant factors. Hull is excluding from consideration living beings who have physiological and psychological systems wholly different from those on earth; but he need not explicitly state this restriction, since it is contained within an implicit *ceteris paribus* clause. The situation is the same as that for the physical sciences. Consider the dynamical law $s = 1/2 \, at^2$. Here there is an implicit gloss saying that the only conditions relevant to its application are the boundary conditions of the Newtonian model. The distance than an object falls freely in some possible universes will be a different function of acceleration and time than that given by the Newtonian formula: but that fact does not count against the Newtonian law, since the model makes it clear that this formula obtains only for the actual universe (and those differing from the actual one only in respect to initial conditions).

In contrast the *ceteris paribus* clause attached to each rule of thumb, whether explicitly affixed or not, cannot be specified precisely. Consider the physical rule of thumb 'Throwing bricks against windows causes them to break.' It is assumed that the window is not made from 'unbreakable' material such as plastic, that the brick is thrown with at least a moderate force, that a sheet of steel does not suddenly drop in front of the window, that a nearby person does not suddenly interrupt the flight of the brick, *and so on*. But there is no clear and precise way to unpack this 'and so on,' since it must exclude indefinitely many contingencies, not all of which can be predicted. The qualification 'all other things being equal' does not provide a precise formulation of the *ceteris paribus* clause; rather this qualification has the force of saying that a precise formulation cannot be given. The situation is the same for psychological rules of thumb. For instance, the generalization 'People automatically compensate for perceptual distortions' has an implicit *ceteris paribus* clause whose force is to exclude cases in which an individual has been attending to an illusion, or is under the influence of some drug, *or so on*. Again there is no precise way to state this qualification.

It is not clear how to explain this difference between the *ceteris paribus* clauses of scientific laws and rules of thumb. One seemingly plausible explanation is that scientific laws are embedded within theories but rules of thumb are not. These theories function in part to set boundary conditions. Sciences consist of sets of theories; but folk opinion consists of mere clusters of generalizations. Though plausible, this explanation is not unproblematic. Folk opinion *might* contain theories. But we cannot definitively decide whether that is the case until we have a clear understanding of the nature of theories, which we do not.

Folk psychology consists not only of rules of thumb, but also conceptual claims about the nature of psychological phenomena. To consider one example, it is a conceptual claim underlying folk psychology that some thinking is imagistic. At the level of common experience it is relatively easy to arouse images: ask a person to think of some well-known object such as the Washington Monument, or to recall some types of information such as the number of faces carved on Mt. Rushmore or the relative heights of lions and giraffes.[6] An analogous case can be made for scientific psychology. Like other sciences, psychology is not exhausted by data collection: it is also concerned with the construction of theories and models. The particular theories constructed are not wholly dictated by the experimental data, since that data underdetermines the theories. The models proposed depend in part on conceptual commitments about the nature of psychological phenomena. For example, recent cognitive models of memory and problem solving presuppose that there are mental representations to which subjects have access.

The conceptual commitments underlying folk psychology are not different in kind, and sometimes not different in substance, from those made by scientific psychology. The folk psychological claim that we sometimes think imagistically, for instance, is related to the claim that there are mental representations we access. Indeed it is in the sphere of underlying conceptual claims that scientific and folk psychology most obviously blend together. The picture that emerges, then, is this. Folk psychology and scientific psychology share a common base, which can be labeled 'conceptual psychology.' (More about conceptual psychology in a moment.) The borders between folk psychology, scientific psychology, and conceptual psychology are not well-defined. But on the whole there is a recognizable tripartite distinction between folk psychological generalizations, scientific psychological generalizations, and the conceptual claims that support and define both types of generalizations.

As a way of fixing these points, it is helpful to compare this picture with an influential view of Wilfrid Sellars's (1963, chapter 1). Sellars distinguishes between the Manifest Image and the Scientific Image. Basically the Manifest Image is that perspective of man and the world provided by sophisticated common sense. It is the viewpoint assumed after considerable reflection by the intellectual community. The Scientific Image of man and the world is the perspective provided by the physical and special sciences. Sellars does not commit himself to the thesis that science is unified; he claims only that a scientific perspective in any sphere is distinguishable from a commonsensical one.

Sellars stresses that these perspectives concern modes of explanation. He says,

> the contrast I have in mind is not that between an *unscientific* conception of man-in-the-world and a *scientific* one, but between that conception which limits itself to what correlational techniques can tell us about perceptible and introspective events and that which postulates imperceptible objects and events for the purpose of explaining correlations among perceptibles. (1963, p. 19)

That is, according to Sellars there is a significant difference and a significant similarity between explanations within the Manifest and Scientific Images. The difference is that explanations within the Manifest Image contain only terms referring to observable events, including introspective ones, but explanations within the Scientific Image contain terms that do not refer to observable events. The similarity is that explanations from both perspectives have the same form, in that, presumably, they appeal to covering laws and use the same canons of evidence, such as Mill's methods.

Sellars's distinction between the Manifest and Scientific images does not correspond to the distinction between folk and scientific psychology. Generally speaking, scientific psychology attempts to explain observable behavior and introspective events in terms of models that contain some terms referring to nonobservable, nonintrospective events. The early behaviorist program of Watson attempted to construct psychological theories that contained only terms referring to observable inputs and outputs. But as Watson's followers quickly found, successful models required terms referring to events intervening between the initial stimulus and the ensuing response that were not wholly definable by means of terms referring only to overt behavior. Recent cognitive psychology contains models not all of whose terms refer to observable or introspective events. To revert to an earlier example, it has been proposed that selective attention is to be explained by an information processing model in which some of the sensory input is filtered out. This filter mechanism selects inputs for full processing, partial processing, and perhaps in some cases no processing. The existence and function of this filter mechanism is an inference from the behavioral outputs and is not literally observable. To be sure, not all contemporary psychologists are unified in the belief that adequate models must include some terms referring to nonobservable events. Preeminent among those who disagree are Skinner and his followers. But on the whole, it is a conceptual commitment of scientific psychology that successful models will contain terms that do not refer to observable events. In contrast it may seem that folk psychology makes use only of terms referring to observable events. But upon closer inspection, terms referring to nonobservables are seen to appear in folk psychological explanations. Voluntary action is often explained by means of a person's act of will; conflicts in desires are often explained in terms of parts of the mind; guilt is sometimes explained by personified forces within a person, and so on. 'Act of will,' 'part of the mind,' 'the father within me' do not refer to observables. Folk psychology is in part naive scientific psychology, and as such, the explanations it provides contain theoretical terms.

In sum Sellars's distinction between the Manifest and Scientific Images does not correspond to the distinction between folk and scientific psychology because the Manifest Image disallows prescientific theorizing. Sellars construes the Manifest Image as a description of the world derived from sophisticated, but nonscientific, common sense. But folk psychology is in part naive scientific psychology. In terms of our earlier picture, Sellars has collapsed folk psychology into conceptual psychology.

4. Conceptual Psychology

Conceptual psychology, the common base of scientific and folk psychology, can itself be modeled by a three-dimensional space, where points in the space are statements. Let us specify that the x-coordinate is the degree of theoretical relevance, the y-coordinate the degree of empirical import, and the z-coordinate time. Theoretical relevance concerns the role a statement can play within a scientific theory. The more highly relevant a psychological conceptual claim is, the more likely it is to be presupposed by a scientific psychological theory. Empirical import is correlated to testability: the higher the empirical import of a statement, the more likely it is to be testable by experimental procedures. The third, temporal parameter is required because the conceptual foundations of psychology change over time.

For illustration, the following statements appear to be contained in conceptual psychology.

(P_1) Rational preference is transitive.

(P_2) If neither duty nor obligation interfere, persons always act on their strongest desire.

(P_3) There is a linguistic internal code in which persons think.

(P_4) Mental events have syntactical (formal) properties.

These statements can be construed as points in conceptual space. For simplicity, assume that the z-coordinates are all equal to the present time. These statements differ significantly with respect to their x-coordinates, the measure of theoretical relevance, and their y-coordinates, the measure of empirical import. (P_1) and (P_2) have relatively low x- and y-values, whereas (P_3) and (P_4) have relatively high x- and y-values. Conceptual statements with relatively low x- and y-values tend to underlie folk psychology; conceptual statements with relatively high x- and y-values tend to underlie scientific psychology. Statement (P_2) and its relatives, for example, played a crucial role in the attempt of the previous chapter to sketch the conceptual foundations of the folk psychological notion of desire. Statement (P_4) and its relatives have played a crucial role in the construction of recent scientific theories about cognitive processes, especially those generated by artificial intelligence.

There is an obvious qualification. This model of conceptual psychology is, at best, approximately correct. No claim is made for these statements having precise theoretical or empirical import. At best, relative judgments are possible. The model nonetheless does have certain features worth emphasizing. Conceptual statements have two dimensions: the role that they play in theories and the degree to which they are bound to evidence. These dimensions can change over time. When new theories evolve, a conceptual statement's role can change; and when new evidence emerges, conceptual statements can become more, or less, plausible. This model is essentially anti-positivistic. There is no sharp, well-defined difference between theoretical and empirical statements. More importantly, the degree to which conceptual statements are theoretical or empirical is a function of extant, accepted scientific models. The foundations of science, including psychology, are not there to be discovered and recorded for time immemorial. But I will not stop and argue for these sweeping claims (cf. Suppe, 1975).

Note that it is not necessary for a statement to be true to be admitted to the space of conceptual psychology. Rather it is only necessary that there is good reason, strong justification, for believing that it is true. The procedure for justifying these statements varies with their presumed location within the space. Statements with high y-values, for instance, are more dependent on observational and experimental evidence than those with low y-values. There is a conceptual physics analogous to conceptual psychology. (There is also a folk physics, though given the development and dominance of scientific physics, folk physics is hard to discern or take seriously.) The criteria for admission to the conceptual foundations of psychology are relevantly similar to those of physics. For instance, the conceptual foundations of physics contained until recently the claim that there are discrete spatiotemporal objects. This claim was for some time highly justified. But it now seems false: quantum mechanical considerations require its replacement by the claim that objects are to be identified with probability distributions of wave packets. The criteria for admission to the foundations of physics, as well as to other sciences, including psychology, concern the accumulation of evidence, theory, and arguments for conceptual coherence.

There is joint interaction and influence among folk psychology, scientific psychology, and conceptual psychology. Conceptual claims and decisions affect the development of scientific experimental psychology; experimental findings influence folk psychology and demand conceptual backing; entrenchment of folk psychological claims constrains scientific models, which in turn has ramifications for experimental design, and so on. Here I want to consider one major type of interaction: the change of conceptual claims underlying folk psychology into ones that underlie scientific psychology. That is, the process by which conceptual claims with relatively low x- and y-values are transformed into ones with relatively high x- and y-values. Call this process 'progressive transformation.' I take it that progressive transformation is an important element in the development of scientific psychology. It is the process by which the conceptual base of scientific psychology is derived from the conceptual base of folk psychology.

The following is an idealized schema for progressive transformation, which I label 'the Method of Case Studies.' It is highly doubtful that this schema reflects actual historical development. It is a relative—probably, a second cousin—to various recent suggestions made by historians and philosophers of science.

Step (1). Isolate some key claim or related set of claims that underlie folk psychology.

A good example for our purposes is

(P$_5$) The cognitive component of intending is believing,

where 'believing' is construed folk psychologically. Recall the earlier arguments against (P$_5$): in particular, the content of belief is a relatively simple proposition, whereas the content of intending is far more complex. Thus (P$_5$) must be replaced by—or rather, transformed into—a justified conceptual claim.

Step (2). Locate conceptual claims related to those isolated in Step (1) and which have significantly higher x- and y-values.

In terms of our example, we are to locate conceptual claims that underlie scientific models that, first, make reference to mental events antecedent to action and, second, specify the cognitive component of these antecedent events.

Step (3). Examine the theories in which the conceptual claims located in Step (2) occur.

The reason for examining the theoretical context is that typically the claims satisfying Step (2) will contain theory-laden terms. A good procedure for examining a theory in which these terms occur is by means of its experimental paradigms, its goals and historical development, and its relationships to other models. That is, a good method to study a theory is by means of a limited philosophical-historical case study. Fortunately exhaustive studies of this type are not required. Such exhaustive studies are appropriate to the charting of the place of that theory within a broad intellectual and historical context, and not to making theory-laden statements intelligible.

In terms of our example one of the relevant claims with high x- and y-values is that the cognitive attitude of a subject who is immediately intending can be modeled by a feedback mechanism of the closed-loop variety. For example, when hammering a nail, my intention to do so consists in my comparing my present stage of the activity with a memory of the completed activity type and, if necessary, making corrections. Later I shall argue that this claim captures, at most, part of the cognitive component of immediate intention. But the main point here is that this claim about the cognitive component of immediate intention is intelligible only in terms of a theory of feedback mechanisms.

Step (4). Compare and contrast the original conceptual claims specified in Step (1) with those located in Step (2), as understood through limited case studies. If competing conceptual claims are located in Step (2), this step also involves comparing and contrasting them.

In our example (P_5) is to be compared and contrasted with the claim that the cognitive component of immediate intention is a correcting activity understood on the model of servomechanisms. This latter claim in turn is to be evaluated with respect to other theory-laden descriptions of the cognitive antecedent to action.[7]

Step (5). Transform the original, unacceptable conceptual claim into one that has higher x- and y-values.

This shift could be severe, in that the original claim is transformed into one identical with a conceptual claim that underlies some particular theoretical model. In that case the folk psychological conception will be eliminated (cf. Churchland, 1979). More likely, and more interestingly, the shift is less severe: the original claim is transformed into one that occupies a position near the center of the conceptual space. In terms of our example, (P₅) is to be transformed into a statement that is more loosely connected with folk psychology and more empirically testable. This new conceptual claim will have higher x- and y-values than (P₅). Action theory is naturalized by bringing its conceptual basis closer to that of scientific psychological theories, not by eliminating it in favor of some particular scientific psychological theory. As a strategy, I counsel conservatism with respect to transformation: transform from folk psychology only so far as necessary to generate a justified conceptual statement.

In using this schema, it is often necessary to repeat the step-by-step procedure. Adjustments are required in virtue of additional issues raised by progressive transformed claims. When this process continues through several rounds, a type of bootstrapping occurs. This process will be illustrated in detail in chapter 8. There the folk psychological notion of prospective intention is transformed by comparing and contrasting it to certain models of large-chunked, schematic mental representations as described by recent theories in artificial intelligence and cognitive psychology.

The Method of Case Studies, in short, is a procedure by which folk psychological conceptual statements with relatively low theoretical and empirical import are transformed into ones with higher theoretical and empirical import by comparing and contrasting them to conceptual statements underlying well-supported scientific models. A related, converse interaction between folk and scientific psychology is that some scientific models are evaluated by means of their relationships with these transformed conceptual claims. Imagine that there are several competing scientific psychological models. As often happens, there is no crucial experimental design to decide among them: each model can be adjusted, if necessary, to account for the data. The data typically do not determine a unique scientific model. However, if the underlying conceptual claims of one or more of these models is incompatible with the transformed conceptual claims of folk psychology, then that constitutes a good reason to reject that model. In its strongest form the claim is this: a scientific psychological model is adequate only if it is compatible with the transformed conceptual claims of folk psychology. Let us label this claim 'the Dependency Thesis,' since its force is that scientific psychology is dependent in part on folk psychology.

The Dependency Thesis is at least initially plausible. It appears, moreover, to be assumed by some recent cognitive scientists, though it played little or no role in the development of the neobehaviorism of several decades ago. The Dependency Thesis tends to moderate conceptual change in scientific psychology. Conceptual claims with low empirical and scientific import are transformed by means of extant scientific models. These transformed conceptual claims are then used to evaluate other models. If there is a radically different scientific model, it will fail this test. A single radical explanatory model will not curry favor, though a series of models with a shared conceptual base explaining a wide range of phenomena might do so.

The Dependency Thesis is the mirror image of the Method of Case Studies. The Dependency Thesis tends to move the conceptual base of scientific psychology toward the center of the conceptual space, while the Method of Case Studies tends to move the conceptual base of folk psychology toward the center. If the Dependency Thesis is true, then these two processes, operating jointly, suggest that the basis for an adequate psychology will be 'midway' between folk psychology and scientific psychology. Put another way, *if* the Dependency Thesis is true, the conceptual base of folk psychology is not wildly mistaken. It then follows that the conceptual base of folk psychology, when transformed by repeated applications of the Method of Case Studies, provides an approximation to an adequate foundation for psychology.

In the next part, I make use of this Method of Case Studies. Chapters 7 and 8 are concerned with transforming the folk psychological account of the cognitive components of intention and intentional action, respectively, into ones with greater empirical import and scientific relevance. Chapter 9 applies the method to the conative components of intention and intentional action. There I discuss motivational psychology, and its relation to recent work in cognitive psychology. The folk psychology of human action, as I argued in part 1, makes it clear that the antecedent to action has a conative property, that is, a property such that that mental event moves the agent to act. From the Dependency Thesis it follows that any theory that excludes conative constructs is inadequate. Theories that take the antecedent to action to be purely cognitive fail to be compatible with the transformed conceptual claims of folk psychology.

Part IV
TOWARD A NATURALIZED ACTION
THEORY

7

Intention and Cognition

The cognitive component of immediate intention is the guidance and monitoring of ongoing activity. In reaching for a glass of water my hand and fingers are guided in their specific movements and this guidance is in turn dependent on perceptual monitoring. The goal of this chapter is to articulate the folk psychological concepts of guidance and monitoring by transforming them into scientific psychological concepts.

I proceed by the Method of Case Studies. In section 1 I will discuss an approach recently defended by, among others, Greenwald (1970), a psychologist, and Goldman (1976), a philosopher. According to it, guidance and monitoring are to be understood in terms of response images of the action types to be performed. This approach is based on William James's (1890), though it differs in several respects. (James's views on this topic are both influential and misunderstood. I attempt to set the record straight in the Appendix.) In section 2 I consider a computational model of guidance and monitoring. The foundational work here was done by Miller, Galanter, and Pribram (1960). I discuss their model, and then illustrate recent progress on this front by means of a proposal by Rumelhart and Norman (1982). This second approach is more abstract than the first in that particular neurophysiological mechanisms are not relevant, only the organizational 'programs.' I take it that these two limited case studies of guidance and monitoring represent the most plausible approaches for dealing with these issues in the literature.

Intentional action is action that has a mental antecedent consisting of immediate intention plus some additional cognitive feature. I argued in chapter 1 that that additional feature involves being part of a plan. In particular an intentional action is initiated by an event that includes a representation specifying the role of that action in the context of related actional and environmental conditions. From the philosophical perspective intentional action is important because it is tied to the key issues of freedom and responsibility. Nonintentional action, especially reflex and automatic action, has been the main object of interest for behavioristically oriented psychologists. The emphasis on this type of action results from the assumption that complex intentional activities can be constructed in a reasonably straightforward way from simple, reflexive ones. But if I am correct in claiming that intentional action involves an additional cognitive feature, then this assumption is untenable. The analysis of complex, intentional action would not be a trivial matter, even if simple, nonintentional action were well understood. In the next chapter I discuss this additional cognitive feature of intentional action. In this chapter my focus is the cognitive feature common to all action, intentional and nonintentional alike.

Before proceeding, let me reemphasize two points. First, 'intention' is given a quasi-technical use. It refers to *whatever* event or complex of events is the proximate causal antecedent to action. The detailed explanation of intention will go beyond that provided by folk psychology; in particular, it will be in scientific psychological terms. This leads to the second point. Despite the appeal to scientific psychology, my goal is not to explain intention by advocating particular scientific theories. That goal is not appropriate: this is not an essay in empirical psychology. Rather the goal is to formulate the conceptual basis for an adequate action theory. That goal is to be accomplished by the progressive transformation of folk psychology into scientific psychology. The discussion of specific scientific theories is meant to be illustrative of the issues and approaches; it is not intended to resolve conflicts between competing scientific theories and models.

1. The Ideo-Motor Theory

Suppose that Richard intends to knot his tie. The cognitive component of his intention, it might be said, involves his memory of performing past actions of the type knotting one's tie. It does not involve a representation of the particular tie-knotting to be performed. When he intends to knot his tie, without yet having completed the action, there are many details, such as the precise moment when the action begins and the rate at which it unfolds, that are not fixed. Generally speaking, the cognitive component of intention involves a memory image of the type of action to be performed. This memory image guides the particular action to completion.

Let us restate this view more carefully. Rather than speaking of memory images, we will follow contemporary proponents of this view and say that information about action types is stored as response images. Thus

(IM) *S* intends to *A* during *t* *only if* (i) *S* has a response image during *t* of his performing prior actions of type *A* and (ii) this response image guides his *A*ing during *t*.

Statement (IM) reformulates the ideo-motor theory. This theory defines the cognitive component of immediate intention; it does not define the additional cognitive feature of the antecedent to action that makes it intentional.

There is an interesting consequence of (IM)—indeed a consequence of any theory that identifies the cognitive component of immediate intention with the guidance and monitoring of activity. Intention initiates action. On the widely held view that causes precede their effects, intention therefore precedes action.[1] But intending need not terminate with the onset of action. When one event causes another, the first need not terminate when the second begins. Indeed it is consistent with the claim that causes precede their effects that these causes and effects terminate at the same time. Given that intention is in part guidance and monitoring of activity, the intention continues as long as the guidance and monitoring continues.[2]

In cases of mere bodily action, such as touching one's toes, the intention continues for the duration of the bodily movement, since guidance is required for successful completion. Cases in which the action reaches into the world, as it were, present a problem. Suppose that Pat throws a penny into the well. The penny's hitting the water is part of her action. But it is nonbodily; the penny's hitting the water is an effect of her bodily movements. Does her intention continue for the duration of the action? Only if the guidance and monitoring endure for that period. The guidance ceases when the penny is released. Similarly, monitoring ceases, even though Pat continues to observe the penny's hitting the water. Persons monitor only those activities they guide. Monitoring is perceptual processing parasitic on guidance; observing the effects of one's bodily movement is not sufficient for monitoring, since the subject can have no further control of these effects.[3] The primary cognitive feature is guidance, as (IM) correctly indicates.

Monitoring and guidance are also involved in mental action. Consider the action of solving a mathematical puzzle mentally, in one's head, as it were. The guidance and monitoring begins with the onset of the activity and continues throughout its lifespan. In this case guidance does not involve motor effects, but rather changes in the tactics and strategy of problem solving. And similarly, monitoring does not involve perceptual feedback; rather it is attending to the ongoing mental events.

The ideo-motor theory received its initial formulation by William James (1890). There is, however, a significant difference between James's action theory and the reformulated thesis (IM). James held that memory images (response images) are necessary *and sufficient* for action. Thesis (IM) claims only that response images are necessary for action: it is consistent with (IM) that there is a noncognitive feature of intending. James, to the contrary, held a purely cognitive view about action initiation. (At least this is James's 'official' position. See the Appendix.)

James's version of the theory is too strong. As I pointed out, it is a deep insight of folk psychology that action is initiated only by events with noncognitive, motivational features. A person can focus his full attention on a possible future activity, such as jumping up and touching the ceiling, or getting out of bed on a cold morning, without acting. Unless he is *moved* to perform an action of that type, he will not do so, no matter how completely memories of similar past actions occupy his consciousness. Contemporary defenders of the ideo-motor theory for the most part recognize this point. Greenwald, for example, says:

> In order not to leave an undue impression of the accomplishments of the ideo-motor analysis, it must be noted that no solutions have been suggested for mechanistic problems for performance that might be classified as "motivational." In the analysis of complex performance, for example, no account has been offered of the processes that may be involved in selecting one sequence of images as a more useful program than another, or of processes involved in converting an image sequence into overt action once the programming process is completed. (1970, p. 93; also cf. p. 96)

Goldman (1976) mostly follows Greenwald's development of the theory, though he makes some modifications that bring him closer to James. According to Goldman, actions are divided into involuntary and voluntary ones. Involuntary actions such as habitual and reflex ones are caused by volitions, which he construes as response images of past performances. Voluntary actions are caused by a mental event consisting of a response image plus a noncognitive feature. I would take issue with Goldman about whether any action can be initiated by a purely cognitive event and about the analysis of the noncognitive component. Goldman (1970) claims that this noncognitive feature is desire, which he unpacks in terms of pro-attitudes. But as I argued earlier, having a pro-attitude does not capture the conative aspect of the mental antecedent. These quarrels aside, neither Goldman nor Greenwald adopt James's strong stance that all action is initiated by purely cognitive events.

Greenwald focuses on skilled perceptual-motor activity, such as hitting a golf ball and knotting a tie. These activities involve corrective procedures during the course of performance. For example, in knotting a tie, adjustments and corrections must be made for the length of the tie, the shape of the knot at the cross-over stage, and so on. The most widely held account of these activities involves closed-loop feedback mechanisms. Sensory feedback from each stage in the activity is compared with a representation of the correct performance, and adjustments in the remaining stages of the activity are made accordingly. Greenwald (1970b) marshals evidence to show that some actions within sequences occur too rapidly for error correction on the basis of sensory feedback. He presented visual and auditory letters and digits to subjects who were to write or repeat them. His data show that written responses to visual stimuli and spoken responses to auditory stimuli were more rapid than could be predicted on the basis of effects due only to stimulus modality. On the assumption that the feedback modality for written responses is vision and for spoken responses audition, Greenwald reasoned that a visual image mediated in the visual-written case and an auditory image mediated in the auditory-spoken case. Responses were selected on the basis of *anticipated* sensory feedback, not actual feedback as the closed-loop explanation requires. The source of these anticipated response images is the memory of relevantly similar responses. Images of future stages of the activity—not feedback from that part of the activity that has already occurred—guide bodily movement. In sum the cognitive component of intention, according to the ideo-motor theory, is the guidance of ongoing activity by stored response images.

There are, however, difficulties for the ideo-motor theory—though, it seems, only the final one that I will discuss is serious. The first difficulty concerns the status of response images. Greenwald, generally speaking, provides a model within the framework of contemporary neobehaviorist learning theory. He is somewhat permissive in his approach: he uses intervening variables liberally; and he appeals to information processing constructs. But on the whole it is fair to say that this work is in the neobehaviorist tradition. Now within that tradition, response images are not to be construed as mental imagery, since the guiding rationale of the tradition is to explain behavior without an appeal to explicitly mentalistic constructs, in particular, without an appeal to events that are accessible primarily through introspection. Thus at one point Greenwald suggests that a response image is an abstraction. He says: "the terms 'image' or 'idea,' as applied to responses, refer to central representations of sensory feedback from responses. Response images are reasonably regarded as somewhat abstract entities, representing functional response classes, rather than specific instances of such classes" (1970, p. 84). But in his experimental work Greenwald (1970b, 1970c) suggests that response images consist in particular visual and auditory images. The existence of particular sensory images is part of the explanation for the rapidity of visual-written and auditory-spoken responses. There is then a tension between the theoretical description of response images and the supposition used in describing the experimental results: for a response image cannot be both something abstract, such as a functional response class, and a particular event, an individual visual or auditory image.

One possible reply is to delimit response images to particular imagistic events. Intuitively this reply is attractive. In knotting my tie, for instance, I have a mental 'picture' of what that activity should look like at each stage. Because knotting a tie is habitual for me, I do not attend to the mental images at each stage of this activity; but with appropriate cues I can attend to them and accurately report my mental image of each stage.

This reply would push Greenwald more toward cognitive psychological modeling than his neobehavioristic theoretic framework would easily admit. But even allowing this reconstruction, an issue would remain: the reply presupposes a controversial claim about mental imagery. As I noted earlier Pylyshyn (1973, 1978, 1981) and others argue that high-level cognitive processing is best modeled by propositional networks. They seem not to deny that persons introspect mental images; it is rather that mental imagery is epiphenomenal, that it lacks a functional role in cognitive processing. On the other side of the debate Kosslyn and his colleagues (1980 and Kosslyn and Pomerantz, 1977) point to reaction time experiments in which a strong correlation has been found between the time required to judge whether two figures are identical and the degree to which they are rotated with respect to each other (see Shepard and Cooper, 1982). A natural explanation is that subjects mentally rotate one figure until it is positioned identically to the target figure. In short Greenwald could adopt this reply to the difficulty about the status of response images only by agreeing with Kosslyn and others that mental images have genuine functional roles: for response images are to play a causal role in the production of behavior, and they can do so only if they are not epiphenomenal. However, as far as I can determine, this controversy about mental images remains unresolved.

Another difficulty concerns the function of response images. Actually this is not really a difficulty for the ideo-motor theory, but rather one that results from a tendency on the part of some authors to misconstrue the function of response images. Their function is to guide ongoing activity. Response images are not representations of the completed activity that are initiatory. They are rather the cognitive part of the motor control mechanism. In the case of intentional action a plan, or similar representation, plays a role in the initiation of the activity. In the case of action that is not intentional the only cognitive feature is guidance and monitoring of the ongoing activity. The point is, again, the ideo-motor mechanism functions to guide and correct individual stages of ongoing activity, not to initiate it.

Goldman (1976) confuses these two functions when he identifies a volition with a response image. The confusion occurs in James, and is sometimes repeated by Greenwald (e.g., 1970, p. 96). In the case of intending to perform some very simple action, such as winking, guidance might not appear different from initiation. Once begun, these actions are completed automatically and without apparent midcourse corrections. Indeed they do not seem to consist of distinguishable stages between which corrections can be made. Some relatively simple actions do consist of stages. These action types are short-lived, overlearned, and proceed automatically. Nevertheless guidance and initiation are distinguishable. In more complex actions there is little doubt that guidance and initiation are distinct. In reaching across the table for the water glass, for example, midcourse corrections are made in virtue of perceptual and kinaesthetic information about the location of the glass and the relative location of one's hand. The difference between guidance and initiation becomes clearer as the complexity and duration of the action increase. In highly complex actions such as getting dressed in the morning or eating dinner in a restaurant, there is absolutely no question that the cognitive states involved in initiating the activity are distinct from those involved in guiding the multiple, minute stages.

The third and most serious difficulty for the ideo-motor theory concerns its scope. Advocates of the theory hold that it covers a wide range of activities; Goldman (1976) in fact conjectures that it includes the entire range of human action. The main reason for attributing wide scope to the theory is that it then provides a solution to the problem, emphasized by Ryle (1949), about the number of antecedent mental events required for an action. If each stage in an action required a separate antecedent mental event, then the subject would be overwhelmed. If a separate antecedent mental event were required for each phoneme in ordinary speech, for example, a subject's mental life would be implausibly complicated. The ideo-motor theory deals with this problem by denying that separate antecedent mental events are required for each stage in an activity. Rather there is a single mental event that initiates the activity; the activity is then guided to successful completion by a response image.

It is surely correct that separate antecedent mental events are not required to initiate each stage in a complex activity. The activity is initiated by a single mental event and then guided to completion. The problem arises, however, whether a response image is the appropriate kind of mental event in *all* cases to conduct guidance. It would seem not to be so . The ideo-motor theory is most plausible for highly learned actions that involve rapid midcourse corrections such as knotting one's tie. But not all actions are of this type. Some cases of overlearned, highly routinized activity, such as reciting the alphabet, involve no midcourse corrections. Rather each stage of the routine triggers the next one. These activities seem best explained in terms of serial chaining mechanisms. Moreover, some activities, though highly learned and requiring midcourse corrections, depend heavily on perceptual feedback; and thus future stages cannot be easily predicted. For example, when driving a nail in soft wood, the position and depth of the nail must be assessed with each swing of the hammer; except perhaps for the most skilled carpenter, it is not possible to anticipate future stages of the activity. These cases seem best explained in terms of closed-loop feedback mechanisms.[4] In short the ideo-motor theory is most appropriate in cases of routinized, sequential actions. But even here some types of sequences are probably best explained by either serial chaining mechanisms or closed-loop mechanisms, not ideo-motor ones.

But matters are far worse. Greenwald presents experimental evidence for the ideo-motor mechanisms for simple actions such as writing or naming a digit. Like James before him and Goldman after him, Greenwald holds that these results can be extrapolated to long-range, complex activities. However, it is not clear that that is the case. Such activities often include many routines and subroutines for which there does not seem to be a single, covering response image. For example, in cases of grocery shopping or driving across town, it is implausible to think that a single response image is operative. The implausibility of this grows as the activity involves options that cannot be predicted in advance. It is highly implausible to think that there is a single response image that guides a person when playing a chess game, writing a paper, or even engaging in casual conversation.

Greenwald (1970, p. 93) briefly discusses complex activities. He draws attention to the analogy between forming complex sentences given a finite natural language vocabulary and grammar and undertaking complex activities. I will not entirely rule out the possibility that response images for simple and skilled actions can be joined to form one for a complex activity. But it is important to observe that this extension is not trivial. Accounts must be provided for the recursive rules of sequence combination—the 'grammar'—and for the units to be combined—the 'vocabulary.'

In sum (IM) is most appropriate in cases of highly learned, motor-perceptual activities involving routinized interaction with the environment. Otherwise it seems implausible. Some sequences do not involve midcourse correction yet proceed rapidly; and some sequences involve midcourse correction on the basis of afferent feedback from completed stages, not from anticipated stages. Most important this model cannot easily account for the guidance of highly complex nonroutinized activities.

The ideo-motor theory hypothesizes a mechanism for the guidance of some types of sequential activity not explained by other mechanisms. Guidance, apparently, is not a unitary phenomenon; there are a number of mechanisms operative, depending on the degree of automaticity and predictability of future stages. Taken together, these mechanisms explain a great deal of the guidance of ongoing activity—though probably not all of it.

2. The Program Theory

The ideo-motor theory is an attempt to explain guidance and monitoring by a mechanical model. Although this theory has been attractive to a number of psychologists and philosophers, additional mechanisms appear required to explain the entire range of human action. But leaving aside this objection, the underlying rationale of this model is clear. It is that guidance and monitoring of ongoing activity is to be understood by a theory about the physical systems of persons and other animate beings.

There is another approach to understanding guidance and monitoring that is more abstract. It does not focus on particular mechanisms. Rather it attempts to delineate the structure, or functional organization, of guidance and monitoring systems. This approach draws on the analogy to computers. The mechanistic approach con-

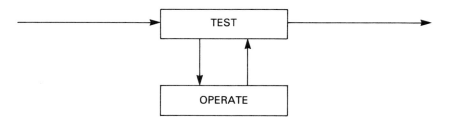

Figure 7.1
The TOTE unit. Based on Miller, Galanter, and Pribram (1960, p. 16).

cerns the hardware of persons, as it were. This second approach concerns the software.

Let us label this second approach 'the Program Theory of Guidance.' An historically important version is Miller, Galanter, and Pribram's (1960) model. This model was originally intended not as an instance of the Program Theory of Guidance, but rather as a depth scientific functional account of action itself. (A theory is depth scientifically functional if it decomposes complex events into primitive operations and gives a functional account of these operations by means of a scientific psychological theory.) I will argue that, to the contrary, this model is best interpreted within the more limited context of the Program Theory of Guidance. Miller, Galanter, and Pribram's attempt to provide a functional account of action, incidentally, is unusual. There have been numerous attempts in recent years to provide scientific functional accounts of input systems and central systems; but scientific functional accounts of output systems are rare. Functional accounts of output systems have tended to be folk psychological, coming from philosophers and not psychologists (e.g., Toumela, 1977 and Davis, 1979).

Miller, Galanter, and Pribram's key idea is that action can be understood in terms of Test-Operate-Test-Exit (TOTE) units. This is the basic or primitive unit of analysis. See figure 7.1. The arrows represent the flow of information. In a physical system that instantiates this unit the arrows depict the transfer of energy (Miller, Galanter, and Pribram, 1960, pp. 27 ff.). Suppose that I grasp a nail. Thus my action consists of the following: I locate my hand and the nail in my perceptual field (Test); I close my fingers around the nail (Operate); I again locate my hand and the nail in my perceptual field (Test); and I terminate my activity (Exit).

TOTEs can be arranged hierarchically to, presumably, indefinite complexity. Miller, Galanter, and Pribram give the example of driving a nail as a two-tiered hierarchy. In driving a nail the subject tests the nail to see whether the head sticks up, tests the hammer to see whether it is in the correct striking position, strikes the nail, tests the hammer and nail again, raises the hammer, and so on until the test of the nail reveals that it is flush, in which case the activity terminates. Miller, Galanter, and Pribram introduce a technical usage of 'plan': a plan is a mental representation of a hierarchy of TOTE units (and in the trivial case, a single TOTE unit). They say: "A plan is any hierarchical process in the organism that can control the order in which a sequence of operations is to be performed" (p. 16; italicized in the text). The hierarchical process to which they refer is the series of interrelated feedback loops constituted by TOTE units: "the TOTE represents the basic pattern in which . . . Plans are cast" (p. 31).

Plans can involve a single activity, such as grasping a nail, or a sequence of activities, such as driving a nail, or building a table, or even building a house. To perform an action is to execute a plan, on this model. Thus driving a nail and building a table are each actions, the former presumably being part of the latter. Intentions concern the completion of actions within a plan in progress: "the term ['intention'] is used to refer to the uncompleted parts of a plan whose execution has already begun" (p. 61; italicized in text). If driving the nail is the nth step in the plan of building a table, and if that plan has already begun but not yet proceeded to the nth step, then the subject intends to drive the nail. Note that plans are not intended; rather it is actions within plans that are intended. Notice also that Miller, Galanter, and Pribram are committed to (IT), the thesis that all intended action is intentional action. To be intentional an action must be part of a plan; and for Miller, Galanter, and Pribram, *all* action is part of a plan.

There remains one more ingredient. Plans are programs. Persons, like computers, store these programs. But how is a stored program selected for execution? Miller, Galanter, and Pribram base their answer on Kurt Lewin's work. During most of the day persons can execute one of many plans. Lewin (1935, 1938) argued that future activities have *valences* in relation to the range of alternatives available to the subject. Miller, Galanter, and Pribram take a positive valence to be a value. It is values that control which program is to be executed. Unfortunately they say little about values, other than that they are not to be understood in terms of needs, as Lewin claims.

Miller, Galanter, and Pribram are proposing a *dynamic* theory of action. Persons are always engaged in one activity or another. The central problem for a dynamic theory is not to explain why persons act, but rather why they perform the particular actions that they do. Miller, Galanter, and Pribram hold that acting is executing a plan and the plan to be executed is the one with the highest value. They say: "so long as people are behaving, *some* plan or other must be executed. The question thus moves from *why* plans are executed to a concern for *which* plans are executed. And to cope with this problem of choice we . . . need some valuation concepts" (p. 62). Dynamic theories of action are to be contrasted with static theories. On a static theory a subject is assumed to be at rest until an activity is initiated. There is no assumption that subjects are continuously performing actions. On a static theory the key question is why is a type of activity initiated.[5]

Dynamic theories misdescribe human action. They fail to distinguish actions from other activities in which persons are engaged. On Miller, Galanter, and Pribram's model, subjects are assumed to be constantly active, constantly executing some plan or other. But clearly persons are not constantly performing actions. Surely they are not acting in the philosophically interesting sense of 'acting' when having their hair cut, or generally, when being victimized by others; they are not acting when sitting quietly and daydreaming, or when asleep. In order to make a dynamical theory a plausible account of human action, it must be supplemented in a way that distinguishes activities that are actional from those that are nonactional. But to make this revision requires an explanation of action initiation. There is no gain then in opting for a dynamic theory, since the key problem with which a static account is faced is also a problem for a dynamic account. Indeed there is a loss, since a dynamic theory incorrectly presupposes that persons are always acting.

Aside from Miller, Galanter, and Pribram's dynamical stance—which in any case is not an essential feature of their model—they present an attractive picture. Action is to be understood computationally, built from basic feedback units. A computational model of activity has at least two advantages. It is consonant with computational models for high-level cognitive phenomena such as memory and inference, and thus holds out the promise for a unified psychological theory. Moreover it is unrestricted in scope. It is plausible that creatures physically very different from us can guide and monitor their movements. Aliens or robots made of silicon might have guidance and monitoring systems at least as well-developed as ours. A computational model of guidance can explain these possibilities.

However, this picture is not without difficulties. First, Miller, Galanter, and Pribram's model purports to be a depth scientific one.

But it is neither fully scientific nor fully depth functionalistic. It is not fully scientific because some of the key terms are used folk psychologically. 'Plan' and 'value' are taken from folk psychology, and while there is some attempt to imbed them in scientific psychological theory, that attempt is far from complete or successful. The notion of a TOTE unit is not folk psychological, though it suffers from not receiving precise and systematic development. The model is not fully depth functionalistic because the basic unit of analysis, a TOTE, is itself in need of decompositional analysis. The test phases must be further broken down into informational processing constructs. And the operate phase—to which I will return—is itself complex.

In defense of the model it seems that it can be supplemented in a way that makes it depth scientific functionalistic. The concepts of plan and value can be transformed into legitimate scientific ones. And the notion of a TOTE unit, it appears, can be further decomposed into primitive computational operations. Miller, Galanter, and Pribram conducted their investigation at a time when functionalism was not yet an entrenched mode of explanation in psychology. It is difficult to fault them for failing to complete their project, since their primary goal was to argue for a computational, nonbehavioristic approach to action.

Second, there are problems about the completeness of the model. Miller, Galanter, and Pribram hold that guidance and monitoring can be explained in all cases by hierarchical structures of TOTE units. TOTE units, either singly or hierarchically ordered, represent closed-loop feedback mechanisms. But not all activities involve these mechanisms. As I pointed out in the previous section, there is good evidence for other types of mechanisms. In overlearned, relatively simple activities such as reciting the alphabet, serial chaining mechanisms are operative. Moreover some activities appear to utilize ideo-motor mechanisms, in which corrections in the activity are made on the basis of anticipated results, not feedback from the actual situation.

This difficulty necessitates considerable change in the model. But its spirit survives. There appears to be no reason in principle that precludes there being a single computational model of serial chaining, ideo-motor, and closed-loop mechanisms. There will be problems about the nature of the hierarchical structures; in particular there will be problems about integrating diverse mechanisms into unified structures. But these problems appear not to be insuperable. Miller, Galanter, and Pribram's primary goal was to argue for a computational model; it is excusable that their particular proposal was incomplete with respect to the computational operations required for action guidance.

The third difficulty is more serious. The model is viciously regressive. All action is to be analyzed in terms of hierarchies of TOTE units. The basic unit is the TOTE. But one stage of a TOTE is Operate, and Operate is itself an action. Consider the case of grasping a nail again. I locate my hand and the nail in my perceptual field (Test); I close my fingers around the nail (Operate); I relocate my hand and the nail (Test); and I terminate the activity (Exit). But closing my fingers around the nail—the Operate stage—*is* an action. Since all actions are to be analyzed in terms of TOTEs and since one stage of any TOTE is an action, an infinite number of TOTEs must be completed for an action to be performed. The regress is vicious because TOTEs take real time.

There is a related fourth difficulty, which is the most important one. At the outset of their discussion Miller, Galanter, and Pribram raise the fundamental question of action theory with which we are concerned. While discussing Tolman's ideas about cognitive organization, they say, quoting in full:

> It is so transparently clear to [cognitive theorists] that if a hungry rat knows where to find food—if he has a cognitive map with the food box located on it—he will go there and eat. What more is there to explain? The answer, of course, is that a great deal is left to be explained. The gap from knowledge to action looks smaller than the gap from stimulus to action—yet the gap is still there, still indefinitely large. Tolman, the omniscient theorist, leaps over the gap when he infers the rat's cognitive organization from its behavior. But that leaves still outstanding the question of the rat's ability to leap it. Apparently, cognitive theorists have assumed that their best course was to show that the reflex theories are inadequate; they seem to have been quite unprepared when the same argument—that things are even more complicated than they dared to imagine—was used against them. . . . [F]ar from respecting Occam's Razor, the cognitive theorist must ask for even *more* theoretical luggage to carry around. Something is needed to bridge the gap from knowledge to action. (1960, pp. 9–10)

This criticism can be put another way. Suppose that a subject has several courses of action available. Suppose also that he has equally good cognitive maps for each course of action; that is, he can represent to himself each course with equal clarity and precision. But the subject will not act. It is only when he is moved to act—however that is to be translated into theory—that a response ensues. Knowledge of alternatives is not sufficient for action.

This criticism of Tolman, we shall see in chapter 9, is not fair. Tolman recognizes the need for a motivational construct. But that is not the point I want to press now. Rather it is that Miller, Galanter, and Pribram are themselves guilty of the error that they attribute to Tolman. There is no motivational construct in their model: the model does not explain how action is initiated.

Consider once again the simple case of grasping the nail. At the first test stage I locate the nail in my perceptual field. The next stage, Operate, consists in my behavioral response of grasping the nail. Where, however, does the conative element enter into this picture? It appears that Miller, Galanter, and Pribram claim that the behavioral response follows directly from the cognitive event of locating the nail in one's perceptual field. They argued against Tolman by pointing out that action is not possible unless the antecedent to behavior includes a conative feature. But there is no conative feature in their model! The gap between knowledge (cognition) and action remains.

It might be thought that there is a conative feature in the model, represented by the downward arrow connecting Test and Operate in figure 7.1. However, Miller, Galanter, and Pribram make no distinction between the kinds of connections between elements in the model. If that downward arrow represents a conative feature, then they all do. But the upward connection between Operate and Test, and the horizontal arrows indicating Start and Exit, do not represent processes or events having conative properties. Only the mental event initiating the behavioral response is conative.

In fact there is nothing in figure 7.1 that could depict the conative feature of action. A TOTE unit, whether singly or in an hierarchical structure, represents the sequence of events making up the action. It does not depict those features that initiate the action. Miller, Galanter, and Pribram are too ambitious in their claims. They have not produced a model of *action;* rather they have constructed a model of the guidance and monitoring of ongoing activity. Their model is purely cognitive, and does not capture the conative feature of action. Additional theoretical constructs are required for this motivational feature.

Thus despite their claims to the contrary, Miller, Galanter, and Pribram's TOTE model deals only with the cognitive guidance and monitoring of action. Viewed in this more limited way, the last two criticisms against the model are not defeating. If the model is used only to depict the guidance and monitoring of activity, then it is not a criticism to point out that it does not also explain the initiation of action. As to the problem of a vicious regress, it does not get started under this limited interpretation. A premise in that argument is that Operate is an action. But Operate is not an action; rather it is part of an ongoing sequence of events that guide the bodily movements to successful completion. Consider the activity of reaching for a nail. Operate is one of the ongoing series of events constituting the movement of the arm toward the nail. The closed-loop feedback mechanism involved in reaching for the nail is depicted abstractly by a hierarchy of TOTE units.

In review Miller, Galanter, and Pribram hold that human action can best be understood in terms of an analogy with computer programs. But care is required in interpreting this model. Although they recognize the need for a conative feature in action, the TOTE model has no room for this feature. Contrary to their claims, the model does not explain action. Rather it provides a computational account of the guidance and monitoring of action. Or better, it provides, when supplemented by additional mechanisms, a first approximation to a computational account of the guidance and monitoring of ongoing activity.

Miller, Galanter, and Pribram's TOTE model is over two decades old. Since that time, as we are all aware, there has been a computer revolution. As a consequence the idea that motor activity can be explained by the Program Theory has gained currency—though not universal acceptance. The main difference between the status of this theory in 1960 and now is that it has changed from an interesting general conjecture into a theory that generates particular testable models. Testing consists in instantiating specialized programs and comparing the resultant simulations with real human behavior. Human actions can be highly complex. The construction and testing of models for such activities had to await appropriate technological developments. In the remainder of this section I want to give a feeling for the current state of this art by briefly describing an attempt to simulate skilled typing by Rumelhart and Norman (1982).

Typing is a good case to consider. This activity is sufficiently skilled and complex so that an adequate model is not trivial. For all the inventiveness of Miller, Galanter, and Pribram's TOTE model, its primary application was to relatively simple activities, such as hammering a nail. Extrapolation to complex activities was conjecture at best; thus the model tends to evoke a sense of artificiality, of oversimplification. Skilled typing, by contrast, requires a sophisticated model for successful simulation.

One issue about which Miller, Galanter, and Pribram oversimplify is the organizational structure of motor activity. Typing can be extraordinarily fast. Champion typists achieve rates of 17 keys/sec (200 words/min). This rate tends to preclude guidance solely by servomechanisms. The mean interval between keystrokes is 60 msec; this interval approaches that required for neural transmission between the spinal cord and the periphery, thereby leaving little time for feedback. Rumelhart and Norman reason that monitoring and guidance of typing does not proceed sequentially, but rather overlapping subroutines occur simultaneously. Thus although the mean interval between keystrokes is small, each keystroke actually takes a longer time. Skilled typists, the data indicate, use approximately one second between the moment a letter is perceived and the appropriate key is depressed. In order for subroutines to occur in parallel, there must be an integrative control mechanism. This mechanism is not part of the central processing system of persons; but it is something in addition to the particular servomechanisms hypothesized by Miller, Galanter, and Pribram.

Normal persons use ten fingers with which to type. Because each finger has several joints, a number of movements are possible. Focusing only on extension, flexion, and rotation (side-to-side) movements, and leaving aside movements of the wrists, lower arm, upper arm, or so on, there are 50 separate motions possible. Persons take advantage of multiple means of finger placement to set up future strokes. Thus a model that explains human typing cannot proceed on a key-by-key basis, but rather must utilize letter groupings. Skilled typists use groups as large as words. Typing speeds are indifferent between connected text and random words; but it is slower for grouped random letters than for words (Shaffer, 1976). Rumelhart and Norman hypothesize that there is a parsing mechanism that groups letters into words (or perhaps syllables) and thus guides the selection of possible movements in a keystroke.

The most important issue about which Miller, Galanter, and Pribram oversimplify is the criterion of adequacy for a program of motor activity. Often, it seems, they take this criterion to be success. A program for hammering nails is adequate if it results in hammered nails. But this is halfway backward. Success is not good evidence that the program simulates human activity. In highly skilled activity complete success is rarely achieved. Good evidence, rather, consists in replicating characteristic patterns of errors, relative rates of completion of subtasks, and so on. The criterion for adequacy is, in short, replication of psychologically real processes.

Rumelhart and Norman considered three characteristic typing errors. Transposition errors, which most often involve keystrokes from both hands, are those that exchange two letters, e.g., 'because' is typed 'becuase.' Doubling errors are those in which the wrong letter is doubled, e.g., 'school' is typed 'scholl.' Alternation reversal errors are cases in which the wrong letter is alternated in a sequence, e.g., 'these' is typed 'thses.'

The latter two errors are especially interesting. One way to try to explain the typing of a double letter, such as 'oo' in 'school' is to say that 'o' is typed once and then again. But this explanation would not account for doubling errors. In these errors the wrong letter is typed twice. Rumelhart and Norman propose that there is a repeating mechanism (DOUBLE) that produces a repetition of the letter. A doubling error occurs when this mechanism operates on the wrong letter in a word.

A consequence of Rumelhart and Norman's explanation is that there is a mechanism operating on types, rather than tokens. It is the letter-type which is the input, and the twin appearance of letter tokens that is the output. Here again Rumelhart and Norman hypothesize processes of higher-level than Miller, Galanter, and Pribram. The TOTE model follows the mechanical picture closely. But by hypothesizing operations on types, Rumelhart and Norman move the explanation of motor activity toward central processing systems. It remains to be seen whether motor activity is part of central processing. My guess is that it is self-contained and does not appeal to long-term memory, inferential processing, or so on.

Rumelhart and Norman do not have a satisfactory explanation of alternation reversal errors. It might be thought that there is a mechanism operative here similar to that for doubling. In that case ALTERNATE should take 'es' into 'ese' when typing 'these.' However, the data does not support this explanation. If there were such a mechanism, then alternation reversal errors should occur for spaces and single-letter words, so that '-I-' would, for instance, sometimes come out 'I-I.' But no such errors regularly occur for human typists.

To repeat, the main point at which current program models have advanced past Miller, Galanter, and Pribram's TOTE picture is that in addition to servomechanisms some relatively high-level functions are needed to explain motor activity. They are required to account for parallel subroutines within an activity, for parsing inputs, and for characteristic error patterns. As Rumelhart and Norman put it: "A motor program is not a fixed action pattern of movements. It is a set of specifications or control statements that govern the actions that are to be performed, with considerable flexibility in the specification of the actions" (1982, pp. 7–8). However, it remains to be seen whether this approach to the Program Theory will yield concrete results. In the case of typing, as I noted, Rumelhart and Norman's model is at best a first approximation; it does not explain all the features of skilled typing and it does not have provision for all the degrees of freedom of actual typing.

There are two scientific psychological approaches to explaining the cognitive feature common to immediate intention. One approach is learning theoretic. An instance of this type is James's ideo-motor model, augmented by serial chaining and closed-loop feedback mechanisms. The other approach is computational. One instance of this type is Miller, Galanter, and Pribram's TOTE model, augmented by programming operations that account for parallel processing and relatively high-level control and integrative mechanisms.

Which approach to monitoring and guidance, in the end, should be accepted? That is not a question I will attempt to answer. My objective is to show how folk psychological action theoretic concepts can be transformed into scientific psychological ones. It is not my goal to opt for a particular scientific account when there are viable competing ones. That is part of the scientific enterprise. It might appear to some that the computational approach is clearly the best one. For this approach enjoys the advantages of unrestricted applicability, in that it is not species specific, and integration with computational models for central processing. This approach might in the end be the correct one, but that is not now obvious. Central processes such as memory and inference seem best explained by computational models, since these processes essentially involve formal symbol manipulation. But it is not clear that other processes are also best explained computationally. On the input side the primary processes are perceptual; and on the output side the primary processes are those of guidance. It is not clear to what extent these processes involve symbol manipulation. To the degree that they do, they are to be explained in terms of computational models. But to the degree that they do not, such processes are to be explained in terms of the causal laws they instantiate. The learning theoretic approach purports to be closely tied to a causal explanation of guidance. If that is so, then, to the extent that guidance is to be explained by brute causal law, it can be understood by that approach. An explanation of guidance would then be integrated with other psychological causal explanations, but not with computational models of high-level, symbol manipulating processes. There may not be a completely unified psychological theory. The jury remains out.

Appendix: James's Theory of Action

James, writing almost a century ago, claimed that there was an intimate connection between philosophy and science. During the reign of twentieth century positivism, however, scientific and philosophical theories were taken to be antithetical. If empirical considerations supported or cast doubt upon a theory, it was thought not to be philosophical. But the pendulum has begun to swing back. In the last two decades or so many have thought that there is a continuum between scientific and philosophical theories, and that in the large middle portion of this continuum there is interaction between the conceptual and empirical. This view has been especially well-received by those concerned with the nature of mind. Among both psychologists and philosophers of mind, James's views have attracted wide attention. James's work on action, I want to argue, also merits notice. In *The Principles of Psychology* (1890, especially chapter 26) James defends a naturalized action theory.

There is a key passage in *The Principles* that in James's words, "seems . . . to contain in miniature the data for an entire psychology of volition" (1890, v. 2, p. 525).

> We know what it is to get out of bed on a freezing morning in a room without a fire, and how the very vital principle within us protests against the ordeal. Probably most persons have lain on certain mornings for an hour at a time unable to brace themselves to the resolve. . . . Now how do we *ever* get up under such circumstances? If I may generalize from my own experience, we more often than not get up without any struggle or decision at all. We suddenly find that we *have* got up. A fortunate lapse of consciousness occurs; we forget both the warmth and the cold; we fall into some revery connected with the day's life, in the course of which the idea flashes across us, "Hollo! I must lie here no longer"—an idea which at that lucky instant awakens no contradictory or paralyzing suggestions, and consequently produces immediately its appropriate motor effects. It was our acute consciousness of both the warmth and the cold during the period of struggle, which paralyzed our activity then and kept our idea of rising in the condition of *wish* and not of *will*. The moment these inhibitory ideas ceased, the original idea exerted its effects. (1890, v. 2, pp. 524–525)

On the basis of this passage as well as other remarks, James is an Oldtime Volition Theorist. He thinks that the mental antecedent is a purely cognitive event and that the effect is a mere bit of behavior. In particular the mental antecedent is a memory image of an action type, and the effect is a bodily movement. He says that an uninhibited memory event "produces its appropriate motor effects." This is his 'official' position—though, as I shall mention momentarily, in some other passages he appears committed to a Mental Action Theory.

James holds that there are three types of actions: reflex and instinctive actions; ideo-motor actions; and actions involving a *fiat*. The last two categories mark the class of voluntary actions, and it is these that concern us. James does not think that there is a clear line of demarcation between these types, though for the most part classification is clear. Orthogonal to the distinction between the two categories of voluntary action is one between simple action in the sense of being a simple movement, and complex action in the sense of being a sequence of movements. (Note that there is potential for confusion between a restricted and unrestricted use of 'ideo-motor.' In its restricted use 'ideo-motor actions' refers to a subclass of actions. In 'the ideo-motor theory' 'ideo-motor' is used unrestrictively; it pertains to the general theory that *all* action consists of a memory image causing motor effects.)

The mental event in the causal sequence making up a voluntary action is a memory image, sometimes referred to by the apt term 'Effectsbild.' James devotes considerable effort to defeating the view, attributed to Wundt, Helmholtz, Mach, and others, that a feeling of innervation causes the bodily movement (1890, v. 2, pp. 492–522). This feeling or sensation of efferent nerve impulse occurs *prior* to the movement and cannot be detected through either introspection or indirect experiments. In addition to this empirical argument James gives an *a priori* one. Consciousness tends to minimize thoughts and feelings. For example, routine activities such as tying one's shoelaces, though initially learned by concentrating on each step in the routine, are performed by focusing on the entire routine. Memory images of movements already occupy consciousness. Hence additional feelings of innervation are superfluous, and would be excluded from consciousness. Proponents of the view that feelings of innervation are efficacious have, James claims, misidentified feelings of afferent impulses resulting from bodily movements with the antecedent mental event leading to the bodily movements.

Since memory images cause movements, the first time a kind of movement occurs, it cannot be voluntary. The movement during its first occurrence (or first few occurrences) would be haphazard, accidental, or reflexive. Once a movement of a particular kind has been made, there is a memory trace available for bringing about that kind of movement voluntarily. The more often a kind of movement occurs, the stronger the memory trace. James notes that this memory trace can be caused by someone else moving parts of one's body or by observing another person moving his body. The mechanisms for memory traces of these latter sorts, I strongly suspect, play different roles in action. Neither learning by someone else moving one's limbs nor learning by observation can be easily assimilated to learning by doing. Coming to know how to do something by observation or passive movement likely involves mechanisms different from those involved in trial-and-error learning.

Memory images of movements may be either of resident sensations or remote sensations. Resident sensations result from the moving parts themselves, for example, the muscles or joints; remote sensations are kinaesthetic, and include, among others, visual, tactile, and auditory impressions. Some sensations can be very remote, sometimes being of the end-state of the activity. Memory images of resident sensations tend to play a role in ideo-motor action, and memory images of remote sensations tend to play a role in actions containing a fiat.

Ideo-motor actions are performed without attending to what is being done. In general these are the minute actions contained in complex actions, where again a complex action is a sequence of simple actions. Consider the action of getting out of bed. That action is identical with the sequence of minute ideo-motor actions of placing one hand on the blanket, grasping the blanket, lifting the blanket, swinging one's feet around, moving one's feet toward the floor, and so on. Each action in the sequence is performed without attention or reflection, and does not occupy consciousness. One indication that they are not objects of consciousness is that they are performed *in* doing the complex sequential action. *In* getting out of bed, I lift the blanket, turn my body, lower my feet, and so on.

Some voluntary actions involve a fiat. Among these are complex actions, taken as a unified sequence. In rising on a cold morning, the fiat (or, as James sometimes says, the consent) consists in a memory image fully occupying consciousness. There is no special act of will. Indecision, or lack of activity, is not a state in which the agent has yet to will; rather it is a state in which one memory image inhibits another. Prior to rising on the cold morning, the image of remaining in bed inhibits the image of rising. When the former fades, the subject gets up.

James discusses in detail the mechanism by which an uninhibited memory image brings about a learned sequential action (1890, v. 2, pp. 579–592). Consider the learned sequences involved in reciting the alphabet or hammering a nail. As I mentioned in the first section of the chapter, it is often thought that these sequences proceed by serial chaining and closed-loop feedback mechanisms. Serial chaining is involved in reciting the alphabet; afferent feedback from one movement acts as the stimulus for the next movement. A closed-loop mechanism is involved in hammering a nail. Afferent feedback is compared with representations in memory of the correct movements, and responses are made to bring future movements into line with the represented correct movements. James suggests a different kind of mechanism for explaining all these activities. He claims that movements in a sequence are caused by anticipated sensory feedback. The initial sensation causes the first movement in the sequence and at the same time causes a second sensation; that second sensation causes the second movement in the sequence and at the same time causes a third sensation, and so on.

The ideo-motor mechanism, however, seems better suited for routine activities than it is for those involving corrective procedures. In the case of routine activity anticipation of future elements in the sequence can hasten their onset, since there is no waiting period for feedback from one element to the next. But in the case of some types of corrective activity, anticipated responses can be counterproductive. If future elements in a sequence are based on a prior established memory image, and not feedback from the actual, ongoing activity, then it is difficult to see how those future elements will be responsive to alterations required by the environment and other factors affecting the activity.

Consider fiats again. The thought to, say, clap one's hands becomes causally efficacious when it fully occupies consciousness. That is accomplished by attending to it. The attending *is* the fiat. By focusing attention on a memory image of a kind of movement, we create a fiat, thereby making that thought efficacious. James says: "The essential achievement of the will . . . when it is most 'voluntary' is to attend to a difficult object and hold it fast before the mind. The so-doing is the fiat" (1890, v. 2, p. 561, italicized in text). Return to the example of getting out of bed on a cold morning. When a person has competing thoughts so that one inhibits the other, he is not wholly attending to one thought. As the thought of remaining in bed diminishes and he attends to rising, the memory image of rising fully occupies consciousness, thereby becoming efficacious, and he rises.

Recent attention by psychologists to James's theory has for the most part concentrated on ideo-motor action and excluded consideration of those actions involving a fiat. For example, in summarizing James's view, Kimble and Perlmuter (1970) say:

> [T]he theory requires no special mental fiat or act of will for behavior of the type we call voluntary to occur. In James's own terms, the purest form of voluntary behavior is one in which the

image of the consequences of an act automatically lead to that act. Such *ideomotor* action thus differs from ordinary involuntary behavior only in the type of stimulus producing it. (p. 366)

Curiously, Kimble and Perlmuter recognize the need for focusing attention in performing unlearned sequences of acts, not realizing, apparently, that focusing attention is for James a fiat. There is the suggestion in much of this recent work on James by psychologists that all voluntary action can be understood as ideo-motor action, or at least as not involving any mental fiat. But James himself thought that some voluntary action does involve fiat, where a fiat, again, is the focusing of attention on a memory image.

James distinguishes between two competing theories of attention, the Effect Theory and the Cause Theory. He gives the following vivid characterization of the Effect Theory of attention.

> The stream of our thought is like a river. On the whole easy simple flowing predominates in it, the drift of things is with the pull of gravity, and effortless attention is the rule. But at intervals an obstruction, a set-back, a logjam occurs, stops the current, creates an eddy, and makes things temporarily move the other way. If a real river could feel, it would feel these eddies and set-backs as places of effort . . . Really, the effort would only be a passive index that the feat was being performed . . . Just so with our voluntary acts of attention. They are momentary arrests, coupled with a peculiar feeling, of portions of the stream. But the arresting force, instead of being this peculiar feeling itself, may be nothing but the processes by which the collision is produced. (1890, v. 1, pp. 451–452)

In attending, on the Effect Theory, representations come to us by the psychological laws of association: there is no actional input; we are passive. The feeling of effortful attending is a natural concomitant of this process, but does not signify any creative or initiatory activity on the part of the subject (cf. 1890, v. 1, pp. 449–451).

The Cause Theory is like the Effect Theory, except that it includes an impetus, controlled by the subject, that directs and sustains attention. James argues for the Cause Theory. He observes that it accounts for our strong intuition that persons have input into what they attend to, and hence what they do. "The whole feeling of reality," he says, "the whole sting and excitement of our voluntary life, depends on our sense that in it things are *really being decided* from one moment to another, and that it is not the dull rattling off of a chain that was forged immemorable ages ago" (1890, v. 1, p. 453).

In defending the Cause Theory of attention, James has shifted his ground from an Oldtime Volitional account to a Mental Action Theory. Or at least he has adopted a Mental Action Theory for that class of actions involving fiat. Attending, he argues, begins with active deciding; and active deciding is a mental action.

James's underlying reason for adopting the Cause Theory of attention is metaphysical. The Effect Theory, he thinks, yields the result that persons do not act freely, that their actions are the result of a "dull rattling off of a chain." He thereby bases his psychology of action on metaphysical considerations.

While in general James is correct in not divorcing empirical issues from conceptual ones, in this particular case no advantage is gained. He cannot argue for the Cause Theory of attention by saying that it alone allows for free action. For the Cause Theory fares no better (or worse) than the Effect Theory in this regard. Suppose that bodily movements were initiated by mental actions of deciding. It is consistent with this supposition that all actions are caused by events beyond the agent's control, that in all cases the agent could not have done otherwise. Active decisions need not be free; they could be compelled or coerced. If an unsavory character were to threaten me, asking for my wallet or promising dire harm, I would no doubt decide to give him my wallet. It is something I actively decide to do, but also something I am coerced into doing. Generally speaking, nothing about freedom or determinism follows from the claim that bodily movement is initiated by a mental action. A person acts freely only if he could have done otherwise. And he could have done otherwise only if he was neither coerced nor compelled. If deciding is part of the event initiating his activity, then he could have done otherwise only if his deciding was neither compelled nor coerced. Decisions construed as actions can be compelled or coerced, depending on the circumstances leading to the decision. Thus a person can actively decide and yet not act freely. The free will issue concerns the types of causes that the mental events initiating actions have; it does not, as James thought, concern the actional status of these mental events.

To repeat the point, the Cause Theory of attention is independent of the claim:

(1) Persons sometimes act freely.

The Cause Theory entails that active decision is an element in at least some cases of attention. Attention in turn initiates high-level action.

Since a person acts freely only if he is not compelled or coerced, the truth of (1) depends, then, on whether every active decision is compelled or coerced. The Cause Theory of attention, however, does not yield an answer to that question. Persons making active decisions could be in all cases compelled by internal psychological states or hereditary factors or coerced by external circumstances or other persons. The Cause Theory is silent on this issue. Thus, contrary to James's claim, the Cause Theory of attention does not ensure the truth of (1).

The Cause Theory of attention is the Effect Theory with the addition of acts of deciding. We can think of the Effect Theory as being purely cognitive, whereas the Cause Theory includes in addition some actional element. James holds that the experimental data is equally well explained by both theories. It is not clear that that is true.[6] But suppose that it is. Then the Effect Theory is preferable, since it is simpler. To this argument James makes a startling reply: "Occam's razor, though a very good rule of method, is certainly no law of nature. . . . Nature may . . . indulge in these complications, and the conception that she has done so in this case is, I think, just as clear (if not as 'parsimonious' logically) as the conception that she has not" (1890, v. 1, p. 453). This reply is extremely curious made by someone who argued against a feeling of innervation causing movement by pointing out that there is a simpler explanation. Moreover it is surely correct in this case to choose the simpler of the two theories, since they have the same explanatory power. James seems to have been driven to this heroic defense of the Cause Theory because he thought it alone provided a place for free will. But this is a confusion: freedom is not dependent on active deciding being part of attending.

In summary James 'officially' opts for an Oldtime Volitional Theory. An action is a memory image causing bodily behavior. But he also commits himself to a Mental Action Theory for a subclass of actions. Some actions include a fiat, which is an attending to a memory image. Attending, he claims, begins with active deciding. However, James offers no good reason for adopting this view of attending over a purely cognitive, nonactional account. The data, he holds, underdetermines the theory. He should then have opted for a purely cognitive theory of attending, in which case he would not have had to shift his ground to a Mental Action Theory. He could have remained faithful to his Oldtime Volitional Theory. Of course as I argued in the first chapter, Oldtime Volitional theories are problematic. They cannot sustain their reductive status, and, reformulated nonreductively, they are unnecessarily convoluted. But that is not the most interesting aspect of James's action theory. It is rather that conceptual and empirical considerations comingle, and that empirical claims by and large constrain conceptual ones. James's advocacy of the ideo-motor theory of action, which is a type of Oldtime Volitional Theory, is based on empirical evidence. This is the attempt to naturalize action theory.

8

Intentional Action and Cognition

In the previous chapter I discussed the cognitive feature common to the antecedent of all action. The folk psychological characterization of that feature is the subject's guiding and monitoring ongoing activity. The discussion proceeded by considering transformations of this folk psychological notion into the neobehaviorist learning theoretic concept of a response image and the computational idea of an abstract structural hierarchy of servomechanisms. In this chapter I will focus on the distinctive cognitive feature antecedent to intentional action. The folk psychological characterization of that feature is, essentially, an action being part of a subject's plan. Intentional action then has dual cognitive components: in terms of folk psychology an intentional action is an action both planned and guided to completion. In chapter 1 I provided a folk psychological sketch of following a plan. Here I want to transform this concept into a scientific one grounded in the computational framework.

My point of departure is the recent work in artificial intelligence and cognitive psychology on the representation of stereotypic situations. In particular I shall propose that, with modifications—some of which will be serious—the notion of scripts and plans as developed by Schank and Abelson (1977) captures the distinctive cognitive feature of intentional action. This conceptual point could also be made in the context of some other related models, for example, Minsky's (1975) frame theory, Rumelhart's (1975, 1979) story grammar, or Neisser's (1976) schemata, since all these models approach being notational variants of each other. I selected Schank and Abelson's 1977 script theory because it is accessible and it explicitly has properties well-suited to our purpose.

In more detail section 1 describes Schank and Abelson's model as presented in their *Scripts, Plans, Goals and Understanding* (1977), and relates it to the folk psychological notion of intentional action. In the following sections I consider problems, qualifications, and modifications for this model. Section 2 is concerned with the issue of self-referentiality; section 3 is concerned with goals, section 4 the range of intentional action, section 5 the representational language of the model, and section 6 the constituent units of plans and scripts. Section 7 briefly discusses a revised version of the 1977 model developed by Schank to deal with some of these problems. Finally, in section 8 I discuss a major difficulty that confronts any computational theory of intentional action.

1. Schank and Abelson's 1977 Script Theory

Neobehaviorist learning theory on the whole follows a bottom-up methodology. It starts with the basic units of stimulus and response, plus an assortment of intervening variables and hypothetical constructs, and attempts to explain behavior. For example, Greenwald's (1970) version of the ideo-motor theory, discussed in the previous chapter, falls within this general approach. One of the notable failures of neobehaviorist learning theory is its inability to account for the long-range complex activities of persons. In contrast there is a strong and growing interest in explaining human activity by top-down methodologies. This methodology has been used in computer simulation models. For instance, it was adopted by Norman and Rumelhart (1982) in their design of a model to simulate skilled typing. Generally speaking, abstract units of analysis are introduced to explain complex activities or states; simple, constituent activities or states are explained by their roles within these complex structures.

Dennett (1978, chapter 7) has argued that the underlying rationale for computer simulation or artificial intelligence (AI) is a transcendental argument.[1] First, a model is constructed that meets the conditions presumed necessary for the possibility of some activity. Then this model is instantiated in a computer program. The program is the testing ground for the model. In constructing the program, all the details of the model must be provided, some of which might be otherwise inadvertently ignored. And in running the program, the limitations and faults of the model are made obvious. If the abstract model successfully passes the programming test, it simulates that activity in persons.

That, at least, is the ideal. In practice there are difficulties. It is not trivial to write programs to test these models. Moreover there exists the serious danger that the contingencies of successful programming will influence the final theory; and thus the theory will not reflect actual processing in persons. Also there are constraints on theory construction beyond that of testability through computer simulation that might be ignored—in fact often are ignored, such as depth of analysis and coherence with related theories. But despite these difficulties in practice, this approach is attractive and has generated some interesting results.

One fruitful idea that has emerged in the AI literature is that high-level cognitive processing sometimes involves representations of stereotypic situations. When undertaking a complex activity such as getting dressed in the morning and going to work, it is not necessary for one to think about every minute step as if it were an entirely distinct activity. Rather a person has a stored master representation of the entire activity such that he need focus only on those features that are unique to the particular occasion. This notion of a representation of stereotypic situations, I will argue, is useful for explaining the cognitive feature common to the antecedent of intentional action. It is superior to the folk psychological notion of belief in that it permits the requisite representational complexity.

I take as my point of departure Schank and Abelson's model in *Scripts, Plans, Goals and Understanding* (1977). Other authors have also appealed to stereotypic representations in cognitive processing. Indeed it can be found as early as Bartlett (1932). Within the AI community the godfather of this notion is Minsky (1975), who labels such representations 'frames.' (See Abelson, 1981, for a brief review of the literature.) I concentrate on Schank and Abelson's work because they have provided a sophisticated and relatively well-developed yet accessible theoretical model, which has, in collaboration with others, received some testing through working programs and psychological experimentation. Moreover their characterization uses representations of event sequences, a mode amenable to our goal of clarifying the cognitive feature of intentional action, whereas some other accounts of stereotypic activity use representations constructed from propositional networks or other nonevent-like abstract structures.

The ostensive objective of Schank and Abelson (1977) is to provide a theory of understanding stories about complex human activity. These narratives might appear in newspapers, fairy tales, verbal reports, or so on. Characteristic of stories is that information about intermediate steps and about the goals of the actors is unstated and must be inferred. Understanding a story consists in being able to provide an account of these missing steps and goals, and the test for understanding is being able to answer questions about these missing items. Schank and Abelson argue that the understanding of stories is achieved by assimilating the stories to past ones in which the details are known. These stored stories are made up of routinized sequences, called 'scripts,' and nonroutinized sequences of limited extent, called 'plans,' and of broad extent, called 'themes.'

Schank and Abelson focus on narratives in part because they provide a definite and unchanging transcript of an activity. Problems of interpretation of the text are kept at a minimum, and providing the computer with an instance to test the underlying theory is relatively straightforward. To think, however, that Schank and Abelson's work is only concerned with narratives is to read them too narrowly. A wider and natural reading is that they are concerned with understanding human activity in all contexts. Their theory, if correct, should shed light on understanding observed past, present, and future behavior of oneself and others. The theoretical terms Schank and Abelson use, especially 'script,' 'theme,' and 'story,' are most appropriate in the context of narratives. I will use these terms in an extended sense that applies to all contexts. A story, for instance, is any complicated incident involving one or more persons performing actions.

I suggest that the folk psychological notion of following a plan can be transformed into a species of having a representation of the kind Schank and Abelson discuss. More exactly I conjecture that the following hypothesis is very highly plausible.

(S) S's Aing is an intentional action *only if* S has a representation for understanding a story in which he plays, with self-awareness, the lead role and in which he performs an action of type A.

(The temporal parameter in (S) is surpressed for simplicity.) The details of this conjecture, including the concomitant modifications it requires in Schank and Abelson's 1977 model, will become clear as I proceed.

In order to understand human activity, it must be organized into units. The leading idea in Schank and Abelson's 1977 model is that the unit of analysis is a *script*. A script is a complex routine. As they put it, "a script is a predetermined, stereotyped sequence of actions that defines a well-known situation" (1977, p. 41). The unit of analysis here is macroscopic when compared with the neobehaviorist stimulus-response unit or with the philosophical action theoretic unit of basic action.

Scripts have variations, called 'tracks.' They have settings, involving props and characters. There are entry conditions when the script begins and exit conditions when it concludes. Scripts have internal complexity and are divided into scenes. Scripts often involve interpersonal situations, but they may concern only one person. Consider the Coffee Shop track of the restaurant script, developed in detail by Schank and Abelson (1977, pp. 42 ff.) and now well-known in the literature. The props are tables, a menu, food, a check, and money. The characters (or role players) are the customers, the waiter, cook, cashier, and owner. The script begins when the customer is hungry and has money; and it concludes when the customer has less money and is not hungry, and the owner gains money. The first scene involves the customer entering the restaurant. His actions consist of the sequence of walking into the restaurant, looking at the tables, deciding where to sit, walking to a table, and sitting down. The second scene concerns ordering. There are several alternative scenarios here: one of which is that the customer picks up the menu on the table, considers the choices, chooses one food, signals the waiter; the waiter walks to the table; the customer orders the food from the waiter; the waiter walks to the chef, places the order with the chef; and the chef prepares the food. I will not describe the alternate versions of this scene, nor the remaining scenes in which the customer eats and then exits.

The main advantage to organizing activity into scripts is that it permits representation without attention to the myriad details. If a person attended to all the detailed actions when thinking about the script, he would be overloaded with information and could not represent to himself the larger structure of which the script is a part. A person can, however, focus on a scene in a script, or an action within a scene, and thereby access the details.

Plans resemble scripts, though they exclude much of the elaboration. Schank and Abelson say: "[P]lans are where scripts came from. They compete for the same role in the understanding process, namely as explanations of sequences of actions that are intended to achieve a goal. The difference is that scripts are specific and plans are general" (1977, p. 72). If eating in a restaurant is a rare occurrence in someone's life, as it might be for a poor rural farmer, then he has a general plan for doing so but not a stereotyped script. For such persons parts of the activity would not be routinized.

Plans and scripts, though dealing with complex activities, are nonetheless limited in scope. Plans and scripts are organized under themes. Themes are long-range predispositions to act in certain ways; they contribute to the development of scripts and plans. Schank and Abelson (1977, pp. 131 ff.) recognize three types of themes: role themes, such as being a waiter; interpersonal themes, such as being an employee; and life themes, such as being an honest person. They do not provide a thorough analysis of themes, and I shall not take up the issue. The study of themes lies at the periphery of action theory, where it intersects with social psychology.

In understanding a story, a subject forms a representation. This representation has two parts: there is a representation of what hap-

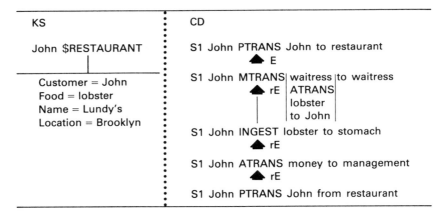

Figure 8.1
John's eating in a restaurant. From Schank and Abelson (1977, p. 153).

pens in the world, that is, the sequences of events and the connections among them; and there is a representation of the goals of the subject. To illustrate the full representational structure, consider two stories, the first involving a script and the second a plan.

The first story is this:

> John went to Lundy's. He ordered lobster. He paid the check and left.

(Schank and Abelson, 1977, pp. 152–153.) The story is diagramed in figure 8.1.

The left-hand side of the diagram, labeled 'KS' for 'Knowledge Structure,' indicates John's goals. Here John is following a script, indicated by '$Restaurant,' and thus is taken to have one overall goal. The right-hand side of the diagram, labeled 'CD' for 'Conceptual Dependency,' indicates the representation of event sequences in the world. The symbol 'S1' relates this conceptualization to the first (and here only) script in the Knowledge Structure.

In the Conceptual Dependency part of the diagram the predicate 'Ptrans' abbreviates 'physically transfers,' the predicate 'Mtrans' abbreviates 'transfers mental information,' and 'Atrans' abbreviates 'transfers an abstract relationship (e.g., ownership).' These abbreviations derive from an artificial language written by Schank (which I will discuss later). The arrows between lines on the Conceptual Dependency side stand for representations of connections between events. Schank and Abelson hold that all connections between events are causal, though differing with respect to the arguments of the re-

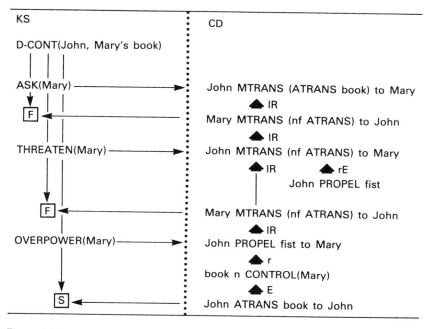

Figure 8.2
John's taking Mary's book. From Schank and Abelson (1977, p. 157).

lations. '①◆E②' is read '① enables (is a condition for) ②,' where ①
is an event and ② an action, and '①◆rE②' is read .'① results in ②,'
where ① is an action and ② is a state that enables (is a condition for)
an action. (In the diagrams, the argument ① appears above the arrow
and ② appears below it.)

The second story is this:

> John wanted Mary's book. He asked her for it and she refused.
> He said he would hit her if she didn't give it to him. She still said
> no. Finally he hit her in the head and took the book.

(Schank and Abelson, 1977, pp. 157–158.) This story is diagramed in
figure 8.2.

Since John is following a plan in this case and not a routinized
script, his individual goals must be represented in the Knowledge
Structure. 'D-Cont (John, Mary's book)' signifies a change in control
of Mary's book to John. The boxes represent the outcomes of goals:
'F' within a box means failure and 'S' success. The downward arrows
are read backward as 'in order to.' Note that there is interplay
between the two parts of the representation. On the Conceptual Dependency side there are several new abbreviations. '①◆IR②' abbre-

viates '$_①$ initiates $_②$,' where $_①$ is an action and $_②$ a thought that is a reason for the action, and '$_①$◆r$_②$' abbreviates '$_①$ results in $_②$,' where $_①$ is an action and $_②$ an event. The second line, 'Mary Mtrans (nf Atrans) to John,' translates approximately as 'Mary's transferring mental information, but not yet ownership, to John.' And the penultimate line, 'book n Control (Mary),' translates approximately as 'Mary's losing control of the book.'

John's cognitive attitudes when acting intentionally can be read from figures 8.1 and 8.2, though not directly. Intentional action is future-directed. In acting intentionally a person focuses on future activity within the constraints of his plan and the environment. There is also an element of past-directedness in intentional action, namely, a memory of the events that led to the present state of affairs, especially one's contribution to it.

Looking at figure 8.2, for example, it is, read all at once, solely past-directed. It depicts John's representation of a past incident and thus is suited to represent his memory of it. In order to determine John's cognitive attitudes when intentionally performing the various acts in the scenario, attention must be paid to the temporal parameters. The flow of time in the diagram is downward: John intends to gain control of Mary's book; first he asks Mary for it; after that, he threatens her; and after that, he overpowers her. At each stage John's cognitive attitude is depicted by his planned goals plus a representation of external events and their interplay with his past actions. For instance, John's cognitive attitude at the time he intentionally threatens Mary would be depicted by figure 8.3, which is a modification of Schank and Abelson's figure 8.2.

At time t_i, John's cognitive state includes an awareness of his overriding goal to gain control of Mary's book, a memory of his past action of asking Mary for the book, and his goals of next threatening her and, if that fails, overpowering her. At the same time John's cognitive state includes a representation of the relevant external events and their relations and of the interplay between these events and his past actions. *This entire complex representation is the distinctive cognitive antecedent of John's intentionally threatening Mary.* Similarly the cognitive antecedents of John's other intentional actions while carrying out his plan can be depicted by modifying figure 8.2 to include the appropriate temporal parameters. A person's mental representation changes during the conduct of a plan.

Let us call a script that is modified to reflect the temporal location of the subject while the script is progressing an *I-script*. Similarly let us call a plan so modified an *I-plan*. Figure 8.3 depicts an I-plan. Notice that not all action is scripted or planned. For instance, auto-

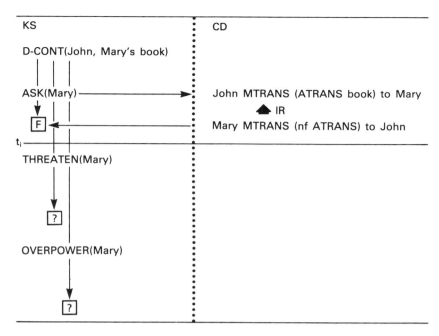

Figure 8.3
A representation of John's cognitive attitude when he threatens Mary.

matic actions, such as putting one's hands forward when falling, are usually neither scripted nor planned. Another class of unscripted and unplanned actions are slips, for example, reversals of word order, that is, spoonerisms (cf. Norman, 1981). In these cases there is no preconceived representation of the type Schank and Abelson discuss. The actual extent of scripted and planned action is of course an empirical matter. This model, when conjoined with (S), correctly entails that not all action is intentional, that is, that the Intentionality Thesis (IT) is false.[2]

2. Self-Referentiality

The hypothesis (S) is a bridge between the folk psychological concept of intentional action and a theory about the representation of stories, broadly understood. Schank and Abelson's 1977 model provides a first approximation to that theory. However, there are a number of problems facing this model. Their resolution will require modifications, qualifications, and elaborations.

The first problem concerns self-referentiality. There is nothing in Schank and Abelson's 1977 model that says that the subject thinks of himself in a first-person, self-referential way. The story depicted by figure 8.2, for instance, is about John, told in the third person. Figure 8.2 is not a representation of John's thinking of a plan in which he himself plays the lead role. Someone's playing the lead role in a script or plan is not sufficient for his being aware that it is he himself who is an actor in the story. The issue is not which role the subject plays in the story; rather it is whether the subject's representation of the story is such that he is aware that it is he himself who is playing the part. Once again, there is nothing in the representational structures used by Schank and Abelson indicating when a subject is aware that it is he who is being represented in the script or plan.

This issue is critical when the model is used to depict the cognitive antecedent to intentional action. For in this case the subject must be aware that it is he himself who is the actor in the script or plan. The hypothesis (S) says that the representational structure must include the element of self-awareness; to that extent Schank and Abelson's 1977 model does not succeed in articulating (S).

This issue is also important if Schank and Abelson's 1977 model is to have wide psychological applicability. While it is plausible to hold that underlying cognitive schemata for understanding narratives and for memory of routinized activities are identical, as in Rumelhart (1977), for example, it is not plausible to think that generalized memory structures for routinized activities are identical to processing structures for ongoing activity. For the processing structure must be such that the subject knows that it is he who is undertaking this activity; but in general memory structures have no such constraint.

With regard to this last point the schemata appropriate for understanding most narratives are not person-specific. Consider

(1) Richard went to the First National Bank. He wrote a withdrawal slip, collected money from the teller, and went home.

There is a great deal of information not stated in (1) but normally understood to be implicit. It can be safely assumed, for instance, that Richard handed the withdrawal slip to the teller, despite (1) not literally saying that, since our schema for normal bank transactions includes handing a slip of paper to the teller. The schema for understanding (1), however, does not include any factor that says whether the subject realizes that he himself is Richard. Contrast this case with one in which Richard himself has a schema for a bank transaction. The schema *he* uses does include a factor that says that it is he who is undertaking the activity. In short there must be some additional psychological mechanism for self-referentiality if Schank and Abelson's 1977 model is to explain both first person scripted and planned activity and understanding first-person narratives.

Schank and Abelson do not suggest any way to account for the self-referential feature of scripted or planned activity. Nor to my knowledge do other psychologists who discuss action schemata. Of course it is inadequate to say that the subject's instantiated schemata contains an element of self-reference when his name is represented in that structure; for that would fail to distinguish the third-person case from the first-person one. There would, for instance, be no difference between the cognitive structures of my thinking of the story told by (1) and Richard's recalling his activity reported by (1). To make the point another way, suppose that Richard had covertly recited (1). He could nevertheless fail to be aware that that story is about himself, if he did not know that his name was 'Richard' or if he knew that but did not know that he was *that* Richard.

Using the conclusions reached in chapter 4, Schank and Abelson's 1977 model can be modified to include a self-referential factor. Consider scripts, which are large, structured cognitive units.[3] They are macroscopic when compared with cognitive units whose content is that of an individual proposition. The primary psychological claim of Schank and Abelson's 1977 model is that scripts are accessed and processed as a unit. The myriad details of a script are not separately accessed, ordered, and then combined. Self-reference attaches to cognitive units. Because scripts are the cognitive units, self-reference attaches to scripts as a whole. Self-referentiality consists in having the primitive attitude of self-ascription directed toward a property. In the case of scripts the attitude is directed toward playing the lead role in the script. For example, the self-referential element in John's eating in a restaurant would be technically expressed as

(2) John self-ascribes the property of playing the lead role in $Restaurant.

In this script the lead role is that of being the customer. The main points, to repeat, are that the cognitive unit is a script and that self-reference with respect to this unit depends on the self-ascription of a property.

Matters are somewhat more complex for plans. Plans differ from scripts in that they are large cognitive units constructed from smaller ones. Plans are the operative representation when the activity is not sufficiently practiced to be routinized. In the story illustrated by figure 8.2, for example, John, presumably, is not in the habit of force-fully taking someone's goods and so had to form a plan of action. The cognitive units in the case of plans are represented by each line in the Conceptual Dependency part of the diagrams. Since self-referentiality occurs at the level of the cognitive units, it attaches to actions within plans, not to the plans themselves.

The Conceptual Dependency part of the diagrams are representations of events in the world. Each line in the diagram is a singular term expressing a person-independent cognitive attitude of the subject. When the subject is aware that it is he who is following a plan, these singular terms should reflect the self-referential aspect of the subject's attitude. For example, the first line in figure 8.2 reads 'John MTRANS (ATRANS) book to Mary.' This line translates into quasi-English as 'John's transferring mental information to Mary about the abstract transfer of the book,' which translated further into English is

(3) John's asking Mary for the book.

In the terminology introduced in chapter 4 the self-referential aspect of this action is captured by recasting (3) as

(4) John's self-ascribing the property of asking Mary for the book.

That is, the representations in the Conceptual Dependency portion of the master representation are cases of self-ascriptions.

Schank and Abelson do not discuss the ontological commitment of their model. A natural interpretation is that their view commits them to propositions (see Toumela, 1981). I argued in chapter 4 that the objects of attitudes are properties. Schank and Abelson's 1977 model can be recast in this manner. This point is similar to the one made about the folk psychological attitudes in chapter 4. They are ordinarily construed as taking propositional objects; but there is a clear advantage, with regard to the issues of self-referentiality and ontological economy, to recast the folk psychological attitudes as taking properties as objects. For simplicity we can continue to use modes of expression that do not reflect a commitment to property object-assimilationism, provided that we are cognizant that there is this commitment.

3. Goals

In this and the following section I will briefly consider two related and important qualifications for Schank and Abelson's model. The first concerns goals. On this model not only are the subject's cognitive attitudes toward the ongoing course of events represented, but also the subject's goals and the interaction between his goals and external events. After a goal is realized (or not), a representation of that fact is encoded in memory and becomes part of the subject's cognitive attitude associated with the I-script or I-plan to which the goal belongs. It is primarily this feature of systematic parallel processing of goal states and representations of external events that makes Schank and Abelson's model attractive.

There are two *prima facie* distinctions to be made about goals. First, there is a difference between *to-be* goals and *to-do* goals, that is, between state goals and action goals. A politician might have the goal to be a senator, or a farmer might have the goal to plow the back forty (that is, to do the back-forty plowing). Second, there is a distinction between instrumental goals and terminal goals. These distinctions are orthogonal to each other. For instance, the goal to be senator might be instrumental to some other goal, say to be president. Moreover, neither distinction is absolute. A to-be goal is a type of to-do goal. If someone has a goal to be so-and-so, then he has the goal of performing those actions he thinks would result in his being so-and-so. If Teddy has the goal to be president, he thereby has the goal to perform those actions he thinks will result in his gaining that office. A terminal goal for one activity can be an instrumental goal for another, when the former activity is part of the latter. Becoming senator can be the terminal goal in one campaign but instrumental with respect to the larger activity of becoming president.

Goals are intimately related to intentions. They are subjects' intentions to do something in the future, that is, prospective intentions. Goals are not to be identified with the cognitive attitude associated with immediate intention because that attitude concerns in part the guidance and monitoring of ongoing activity. Rather goals concern the subject's representation of what he is setting himself to do.

A subject must see the goal as his goal. Goals are self-referential. This self-referentiality is inherent in prospective intention. Consider again the I-plan depicted by figure 8.3. The goal of John's plan is described canonically by 'D-CONT (John, Mary's book).' In quasi-English this translates to 'John's changing control of Mary's book,' which in English means

(5) John's gaining control of Mary's book.

But (5) is not quite correct: it fails to specify the self-referential element in John's thought. Rather John's goal, his thought of what *he* intends to do in the future, is reported by

(6) John's setting himself to acquire the property of gaining control of Mary's book.

At t_i, John has an unrealized terminal goal to his I-plan. That goal is an intention to do something in the future, his gaining control of Mary's book.

Self-referentiality therefore is to be incorporated into Schank and Abelson's 1977 model at two places. The Conceptual Dependency side of the diagrams depicts representations of external events. When these events directly involve the subject, he adopts the primitive attitude of self-ascribing a property. The Knowledge Structure side of the diagrams depicts representations of goal structures. Goals are future-directed intentions. That is, in having a goal the subject represents to himself what *he* intends to do. Thus in following a plan the subject also adopts the primitive attitude of setting oneself to acquire a property.

A terminal goal is the goal for which a subject undertakes the entire scripted or planned activity. It is the highest-level goal of the script or plan. An instrumental goal is one that occurs within a script or plan as an intermediate step toward achieving the terminal goal. Said another way, future intentions, when directed toward a single script or plan, are hierarchically ordered: some intentions are subsumed under others within a single representation.

Plans can have subplans or scripts as parts. Thus a terminal goal in one plan or script can be instrumental in a more inclusive plan of which it is a part. Another complication concerns the interaction of plans. Two or more plans can proceed simultaneously and be mutually supporting. For example, I might have both the plan to learn to become a cabinetmaker and the plan to build furniture for my living room. These plans proceed in parallel and mutually reinforce each other. But sometimes plans can detract from each other. Suppose I have the plan both to become a cabinetmaker and to become a world traveler. These plans, while not entirely incompatible, tend to interfere. In general, nested plans and interactive plans can be extremely complex; and thus the relationships between instrumental and terminal goals is a matter of considerable complexity.

Instrumental goals are related to terminal goals by the in-order-to relation. In the I-plan diagramed by figure 8.3, asking Mary for the book is instrumental to gaining control (or possession) of it. The subordination of this instrumental goal to the terminal goal of the plan is expressed by

(7) John's asking Mary for her book in order to gain control of it.

In this context the by-relation is the converse of the in-order-to relation (cf. Thomson, 1977, chapters 11–13). Taking into account the self-referentiality of John's thought, it is to be expressed by

(8) John's setting himself to acquire the property of gaining control of Mary's book by asking her for it.

These formulations of the subject's goals are stated as to-do goals. Schank and Abelson's model concerns representations of subjects' actions. If a subject has to-be goals, these are to be represented in terms of their correlated to-do goals.

4. Intentional Action

In chapter 1, I claimed that from the folk psychological viewpoint an action is intentional just in case it is either explicitly planned or part of a pattern of planned activity. This claim cannot be straightforwardly transformed into Schank and Abelson's 1977 model. Explicitly planned action is action that is included in a subject's plan, defined by the model. In our example, since John's asking Mary for the book is part of his plan, his asking her in fact is an intentional action. Scripted actions are not explicitly planned, but are part of a pattern of planned activity. They are not explicitly planned because a script suppresses their conscious accessibility. The KS representation for $Restaurant, for example, does not explicitly contain the action of sitting at a table. But that action is part of the overall activity of eating at a restaurant. While it is not normally accessed, it can with cues be brought to consciousness. Thus actions that are performed in virtue of following a script are intentional. Unfortunately folk psychology assigns intentionality to actions other than those that are scripted or planned on this model. Some actions are intentional in virtue of being included in a pattern of activity without being preconceived. Schank and Abelson's model thus yields an account of intentional action that is too narrow.[4]

As discussed in chapter 1, there are two ways in which an action can be part of a pattern of activity without being explicitly planned or scripted. An action can be substituted for one when planned action cannot be performed; or an action can be improvised when it is an integral part of a planned activity. In the case of John's reprehensible plan, if Mary were deaf, he could not ask her for the book, but rather would have to substitute an action of signing for it or requesting it in writing or some such. Though not planned, this action substituted at the moment is nevertheless intentional. Or similarly, in order to overpower Mary, John raises his arm. But raising his arm is not an explicit part of the preconceived plan; rather it is an action that must be added for the plan to succeed. This improvised action clearly is also intentional. The folk psychological concept of intentional action, moreover, permits interruption of a plan without negating the intentionality of those actions completed according to plan. If John is distracted during his interaction with Mary, say to kick a dog, his actions toward Mary are intentional even though they did not proceed uninterrupted as originally planned.

It might be thought that as a consequence of this problem the model should be revised. But that is misguided. It would be psychologically unrealistic to increase the complexity of I-scripts and I-plans to include the myriad details and alternative possibilities required by improvised and substituted action. The attractive feature of scripts and other schemata is that they allow for processing and memory without attention to details and alternatives. Rather the appropriate strategy is to alter the bridge statement (S), which connects the model with folk psychology. This approach is similar to that suggested in chapter 1. Recall that in discussing this issue from the folk psychological viewpoint, the definition of 'intentional action' was modified. In contrast to a definition of 'action plan,' which is constrained by empirical considerations, the definition of 'intentional action' is governed to a significant extent by conceptual considerations.

The bridge statement (S) between the model and the concept of intentional action is to be revised to:

(S*) *S's Aing is an intentional action if and only if:*
(i) *S's Aing is action; and*
(ii) *either S* has a representation for understanding a story in which he plays, with self-awareness, the lead role and in which he performs an action of type *A or S's Aing* satisfies (Prin* S), (Prin* Im), or (Prin* In).

(Again the temporal parameters have been suppressed for simplicity.) The principles (Prin* S), (Prin* Im), and (Prin* In) are versions of the substitution principle (Prin S), the improvisation principle (Prin Im), and the interruption principle (Prin In) discussed in chapter 1 modified to cohere with Schank and Abelson's 1977 model.

For completeness let me state these modified principles.

(Prin* S) *If* (i) *S's Bing is an action,* (ii) *S's Bing is a substitutive action for S's Aing with respect to a story T and* (iii) *S is not able to A, then S's Bing is an intentional action.*

For any person S and action types A and B, S's Bing is a substitutive action for S's Aing with respect to story T *iff* there is a story T^* in which S plays with self-awareness the lead role and that differs from T only in containing S's Bing where T contains S's Aing. This principle can be reiterated, so that a number of actions can be substituted in each story. Here a story is of course a script or plan characterized by the Schank and Abelson model.

> (Prin* Im) *If* (i) S's Bing is an action, (ii) S's Bing is not contained in any story of S's about himself, but (iii) S does represent to himself a story in which he A_is and A_{i+1}s, where his A_{i+1}ing depends on his Bing and his Bing depends on his $A_i$ing, *then* S's Bing is an intentional action.

For example, Pat's moving her soup plate closer during a meal at *Pierre's* is intentional even though that action is not a preconceived part of any script or plan she has. For she does have a script for eating in a restaurant which includes the actions of sitting at the table and eating, and her moving her plate closer is a necessary intermediary between these actions. This example is in terms of causal dependencies between events. But, as argued earlier, some event dependencies are conventional. When the conductor lowers his baton, the symphony begins to play. The relationship between these events is conventional, since the baton lowering is a sign to begin. Schank and Abelson (1977) do not include conventional dependencies among events within their framework. Thus (S*) entails an enrichment of that framework.

Continuing with these principles,

> (Prin* In) *If* (i) S represents to himself some story in which he A_is and A_{i+1}s but does not B, (ii) S's Bing occurs between his $A_i$ing and A_{i+1}ing or during his $A_i$ing or A_{i+1}ing and (iii) S's Bing is not dependent on either his $A_i$ing or A_{i+1}ing, or conversely *then* S's $A_i$ing and A_{i+1}ing are intentional actions.

An action, that is, is intentional if it is a preconceived part of some story, no matter whether the story unfolds as represented. All manner of things might go wrong as Pat eats in the restaurant; nevertheless any actions performed according to $Restaurant are intentional.

Supplemented in this way, Schank and Abelson's model yields the correct intuitive results about the extension of 'intentional action.' If that were not the case, the bridge statement (S*) would have to be altered further—in particular the constituent principles would have to be revised. For now, since the goal of this chapter is to provide a general strategy for transforming the folk psychological concept of intentional action into a scientific one, attention can be focused on the simpler (S). In a final formulation of the model, (S*) would be required.

5. The Representational Language

In Schank and Abelson's 1977 model (as well as in a revision of that model to be discussed shortly), information is encoded in the artificial language Conceptual Dependency—hereafter 'CD.'[5] This language was developed by Schank and his colleagues: see especially Schank (1972, 1975).

Schank devised CD as a canonical system in which action types and causal chains can be represented. The language has received semiformal development. It has been formulated with eleven primitives for types of actions, four primitives for types of causal relations, additional primitives for various attribute scales, machinery for tenses, and so on. One advantage of CD is that it is a good implementation language for machine programs. The Yale AI Lab has had success using CD as the high-level language for SAM (Script Applier Mechanism), PAM (Plan Applier Mechanism), and TALESPIN, which is a program that generates narratives for a simulated world. Recently it has also been used in systems that modify memory structures as text is processed; for example, in IPP (Integrated Partial Parser) and CYRUS, a system that simulates exchanges with former Secretary of State Cyrus Vance (see Schank, 1982, pp. 197 ff.). The key question from our viewpoint, however, concerns not computer implementation, but whether CD is the appropriate representational language for psychologically real cognitive structures. There are good reasons to think that the answer to this question is negative.

Schank holds that there is an internal code distinct from natural language in which persons think. He says:

> I claim that there exists a conceptual base that is interlingual, onto which linguistic structures in a given language map during the understanding process and out of which such structures are created during generation. . . . The simple fact that it is possible for humans to understand any given natural language if they are immersed in it for a sufficient amount of time and to be able to translate from that language to whatever other natural language with which they are well acquainted, would indicate that such a conceptual base has psychological reality. (1972, pp. 553–554)

As Schank makes clear, he holds that this internal code is CD. There is reason to agree with him that there is an internal code distinct from natural language (see especially Fodor, 1975). But it is not likely that that internal code is CD. To my knowledge there is no experimental evidence to show that CD is the internal code. More important, it would seem that no such evidence will emerge because of the nature of CD.

As I mentioned, some human information processing may involve imagistic thinking. There is some evidence that persons form and manipulate mental images (see Kosslyn, 1980). It remains open, as I also mentioned, whether imagistic thinking is epiphenomenal. Mental images might be like computer graphics; they play no role in actual processing, but are there for the benefit of 'observers.' But if there is dual processing, that is, if some imagistic thinking is functional, then there are serious ramifications for the nature of the internal code. It would have to contain both linguistic and imagistic modes of representation. With regard to CD, it could only be in that case part of the internal code.

CD is a sparse language, with a small set of semantical primitives. From the formal viewpoint there are advantages to this language in terms of elegance. But from the computational viewpoint it appears disadvantageous. Natural languages have enormous expressive power. Thus there have to be numerous and complex reductionistic translation rules between natural language expressions and those constructed from the primitives of CD. It would appear to be computationally more efficient if the internal code were sufficiently rich to permit straightforward mapping from natural language, without an intermediate reductionistic step.

Leaving aside computational efficiency, there are serious problems in generating reductionistic translation rules. Consider the following example of a translation from natural language to CD that purports to preserve meaning (Schank and Abelson, 1977, p. 31). The natural language sentence

(9) John gives Bill an orange for his cold.

is to be rendered by

(10) John ATRANS orange to Bill
          ◆rE
    Bill INGEST orange to INSIDE (Bill)
          ◆r
    Bill Health (Pos change)

'ATRANS' and 'INGEST' stand for primitive action types, the former for "the transfer of an abstract relationship such as possession, ownership, or control" and the latter for "the taking in of an object by an animal to the inside of that animal" (1977, pp. 12–13). 'HEALTH' stands for a scaled attribute; 'Pos change' means that the value of that attribute increases. As noted earlier, '◆r' stands for a causal relation in which the arguments are an action and a state; and '◆rE' indicates that the causal relation is between a state and a (mental) action.

One problem facing translation is reading content into natural language sentences.[6] The translation (10) contains more information than literally stated by (9). Sentence (9) does not say that Bill ate (ingested) the orange. Strictly speaking it is consistent with (9) that Bill did not eat the orange; he might have put it in his knapsack for a later time, but then forgot about it. Conversely (10) could be true while (9) is false. Suppose that John knows nothing about Bill's cold, but rather gives him an orange in order to repay a debt. Or suppose that Bill does not have a cold at all and John gives him an orange out of friendship. Despite (9) being false in these cases, the causal chain described by (10) nonetheless occurs.

One response might be that the context is adequate to elicit semantical meaning; codifying elided meaning into translation rules is a difficult but largely technical task. In the case of translation from (9) to (10), there is a presumed context that justifies the claim that (9) implicitly contains all and only the semantical information explicitly stated by (10). This response might be correct when all is said and done, but it is not obviously so. There is not now an adequate linguistic theory of how context determines the meaning of a natural language sentence. To point to one issue, contexts will not always disambiguate natural language sentences. Consider the sentence: 'The chickens were ready to eat.' Suppose that the context in which it is embedded is something like this: 'John and Mary arrived at our farm late afternoon. The milk cow and the hogs were fed. The chickens were ready to eat. Everyone was hungry.' The context fails to make it clear whether the people were prepared to eat the chickens or the chickens were prepared to get their dinner. With some ingenuity this context can be elaborated and enlarged, without, however, making specific the semantical import of the sentence in question.[7]

There are additional problems for CD, though I shall not discuss them. For there is one consideration that makes that discussion otiose: the existence of the cognitive structures hypothesized by script theory are independent of claims about the representational language used to encode information within these structures. Again script theory (or some variant of it) can provide an adequate explan-- atory model even if the representational language is very different from CD. One reason to appeal to scripts and plans is that they seem to provide the correct 'chunking' structure; this reason does not also count toward the claim that CD is the representational language of these structures. In this chapter I have discussed script theory in terms of CD, but mainly as a matter of expository convenience.

Let me make this important point another way. There is significant similarity between Minsky's (1975) notion of a frame and Schank and Abelson's (1977) notion of a script. Scripts are a species of frames. Frames can be specific, such as a frame for a particular room, or general, such as one for living quarters; they can concern static arrangements of objects as well as dynamical situations concerning events; they can be used in various cognitive activities from vision to memory and planning. Frames have slots, spaces as it were, to be filled by the particulars of the situation to which they are brought to bear. When not applied on a particular occasion, these slots receive default assignments, that is, they are filled by stereotypic individuals or events. For example, in a frame for a living room the slots for the furnishings might be filled by representations of a stereotypic couch, easy chair, and coffee table. Scripts are frames restricted to stereotypic action chains. As Schank and Abelson originally developed the idea, scripts were both processing structures for understanding narratives and memory structures for these narratives. Like frames, scripts have slots. In $Restaurant, for instance, there is a slot for the customer, waiter, and so on. Also like Minsky's frames, these slots receive default assignments in the absence of specific information.

Minsky (1975) does not propose the use of any particular representational language. There are numerous candidates for the representational language for frames. Indeed Hayes (1980) correctly points out that first-order logic can be the representational language. Hayes's basic idea is that a frame is a bundle of properties. Thus the frame *Living Room* is given by '$(\exists x)(\text{sofa}(y_1,x)$ & ... & coffee table $(y_n,x))$,' where the free variables, $y_1, ..., y_n$, correspond to slots, which would be instantiated in the case of a particular living room. In general a frame for a concept C, with slot-relations $R_1, ..., R_n$ is:

(11) $(x)\{Cx \equiv (\exists y_1) ... (\exists y_n)[R_1(y_1,x)$ & ... & $R_n(y_n,x)]\}$

Though there are complications, for example, the manner in which to treat default assignments, all the information contained in a frame can be encoded in first-order logic. Since scripts are a species of frames, it follows that there are many candidates for the representational language. In particular, as in the case of frames, the information contained in a script can be represented by first-order statements. If C is restricted to scripts and plans, (11) gives their general form. This restriction is accomplished by associating each script and plan with a set of relations $R_1, ..., R_k$. For instance, if $Cx = x$ is a \$Restaurant, the relation set is $\{①$ is a waiter in $②, ①$ is a menu of $②, ...\}$.

To sum up, the issue of the psychological reality of the cognitive structures hypothesized by script theory is largely independent of the issue of the nature and status of the representational language used for encoding information within these structures. There is evidence that persons use large-chunked structures such as scripts; but this evidence says nothing about CD being the representational language. We could combine script theory with first-order logic, or even with Montague grammar. I am not recommending that we do: the point is that the adoption of scripts, or similar constructs, as memory or processing structures does not necessitate the adoption of CD. We can in short accept script theory as the complement of (S) without committing ourselves to Schank's semantically based account of the representational language.

6. The Constituents of Scripts and Plans

The units of analysis for Schank and Abelson's 1977 model are scripts and plans. These units are large-scale representations. They are in turn composed of constituent representations, which we can think of as atomic and molecular. Let me first discuss the elementary, or atomic, constituent representations, and then turn to the issue of the molecular ones and their relationship to the large-scale, master representations.

One possibility is that the constituent elementary representations are isomorphic to events in the world. This suggestion is initially attractive and appears to be the one adopted by Schank and Abelson (1977). Its intuitive appeal derives from the representational theory of mind—that is, the view that cognitive attitudes are *about* external events, at least in a formal way, a view that has had considerable following since Locke.

However, on reflection this suggestion about the atomic constituents of scripts and plans is unacceptable. There are indefinitely many events that take place when someone follows a script. The identity conditions for events, I argued at length, are in terms of necessary spatiotemporal coincidence. These identity conditions are fine-grained. In eating in a restaurant, the actions of raising one's fork for the first time, moving the fork to one's mouth, taking the first bite, the second bite, and so on and so on, are distinct. It is simply psychologically unrealistic to suppose that persons normally divide scripts and plans into units representing each of these many events: to do so would be to suppose that persons utilize an incredible amount of processing capacity in scripted and planned activity. But more important, this suggestion does not do justice to the function of scripts and plans in cognition. In the case of episodic memory of particular planned activities, it might be that the constituent units are representations of particular events. Scripts and plans, however, are also used in memory for types of activities and in projections of future activities. In these cases representations of particular events are not appropriate. In the case of I-scripts and I-plans some of the constituent units must represent future events: since future events have not occurred, they are not particulars, and hence the representations cannot be representations of particular events.

The most plausible suggestion concerning the constitutive atomic units of scripts and plans is that they are representations of basic event types. It is clear that the units must be types rather than tokens, since types are needed to capture generic memory and future action. Mental representation of event types, it would appear, is relevantly similar to representation of object types. Some recent research suggests that representation of object categories does not consist in specifying necessary and sufficient conditions, or definitions, but rather proceeds by means of family resemblance, or some such means (Smith and Medin, 1981). Representation of event types, it would seem, also proceeds by family resemblance.

As to the level of abstraction for the atomic constituents, Bower, Black, and Turner (1979) found that there is considerable agreement among subjects that in scripts actions are stored in memory at the basic level (also see Galambos and Rips, 1982). Bower et al say "what is surprising is how much agreement there is in the 'basic action' language that people use to describe the activities" (p. 181). For instance, subjects were asked to list the actions involved in eating in a fancy restaurant. Bower et al report that "people wrote 'He ate his soup' rather than 'He picked up his soup spoon, dipped it into the cup of soup, lifted it out, blew on it to cool it, raised it to his lips, put the spoon in his mouth . . .' " (p. 183). These results are summarized in table 8.1.

The notion of a psychologically basic action language derives from the work of Rosch et al (1976) on the categorization of objects. Categories are divided into superordinate, basic-level, and subordinate ones. A superordinate category (e.g., animal, furniture, clothing) is the most inclusive; it is one in which subjects find no feature in

Table 8.1
Each asterisk indicates that 25% of
the subjects listed this action (e.g.,
75% of the subjects listed 'Leave').

Open door	*
Enter	**
Give reservation name	**
Go to table	*
Be seated	***
Order drinks	**
Put napkin on lap	*
Look at menu	***
Discuss menu	**
Order meal	***
Talk	**
Drink water	*
Eat salad or soup	**
Meal arrives	*
Eat food	***
Finish meal	*
Order dessert	**
Eat dessert	**
Ask for bill	*
Bill arrives	*
Pay bill	***
Leave tip	**
Get coats	*
Leave	***

Based on Bower, Black, and Turner
(1979).

common among all members of the category; it is, as it were, a disjunctive concept. A basic-level category (e.g., horse, table, pants) is one in which subjects find a substantial number of common features among members; it is, as it were, a weak conjunctive concept. A subordinate category (e.g., quarter horse, dining room table, jeans) is the least inclusive; it is one in which subjects find numerous common features among members; it is a strong conjunctive concept.

Bower, Black, and Turner (1979), it should be said, have not established their case beyond doubt. They deal only with scripts, not with plans. It is possible that subjects represent the atomic units of plans at the superordinate or subordinate levels, depending on the complexity of the plan and the period of time to execution. Moreover, with respect to scripts, they may have biased the data toward reports on the basic-level because of the instructions given to subjects. The instructions for eliciting the lecture script, for instance, were:

Write a list of actions describing what people generally do when they go to a lecture in a course. We are interested in the common actions of a routine lecture stereotype. Start the list with arriving at the lecture and end it with leaving after the lecture. Include about 20 actions or events and put them in the order in which they would occur. (pp. 180–181)

The request for common actions, the examples of arriving at the start of the lecture and leaving after the lecture, and the direction to list about twenty actions might lead subjects to record basic-level actions even if that is not the level at which the atomic constituents are represented.

Turning to the molecular constituents of scripts and plans, Schank and Abelson's model contains two major empirical theses: first, scripts are stored as unified wholes; and second, scripts consist of scenes, which are serially (that is, temporally) ordered. For example, $Restaurant is stored as a single unit, which in turn is divided into the serially ordered molecular scenes Entering, Ordering, Eating, Exiting (1977, pp. 42 ff.). However, there is strong evidence that both of these theses are false.

With regard to the first one, Bower and his colleagues found evidence that scripted stories are stored as separated chunks in memory (Bower, Black, and Turner, 1979, Black and Bower, 1979). They showed that recall of actions within a scene was dependent on the length of the narrative account of the scene but significantly independent of the length of the other scenes in the story. Similar chunking judgments are also made in planning. Byrne (1977) found that in real-life tasks such as planning a meal, subjects divided the projected task into segments. Additional evidence counter to the first thesis concerns recognition confusions between scenes of similar scripts (Bower et al, 1979 and Graesser et al, 1980). In these studies subjects were presented with a number of scripted stories. In a typical case one story concerned a visit to a medical doctor's office and contained a sentence saying that the protagonist sat in a waiting room and read magazines. If another story, which concerned a visit to a dentist's office, contained a sentence saying that the same protagonist sat in a waiting room and read magazines, then recognition confusions appear when the subject is queried about which sentence appears in which story. On Schank and Abelson's 1977 model, scenes are parts of scripts and have no independent status; and hence the model lacks the capability to explain confusions between scenes of different scripts. Put another way, the model is unable to explain that scenes of some scripts remind subjects of scenes in other scripts (see Schank, 1982).

It might be thought that confusions and remindings among scenes of different scripts can be explained by subsuming those scripts under more abstract ones. For instance, in the above example, there would be a visit to a health care professional script in which the scene sitting in a waiting room and reading magazines occurs, and to which the scripts about a visit to a doctor and a visit to a dentist are subsumed. However, this suggestion is implausible. First, Schank and Abelson's 1977 model of cognitive schemata, unlike some other models such as Minsky's, does not permit increased levels of abstraction. Schank says about the possibility of a script for a visit to a health care professional on the 1977 model: "Such a script is beyond our initial conception of what a script was, because it was not specific enough. We had always believed that scripts were rooted in actual experiences rather than in abstractions and generalizations from experience" (1980, p. 258). Second, and more important, recognition confusions are likely to occur at higher levels of abstraction as well as at the more experiential levels. Thus scripts would be pushed to higher and higher levels, until their usefulness in memory becomes questionable. For example, since one waits in a room and reads magazines during visits to attorneys and accountants, a script about a visit to a professional might be the needed level of abstractness. But one also waits in a room and reads magazines when an automobile is being repaired; so a script about a visit to someone who solves problems might be the required level of abstractness. Persons also sit in a room and read magazines while waiting for a boyfriend or girlfriend to get ready for dinner; and so a script about a visit to someone (or other) might be the needed level of abstractness. At this point, however, the purported script has become too general to be directly useful in memory and processing.

With regard to the second empirical thesis, that scripts consist of serially ordered scenes, Galambos and Rips (1982) have provided evidence that schemata are hierarchically ordered.[8] Their primary experimental design involved showing that centrality affected recognition reaction time but temporal order did not. Consider, for example, the script for changing a flat tire. It contains molecular constituents that occur early and are highly central, such as raising the car, that occur late and are also highly central, such as putting on the spare, that occur early in the script but are not central, such as taking off the hubcap, and that occur late and are not central, such as putting away the jack. It was found that, when a molecular constituent name is associated with the script pointer—in this example 'changing a flat tire'—recognition reaction time for whether the constituent was part of the script was dependent on centrality but independent of the temporal (sequential) position.

Abelson (1981) recognizes that centrality is an ordering relation on the molecular constituents of scripts. He distinguishes between weak and strong scripts. Weak scripts are ones in which sequencing properties do not order the molecular constituents. For example, in $Circus, the order of performances by the lion tamer, clowns, trapeze artists, and so on, are immaterial. Strong scripts are ordered on the basis of centrality and sequential properties. $Restaurant is an example of a strong script. Abelson (1981, p. 717) suggests that there are some rare cases of extremely strong scripts in which only sequential properties order the molecular constituents. $Japanese Tea Ceremony, which is highly ritualized, might be an example of this type. I wonder, however, whether there are in fact any extremely strong scripts. It would be interesting to see whether there is experimental evidence for the absence of centrality in ordering the molecules of $Japanese Tea Ceremony and similar scripts.

7. Schank's Revised Model

Schank (1979, 1980, 1980b, 1982) is aware that the 1977 model faces difficulties. He has recently proposed modifications of this model designed to deal with the experimental findings and to give a more useful picture of memory structures. Script theory continues to undergo change, and there is not now a definitive version. Indeed there are variants among those at the Yale AI Lab. The main lines of alteration, however, appear clear.

The key changes from the 1977 model are that, first, the units of analysis are changed from large-scale scripts and plans to smaller and more abstract ones, and second, these new units are typically hierarchically ordered. The units of analysis in the revised model are generalized scene-length structures. A sequence of these units linked together is called a 'MOP' (memory organization packet). Examples of MOPs are Professional Office Visit, Take Airplane, Conduct Meeting. MOPs are like scripts on the 1977 model, except that, where scripts are psychologically indivisible, MOPs are constructed from separable, abstract scene-length units. On this revision of the theory scripts are scene-length units relativized to occasions and contexts. For instance, Waiting Room is a scene, and a corresponding script would be, say, $Waiting Room of Dr. Jones's Office.

Schank's recent work focuses on memory structures. Types of memory structures can be ordered on the basis of abstractness. In the revised theory these structures are, beginning with the least abstract:

  (i) scripts
  (ii) scenes
  (iii) MOPs
  (iv) metaMOPs
  (v) TOPs

MetaMOPs organize MOPs. TOPs—thematic organization points— are structures that reflect themes in MOPs and metaMOPs. An example is the theme Romeo and Juliet, which reflects the similarity between Shakespeare's play and the musical 'West Side Story,' despite very different settings, staging, and dialogue.

Within MOPs and metaMOPs scenes can be organized either sequentially or hierarchically. Temporal Precedence Search imposes serial ordering properties on the scene-length units. Map Search imposes hierarchical ordering properties such as those exhibited by flow charts or by semantic memory systems using ISA links. This revised model is basically top-down, thus bringing Schank closer to the views of other cognitive scientists concerned with schemata (see, e.g., Bower, Black, and Turner, 1979, Mandler and Johnson, 1977, and Rumelhart, 1977).

This revised model is able to explain the known experimental results. Since MOPs and metaMOPs are the stored structures, recall focuses on the constitutive, separable scene-length units.[9] Recognition confusions between scenes of different MOPs and metaMOPs are explained by shared generalized scenes. For example, Waiting Room is a constituent of the MOPs Professional Office Visit and Health Care. The second problem for the original script theory was that reaction time experiments showed that scenes were often ordered hierarchically rather than serially. According to the revised model, MOPs and other high-level structures are typically constructed from scene-length units ordered according to their centrality. Thus the more central the scene, the faster it will be recognized as part of the MOP or metaMOP.

Schank's revision does not pose problems from our perspective. We require a scientific notion of a plan, with a dual representational structure similar to that in the 1977 model. We do not require that plans and scripts be the units of analysis; nothing about the uses to which plans and scripts were put disallows their being replaced by more fundamental scene-length units. Of course, the qualifications and modifications discussed in the previous sections must apply *mutatis mutandis* to the revised model. The revised form of the theory has to be modified to account for self-referentiality and the level of abstraction for elementary representational units. In addition it must be supplemented by an adequate definition of 'intentional action,' and from the viewpoint of psychological reality, divorced from the implementation language CD.

An interesting methodological shift emerges with the transition from the 1977 model to the current one. Schank revised the 1977 model, at least in part, because of experimental results. In his earlier work (e.g., 1972) the emphasis was on the development of intelligent machines without a great deal of regard for the manner in which persons in fact process information. But simulation proved more difficult than initially supposed. As a result attention is now paid to how persons actually process stereotypic information. Schank says: "I do not believe that there is any alternative available to us in building intelligent machines other than modelling people. . . . It may be possible that in the distant future we will build machines that improve upon what people can do. But, they shall have to equal them first, and I mean equal very literally" (1979, p. 95). The gap between cognitive psychology and AI is narrowing.

The following point is worth reemphasizing. The 1977 model is a first approximation to planned activity. Schank's revised model, when fully articulated and when modified and qualified by the conceptual considerations raised here, is a second approximation. But further revision and modification can be expected. The possibility remains, of course, that the model will be beyond repair. If that happens to be the case, a different theory will have to be used to complement (S).

And that indeed might be the case. There is a serious objection to Schank's entire project. Despite his protestations to the contrary, central processing, including memory and plan formation, is not well-understood. Thus to the extent that the transformation of the folk psychological into the scientific depends on a theory of central processing, that transformation will not be successful. Intentional action in that case cannot be understood by means of a schema theory such as Schank's revised script model. This is an important and powerful objection, and warrants detailed consideration.

8. The Scope of Scientific Psychology

Jerry Fodor (1983) argues that some but not all psychological subsystems are modular.[10] Modular subsystems have the following main properties: they are domain specific; their operations are mandatory;

they are fast; they are associated with fixed neural architecture; and they are informationally encapsulated. Fodor focuses his discussion on input subsystems. These include the perceptual subsystems and language comprehension. I take it to be controversial whether language comprehension has these characteristics. But it is reasonably clear that the perceptual subsystems have them. Consider vision. It is clearly domain specific, being concerned with the recognition of color, shape, and other features of the distal array. It is mandatory: an array must be seen as objects distributed in three-dimensional space. It is fast, possibly on the order of 250 milliseconds. And it is associated with specific, locatable neurological mechanisms. Most important, vision is informationally encapsulated; that is, visual processing proceeds without being affected by other subsystems. What we see is independent of feedback from central subsystems, such as memory, and other input subsystems, such as the tactile one.[11] This last claim is not uncontroversial. So-called 'new look' accounts of perception hold that there is interaction between central processes and vision, that what we see is in part determined by what we expect and hypothesize. But Fodor is persuasive. He distinguishes between what we see and the fixation of a perceptual belief. Only the latter is influenced by expectation and hypothesis formation. The speed with which visual processing occurs is to be explained by its being self-contained.

Suppose that, for the sake of argument at least, input subsystems satisfy the conditions for being modules. Fodor barely mentions the output systems in his discussion. Presumably, however, some output subsystems are modular. In analogy to the input subsystems, he might claim that the speech subsystem is modular. But less controversially it would seem that the cognitive component of immediate intention, which is responsible for the monitoring and guidance of ongoing motor activity, is modular. Motor activity, especially when routinized, is domain specific. It is mandatory, at least to the extent that once a specific motor activity is begun, it's difficult to stop. Mandatoriness is clearly the case in automatic action; it is difficult not to put one's hands forward when falling. Guidance and monitoring of ongoing activity is also fast and associated with fixed neural architecture. Most important, monitoring and guidance seem to be informationally encapsulated. They appear to proceed without informational feedback from central processes, without conscious awareness or appeal to long-term memory.

Central processes, by contrast, are not modular. Fodor's primary example of a central process is the fixation of belief. It is not domain specific: beliefs about music, mathematics, or the weather can equally well be fixed. And it is not mandatory: the entertaining of a proposition does not necessarily lead to belief. Belief fixation can be slow, especially when the coherence of the proposition with entrenched beliefs is at issue. There appears moreover to be little or no evidence that belief fixation, or other central processes such as problem solving and memory, are associated with specific neural structures. Rather it is my understanding that, with regard to central processes, the neural structure is relatively plastic; it exhibits equipotentiality. Central processes, most importantly, are *not* informationally encapsulated. The fixation of belief, for instance, is accomplished by drawing on the input subsystems, the output subsystems, and other central processes. Put another way, belief fixation is, first, sensitive to the acceptance of any other proposition, and second, sensitive to global properties of the entire set of beliefs such as coherence, consistency, and simplicity. Central processes in short are not local; they are intimately connected with each other.

Fodor observes that progress in psychology has been limited to modular subsystems. We have some understanding of vision. Similarly we have some understanding of monitoring and guidance mechanisms. Of course, these subsystems are not fully understood; a great deal about them is unknown. But—and this is the main point—progress has been made on explaining these input and output subsystems. By contrast we have little understanding of central processes and seem not to be making progress. The reason is that central processes have global properties and subsystems with these properties resist analysis. With tongue firmly placed in cheek, Fodor summarizes this point as the 'First Law of the Nonexistence of Cognitive Science,' namely, "the more global . . . a cognitive process is, the less anybody understands it" (1983, p. 107). Fodor, note, is not asserting the view that central processes can never be understood, that they are somehow beyond comprehension—though he does not foreclose that possibility. Rather the claim is that current explanatory frameworks in cognitive psychology and cognitive science cannot account for central processing.

Extending Fodor's argument to the case in point, the cognitive component of prospective intention is plan formation. Plan formation in turn connects with other central processes. To have a plan is to have a detailed representation of future activity based on memory of past similar activity and perception about the current environment. The output system extends from the moment of decision to the completion of motor activity. The initial stages of the output system interface with the central system. The terminal stages interface with the completion of motor activity. To the extent that the output system overlaps with the central system, it is not amenable to scientific explanation, since only modules are amenable to such explanation and central subsystems are not modular.

At the risk of being repetitious let me restate this objection. Fodor's complaint about the possibility of scientific explanation of central processes is a version of the frame problem. The frame problem is basically the difficulty of delimiting in a principled way the extent to which central representations are interdependent. If every central representation is dependent on every other one, then combinatorial explosion occurs. If the acceptance of a proposition p depends on the acceptance of every other proposition, including higher-order ones such as the proposition 'the acceptance of p depends on the acceptance of other proposition q,' then accepting p is an impossible psychological process. In that case scientific understanding of central processes, including plan formation, cannot be achieved. Thus the best that can be done to understand prospective intention is turn toward folk psychology, despite its known limitations.

In reply let me first mark the scope of this objection. It does not show that the transformation of folk psychology into scientific psychology fails to articulate the nature of the human output system. Rather, if the objection is correct, it shows only that that part of the output system which interfaces with the central system cannot be explained scientifically. Indeed Fodor's account of modularity, as I noted, is naturally extended to the monitoring and guidance of motor activity. More important, the objection is not forceful with respect to plan formation. Plan formation can be explained in terms of Schank's revised script theory. In the end that theory may be unacceptable— but not for the reasons Fodor suggests. Schank's theory appears to have the resources for a response to Fodor's objection, at least in a programmatic way.

Consider the global properties of interconnectivity among central representations and the interdependence of a single central representation with features of the entire set of representations. These global properties are independent of each other and are gradational.[12] They are independent in that some central representations interact with others but are not sensitive to features of the entire network of representations, and conversely. Plan formation in particular is connected with other central representations, but not, typically, dependent on global features of the total set of representations. These global properties are gradational in that some types of central representations have one or both to a greater extent than others. Fixation of belief, for example, exhibits these global properties to a significant extent. By contrast, plan formation exhibits them to a moderate degree.

This last point is important. There is a difference between deciding whether to undertake something and planning to do it. Deciding whether to undertake an activity is a matter of practical reasoning. Practical reasoning, viewed folk psychologically, is the interaction between the belief and desire matrices. Plan formation is the determination of a course of activity required to realize a decision. Plan formation is less centrally located than practical reasoning. Suppose that John is faced with the decision to reveal Richard's indiscretions. He gives it careful thought, weighing the advantages and disadvantages. Is he to cover up these activities or is he to risk his career? Finally he decides to make public what he knows. He sits down at his typewriter and, after several false starts, types a letter to the editor of the *Washington Post*. He puts the letter in an envelope and walks to the mailbox. John engaged in practical reasoning when he was deciding whether to reveal Richard's indiscretions. Using both current information and that obtained from memory, he drew inferences about likely outcomes and their values to him. This process is clearly centrally located. But once the decision was made, a plan had to be formulated. That plan consisted in typing a letter to the newspaper and mailing it. While memory clearly had a part to play in the conduct of this plan, much of the activity was routinized. Central representations are involved in the formation and conduct of John's plan, but not to the extent that they were involved in determining the course of action. Once the decision was made, John's plan was formed and conducted without consideration of consistency and coherence with the entire set of beliefs and memories and without comparison with every central representation. Plan formation and conduct is relatively self-contained, not as self-contained as vision or automatic motor activity, but more so than practical reasoning.[13]

If this is right, if plan formation is not a highly global process, then the objection has been defused. The frame problem does not arise, at least not with its full fury, in the case of prospective intention. Thus articulating plan formation by transforming it into a scientific psychological construct, such as Schank's revised script theory, is not implausible. Practical reasoning, though, remains subject to the objection, since it is highly global. Of course, the objection might not be definitive. There may be some scientific model, not now in the offing (or at least not known to me), that can be used to successfully transform practical reasoning from a folk psychological concept into a scientific one. Perhaps Bayesian decision theoretic models can be developed for this purpose; or perhaps more plausibly, the experimental work on actual human judgments under uncertainty will yield a theoretical model of the requisite kind. But I leave these speculations to others, since my target is prospective intention, not practical reason.

Despite not being highly global, plan formation has some global characteristics. But no combinatorial explosion threatens. On Schank's revised model, plans, no matter their complexity, are constructed from scene-length units. John's plan to reveal Richard's activities to the *Washington Post,* for instance, has the complexity of a MOP; and this MOP in turn is decomposable into scene-length units such as Typing and Mailing a Letter. Plan formation consists of two operations (which might occur sequentially or concurrently): searches for the appropriate scene-length units and combination of these units into complex representations. The search procedure is manageable because the repertoire of stored scene-length units is finite and not very large, and the search does not proceed sequentially. Scenes are marked with pointers, which are categorized and searched by top-down procedures. As the appropriate scenes are located, they are combined into a complex representation. Construction of these complex representations does not proceed on a random basis, but rather uses guidelines, such as temporal and causal precedency. Even if construction of the complex representations were random, it would not be an unmanageable process, since complex representations are typically constructed from a relatively small number of scene-length units. In short Schank's revised script theory suggests a principled procedure for delimiting those central representations to be accessed and ordered in plans. The original objection is not to the use of models that make reference to central processes *per se,* but to those models that lack systematic and psychologically plausible procedures for dealing with central processes. Schank's revised script theory, construed as a model for the cognitive component of prospective intention, can be formulated to include procedures for processing central representations.

Let us take stock. In order to articulate the role of cognition in intentional action, the folk psychological view was transformed into a scientific one. Chapter 1 briefly outlined the folk psychological view; this chapter undertakes the transformation. Cognitive scientists, often of different persuasions, have hypothesized memory and processing schemata of the type appropriate to reflect the complexity of long-range intentional activity. One of these proposals, Schank and Abelson's 1977 model, appears especially well suited, since it is designed to deal with extended causal chains involving actions while utilizing a dual representational structure, and since there is some evidence for its psychological reality. Using the constructs of this theory and revising it to include temporal parameters, we can say that the distinctive cognitive feature of intentional action is the subject's having a representation of a story in which he performs this type of action. Stories are composed of scripts, which are memory structures for stereotypic activity, and plans, which are structures for activities that have not been sufficiently practiced to become stereotypic.

It is important to be aware that, although the terms 'story,' 'script,' and 'plan' have ordinary senses and referents, they are theoretical terms within Schank and Abelson's model. This model was initially designed to deal with text understanding, and these terms, especially 'story' and 'script,' were borrowed from ordinary language in this domain. But they are theory-laden terms, despite their ordinary appearance.

Schank and Abelson's 1977 model, though initially plausible, requires modification and qualification. On the conceptual side the model must be altered to permit self-reference during ongoing activity and remembered first-person activity. This alteration is accomplished by employing the primitive attitudes of setting oneself and self-ascribing. The concomitant ontological commitment is to properties. The model takes Schank's Conceptual Dependency (CD) as the representational language. Schank holds that CD makes explicit the meaning of natural language sentences. But CD is pragmatically impoverished, as well as being deficient in other respects. These difficulties for CD, however, are not serious from our perspective, since the psychological aspects of the model concerning cognitive schemata are largely independent of the representational language.

On the psychological side there is strong evidence that the units of analysis chunk memory and processing structures too grossly. Scripts are composed of scenes; but these scenes are inseparable from the scripts in which they occur and are invariably ordered sequentially. The evidence points toward separable scene-length chunks that can be ordered hierarchically. In light of these experimental results Schank revised the 1977 model. The new units of analysis are generalized scenes. MOPs (memory organization packets) are constructed hierarchically from these units using contextual information. Scripts are now conceived to be particular, scene-length units. MOPs play the role in the revised theory formerly played by scripts; but, where scripts on the 1977 model could not be decomposed, MOPs are constructed master representations. It appears that this revised model is adequate to the available experimental data. The revised model provides a different interpretation of the theory-laden terms 'story,' 'script,' and 'plan.'

The transformation of folk psychology to scientific psychology is an interactive process. In particular the folk psychological account of the role of cognition in intentional action is improved by the scientific theory of stereotypic representations. The scientific account is in turn subject to revision and qualification from constraints arising from folk psychology and philosophical action theory. The resultant view, when all is said and done, will have conceptual elements derivative of both folk and scientific psychology. To revert to an earlier metaphor, the account will be located toward the center of the conceptual space.

9

Intention and Conation

In formulating the fundamental problem for action theory, I argued that the proximate cause of action is a complex mental event consisting of cognitive and conative components. The cognitive component is itself complex. Chapter 7 dealt with the cognitive feature common to all action, the monitoring and guidance of ongoing activity; and chapter 8 dealt with the additional cognitive feature antecedent to intentional action, namely, the representation of planned activity. Not unexpectedly the conative component is also complex, one part common to all action and another, additional part antecedent to intentional action. This chapter is concerned with both aspects of conation.

The need for a conative component of the cause of action is generated by the conceptual base of folk psychology. Consider again the case in which a person is deciding whether to jump up and touch the ceiling. Assume that he has well-functioning monitoring and guidance systems and has a plan—a master representation of future activity—into which his jumping fits: nevertheless he will not jump unless moved to do so. A cognitive representation of his possible future course of activity, no matter how well articulated and no matter how fully attended to, is not sufficient to initiate action. I take this claim to be a deep truth about the concept of action.

In the case of the cognitive features of the antecedent to action, it is reasonable to think that the development of certain extant approaches to guidance mechanisms and to the representation of planned activity will lead to successfully transformed folk psychological concepts. Unfortunately the situation for the conative features is less happy. There is presently no tenable scientific theory into which this folk psychological concept can be transformed. Motivational psychology at this point in its history is in disarray. The best that can be currently achieved is a partial transformation. A complete transformation of conation must await future scientific developments. Only informed speculation is now possible.

Nevertheless I remain convinced that human action is to be explained naturalistically. If I have been on the right track in previous chapters—even approximately—much of human action can already be explained within the context of scientific psychology. The lacuna in motivational psychology, I expect, will be closed. One way to assist in its closing is to emphasize that there is this real gap in the psychological explanation of human action.

In section 1 I characterize the folk psychological idea of conation. The remainder of the chapter is divided into two parts. The first is largely negative. In the next three sections I show in some detail why extant motivational theories are inadequate. Such negative findings are not exciting; but they must be explicitly stated in order to make secure the point that no extant motivational theory is tenable. Section 2 focuses on Hull's Drive Theory. This theory occupied centerstage in the neobehaviorist movement that dominated motivational psychology from approximately the 1930s through at least the early 1960s. In section 3 I discuss Tolman's Expectancy Theory, an alternative neobehaviorist account that takes seriously the relationship between motivation and cognition. This theory is the basis of some recent psychological and philosophical models; and while an improvement over Drive Theory, it fares only marginally better.[1] The second part of the chapter is less negative. I suggest that a partial solution to the problem of transforming conation already exists in the form of the theory of production systems. This theory falls within the computational framework. In section 4 I examine Anderson's (1976, 1983) version of the theory. In the following section I discuss the possibility of generalizing some recent work in animal learning theory on motivation systems to the human case. That conjecture is highly speculative.

1. The Folk Psychology of Conation

A key folk psychological idea is that the mental antecedent to action is initiatory, that an action is performed only when an agent is moved to act. Restated, folk psychology is committed to:

(C) The mental event causally antecedent to action has conative properties.

As I argued at length, this mental event is an intention.

There is no conclusive argument that folk psychology is committed to (C). Rather the claim is supported by ordinary intuition. Suppose that you were asked to plan a bank robbery that has a good chance of success. You carefully think about which bank to rob, probably 'case

the joint,' and devise an escape route. Imagine that your plan requires some cunning, a little nerve, and is not physically demanding,
and that you have all the necessary abilities. At that point you have a
plan to rob the bank. But do you in fact carry out this plan? Presumably not. Notice that all the cognitive prerequisites are satisfied. You
have a master representation in memory, and you have motor systems
capable of completing the actions within this script. The reason you
do not carry out this plan is that the conative prerequisites are not
satisfied. You are not moved to act. Our ordinary, folk psychological
conceptualization of action requires that the agent be so moved.[2]

Some psychologists have attempted to develop theories of action in
which the antecedent mental events lack conative properties. (James
held this position; for a recent example see Baars and Mattson,
1981.[3]) They attempt to defend purely cognitive theories of action
initiation. All that is required for action is appropriate representations in memory and a well-functioning monitoring and guidance
system. But these theories, no matter their appeal, do not fully explain human action. They do not provide a transformation of the folk
psychological concept of action because they leave out its essential
property of being caused by a conative event. Indeed it is not clear
what purely cognitive theories of behavioral response are in fact
about. But this much is certain: they are not about actions. Folk
psychology is articulated and made coherent by scientific psychology, sometimes through the method of progressive transformation.
But scientific psychology is not free to develop any arbitrary conceptual scheme; it is constrained by the conceptual base of folk psychology. Commitment to (C) is a prime example of constraints on
scientific psychology that are derived from folk psychology.

Throughout this book I have pressed the point that there is a fundamental distinction between intentional and nonintentional action.
Intentional action falls within the pattern of a plan; nonintentional
action does not. This distinction is reflected in a difference between
cognitive antecedents. Intentional action is partially caused by large-
chunked representations in memory; nonintentional action is not.
This distinction is also reflected in a difference between conative
antecedents. An account of conation will have to explain both:

(i) the conative properties of the mental antecedent to nonintentional action;
(ii) the conative properties of the mental antecedent to intentional action.

All action is preceded by an event with conative features. Intentional
action is preceded by an event that has additional conative features.

One way to isolate the conative feature common to all action from that additional feature antecedent to intentional action is to examine nonintentional action. Thus, again, a full account will have to explain both the conative antecedents to nonintentional and intentional action.

With respect to (ii)—the additional conative feature antecedent to intentional action—there are actually two elements to be explained. Intentional action is action that falls within the pattern of the agent's plan. Thus we need to explain both:

> (ii,a) the conative properties of the mental antecedent that result in plan selection;
> (ii,b) the conative properties of the mental antecedent that result in following a plan.

Being moved to select a plan to achieve some goal is distinct from, though related to, being moved to follow the steps in the plan. Intentional action initiation is a two-step process: first, a person is motivated to select a plan; and second, he is motivated to follow the selected plan.

According to (ii,b) the subject is moved to *follow* a plan. Following a plan is to be contrasted with acting according to a plan. This distinction derives from one made by Wittgenstein (1953) between acting according to a rule and following one (cf. Kripke, 1982). Suppose that a child, who knows nothing about chess, picks up a white knight from KKt4 and puts it in the vacant KB6. This child would be acting in accordance with a rule, but not following one. He is unaware that there is this rule, or even, we can suppose, that there is the game of chess and that it is rule-governed. His action, as a matter of luck, conforms to the rules of chess. Similarly an aborigine might open a combination lock fortuitously. He has not learned the combination; he has not, we can suppose, any beliefs at all about locks and their combinations. It was happenstance that he dialed the combination. This person would be acting according to a plan, but not following one.

It is sufficient to act in accordance with a plan that there is an instantiated hierarchical structure of action types. In opening the lock, the aborigine unknowingly instantiates the plan for opening it. Acting in accordance with plans, of course, is not limited to children and aborigines. A well-informed adult might haphazardly hit keys on a computer terminal, not paying attention to what he is doing, and as a result execute a complex program. Following a plan is more complex. The person must instantiate an hierarchical structure of action types, *and* he must be aware, in some sense, of what he is doing. The person must have a mental representation of this abstract structure, and he must know that his actions conform to this representation.

It is possible that a single set of actions instantiate more than one plan. Thus it could be that a person simultaneously follows one plan and acts according to another. Suppose that Gordon, who is extraordinarily fastidious, has devised a complicated plan to prepare and drink tea. As luck would have it, there is a Japanese ceremony that dictates that tea should be prepared and drunk in precisely this way. Gordon follows his plan to drink tea but only acts in accordance with the Japanese Tea Ceremony plan.

To be moved to follow a plan, then, is to be moved to perform knowingly those actions that conform to one's representation of the plan. The motivation to perform an individual intentional action is inherited from the motivation to undertake the plan coupled with the knowledge that that action conforms to the plan. By contrast, being moved to act according to a plan is not inherited from any motive concerning the plan. The motivation to perform an action which would be in accordance with some plan stands apart from the motivation to perform other actions in that plan. If in the odd case a person acts in accordance with one plan but follows another, then his motives to perform these actions are unified, but only in virtue of the plan he is following.

In nonintentional action the conative feature of the antecedent mental event is independent of all plans the subject follows. An example of a nonintentional action is putting one's hands forward to break a fall. A person is normally moved to do this, not because of some plan, but rather because it is a 'natural' response to the circumstances. The 'naturalness' of this action seems to derive from its innateness. It is plausible to think that breaking a fall by putting one's hands forward is 'hardwired' into persons. Certainly this type of action has survival value. Some nonintentional actions, however, seem to be learned. I learned to tug on my mustache, for instance. It isn't something innate. This type of action nevertheless is not filtered through high-level mental representations such as plans.

The chain of events leading to nonintentional action necessarily includes an immediate intention, but necessarily excludes a prospective intention. The conative feature of prospective intention, which precedes intentional action, makes reference to the representational content of that intention. Nonintentional action is preceded (or accompanied) only by immediate intention. Since immediate intention does not have a representational content, the conative aspect of nonintentional action does not make reference to any accompanying representational content.

How then is this conative property of immediate intention to be explained? One answer is that this conative feature is related to the agent's physiological state. There is something about the agent's bodily state that leads him to act. This answer is suggested by folk psychology. But beyond making the suggestion, folk psychology is not informative. It does not contain an explanation for the mechanisms by which the state of a person moves him to act. But that is not surprising. An explanation of this type falls within the domain of scientific psychology. And indeed during the first half of this century, a great deal of effort was devoted to explaining the physiological influences on action initiation. In the next section I want to discuss one such proposed explanation, one that dominated the debate.

2. Drive Theory

The focal idea that shaped early twentieth century psychology was that motivated behavior can be explained in terms of responses to stimuli. Some psychologists took a radical position and proposed a purely mechanistic account. There is no need for intervening variables, not to mention those referring to properties of mental events. Watson at least in his early work and his close followers defended this position (see Mackenzie, 1977). Skinner and his colleagues also seem to advocate it, though it is difficult to be clear about this, since they eschew explicit theoretical commitments. I will not discuss radical behaviorism: it suffices to say that it is without plausibility. Unless intervening variables are utilized, maze behavior of rats is inexplicable; more important, there is no realistic hope that complex human action can be explained solely in terms of input stimuli and output responses (see Chomsky, 1959).

Most psychologists working within the stimulus-response (S-R) framework were not radical behaviorists. They acknowledged that an explanation of action required intervening constructs. The most influential moderate behaviorist—or neobehaviorist—was Clark Hull. On Hull's 1943 account, upon stimulus, behavioral responses result from the organism's habits and drives. Motivation (excitatory potential, E) is a mathematical function of habit and drive, namely,

(1) $E = f(H \times D)$.

Habit (H) is to be understood as a learned action type, where learning proceeds by reinforcement. Habit strength is a function of the number, intensity, and delay of reinforcement. Some learning is accomplished by secondary reinforcement, in particular, instrumental learning. In one classic study chimpanzees were trained to insert tokens into a vending machine to obtain food.[4] The food is a primary reinforcer, and the tokens a secondary reinforcer. The tokens come to resemble the function of food in the development of habits. Drive (D) is the activator of behavior in Hull's system. It is a nonspecific energy source that derives from a physiological deficiency or need, such as hunger, thirst, or so on. Drive, that is, provides the energy for behavior (action) and habit determines the direction. Both these constructs are operationally defined in terms of observable states and activities of the organism.

In his 1951 version of the theory Hull modified his views in two important respects. Miller (1948) showed that drive need not emanate from tissue deficiencies. He placed rats in a two compartment shuttle box. The compartments were separated by a door, with one compartment white and the other black. The animals were placed in the white compartment and then given an electric shock. Escape from the shock was possible by moving to the black compartment. At first the animals had a long latency period before escaping; but with subsequent trials the latency period decreased. After a number of trials the animals ran to the black compartment before the shock was administered. They took steps to avoid the shock: they acted *prior to* tissue deficiency. Hull's reply was to distinguish between primary and secondary drives, in analogy with primary and secondary reinforcers in habit formation. Secondary drives are acquired when neutral stimuli are paired with primary drives and there is rapid diminution of the stimuli producing the primary drive. Thus drive is no longer limited to tissue deficiencies, but can result from any internal stimuli. Secondly, influenced by Spence, Hull elevated incentive from a determinant of habit to an independent factor for responses. It had been shown that response varies if the quality or quantity of reward is varied while drive and habit strength are held constant. Incentive is conceptualized as a 'pull' and drive as a 'push' toward a goal state. Accordingly, in Hull's later account motivation is a function of drive, habit, and incentive (K), namely,

(2) $E = f(D \times H \times K)$.

Spence (1956) himself thought that drive was not necessary for motivation; in the presence of an appropriate habit, incentive was sufficient to motivate behavior. Thus Spence proposed

(3) $E = f[(D + K) \times H]$.

The focal idea, however, remains the same in these alternative formulations. Two factors are required for behavior, an energy source and a learned direction of activity.

Hull's theory is within the spirit of folk psychology and seems to provide a basis for transforming the concept of moving to act into a scientific one. Moving to act is like drive in that it initiates activity. A subject is moved to act in direct proportion to the strength of the drive, which is determined by current physiological conditions. In brief the transformed folk psychological picture of immediate intention that emerges on Hull's Drive Theory is this. The conative feature of immediate intention provides the initiatory energy for action; it is to be understood in terms of drive (or incentive). The cognitive feature provides the direction; and it is to be understood in terms of habit.

The key element in this theory is the drive construct. Unfortunately it is not viable. According to Hull (1943), the primary properties of the drive construct are that:

(i) drive is anchored direcly in the subject's biological needs;
(ii) drive contributes only to the energizing of behavior, not its direction;
(iii) drive is nonspecific, in that there are not different kinds of drive for each type of behavior;
(iv) drive reduction is the basis for all reinforcement.

The experimental evidence has almost totally discredited this construct.

With regard to (i), some or perhaps most behavior seems not to be generated by biological needs. Defensive behavior appears to depend on short-term external stimuli and not conditions within the body. In running or freezing a rat is not reacting to some physiological homeostatic imbalance. Thirst, which would appear to be a prime candidate for need generated behavior, is in fact associated for the most part with an animal's eating and governed by the time of day (Fitzsimons, 1972). Hull relied heavily on the case of hunger in constructing his theory. But even here the evidence does not support a direct connection between need and activity. Consummatory activities, such as eating, involve two mechanisms, one to initiate the activity and the other to terminate it. The precise physiological mechanism that initiates eating is not known: contrary to expectation, it does not depend on muscular stomach contractions. It remains, for the most part, an open question whether need initiates eating. Moreover termination of eating appears to have nothing to do with the alleviation of need. Eating ceases when most of the meal remains in the stomach and prior to the reduction of any homeostatic imbalance that generated the hunger. Evidence points rather to a satiety hormone.

Turning to (ii), in early experiments Perin and Williams showed that food deprivation increased resistance to extinction of a reinforced response (reviewed by Bolles, 1975). Rats were trained to press a bar for food. It was found that resistance to extinction of bar pressing systematically increased when tested under 3-hour and 22-hour periods of deprivation. Hull (1943) reasoned that drive, measured by deprivation, strengthened or energized behavior. He also argued that the energizing effect of drive applies to all types of behavior, including instrumental responses.

Unlike the claim that drive is anchored in physiological needs, the claim that drive energizes behavior has experimental support— though only in a limited way. Hungry or thirsty rats exhibit increased general activity levels, as measured by an activity wheel. However, increased activity also occurs for nonregulatory reasons, for example, appetizing food. In addition it may well be that the rat's activity level follows a periodic 24 hour cycle (see Collier et al, 1972). Generally speaking the activity level in rats appears to result from a number of factors including associative ones. Thus drive provides at best a partial explanation of increased activity in rats. More important, these results have not been replicated in some other species. Hunger, for example, appears to suppress wheel running in guinea pigs. In general increased activity by hungry or thirsty rats is a species-typical response; deprivation probably energizes behavior in other species, but not for all species nor for all types of behavior.

Consider (iii), the nonspecificity of drive. If drive is unitary and not divisible into types, then drives from different sources should be additive and different sources of drive should elicit the same behavior. However, there is little evidence to support either of these predictions. No uniform additive effect has been found; rather the severity and source of drive influence the strength of the resultant behavior. Hungry rats exposed to aversive stimuli, such as bright light, cold water, or shock, appear no better at escaping than satiated ones. With regard to substitutivity of drives, it was initially found that rats trained to run for food did not change their behavior when suddenly shifted to a water deprivation condition. However, these results fail to confirm substitutivity because hunger and thirst cannot be manipulated independently. An animal made thirsty is also hungry, and so the water deprivation condition does not introduce a different source of drive.

Turning to (iv), that drive reduction is the basis of all reinforcement, the evidence again does not confirm the theory. On the contrary, there is evidence that learning occurs when the consummatory response is made, irrespective of whether there is drive reduction (Sheffield, 1966). Naive male rats were permitted to copulate but not ejaculate with receptive females. Thus drive was increased rather than reduced; nevertheless instrumental learning occurred under these conditions. Similarly it was found that hungry rats learn instrumental responses when reinforced with saccharin drinks. But saccharin has no apparent nutritional value, and hence reinforcement does not result from drive reduction.

The status of the drive construct and its relation to folk psychology is nicely summarized by Bolles:

> . . . once the primitive notion [of drive] was put into empirically testable form, primarily by Hull and his students, it did not take long for its inadequacies to be revealed . . . [T]he great enthusiasm with which early researchers sought to connect motivated behavior with automatic, physiological adjustments and needs of the organism has been frustrated time and again. The idea that an animal's motivation reflects its need for this or that commodity in order to establish homeostatic equilibrium has only occasionally been demonstrated experimentally . . . [W]hat the evidence seems to indicate instead is that most of the time an animal's motivation is itself learned and that if we are to explain its behavior, we must do so by using constructs other than drive. (1975, p. 279)

Again there is strong disconfirming evidence for there being a construct with the properties Hull (1943) attributes to drive. There is some evidence for a construct that energizes behavior; but even here it is mixed. This reconstruction of folk psychology is not tenable.

It might be thought that, though drive is problematical, incentive can provide a basis to transform the conative feature of immediate intention. Whereas drive is internal, unlearned, and based on physiological needs, incentive is externally aroused, learned, and not based on physiological needs. Evidence is lacking for a motivational construct anchored in physiological imbalance; incentive, not being so anchored, is not dependent on such evidence.

Spence (1956) provides the most influential development of the incentive construct. Working from an idea in an early paper by Hull (1931), Spence argued that the underlying mechanism for incentive is fractional anticipatory goal response (r_g-s_g). After having been habituated, a rat will exhibit behaviors in a runway, such as licking his lips, chewing, and salivating, that are appropriate to eating in the goal box. These responses are fractional in that the complete goal response is not emitted and they are anticipatory in that they occur prior to the sight or smell of food. The goal response (r_g) produces stimulation (s_g), which in turn energizes further activity toward the goal.

The r_g-s_g mechanism, however, has come under attack. (For reviews, see Weiner, 1972, and Hilgard and Bower, 1975.) Incentive and drive may not be independent. For example, a satiated animal will respond less to a goal object than will a deprived animal. Thus the antecedent conditions determine in part the anticipatory goal response. Moreover incentive and habit may not be independent. There appears to be no operational way to separate incentive and reinforcement. Reinforcement proceeds through rewards and rewards are incentives. Indeed there is some evidence against the r_g-s_g mechanism being an energizer. For animals that have their goal responses, such as salivation, facilitated or inhibited by drugs, the predicted effect on performance does not occur.

A number of psychologists have reacted to these and other seeming difficulties with the r_g-s_g mechanism by disassociating it from incentive (e.g., Mowrer, 1960). Others have tended to develop this construct in a way that is compatible with expectancy models of motivation (e.g., Bolles, 1972). It is clear that Spence's version of the incentive construct is unsatisfactory. But it is not fully clear at this point whether one of these altered versions can be useful in explaining motivated behavior.

In addition to a lack of experimental support, there are two conceptual problems for both Hull's drive construct and Spence's incentive construct that make them unlikely candidates for the basis of a transformation of the conative feature of immediate intention. The first concerns ontological status, and is well-known. Drive and incentive are properties of an organism's physiological state. But moving to act is a property of immediate intention, which is a mental event. An essential ingredient in the folk psychological picture of action is that it is initiated by a mental event; but neither Hull's nor Spence's neobehaviorism captures this part of the folk psychological picture. In most general terms the drive and incentive constructs leave out the mental life of the subject in action.

Neobehaviorists like Hull and Spence would no doubt reply that nothing has been eliminated from the explanation of action. Their approach, they would claim, accounts for action initiation without hypothesizing mental events—or rather it will do so when appro-

priately developed and refined. We should not be misled by introspection, which makes it appear that there are mental events.

However, this response cannot be sustained. It is correct to dismiss uncontrolled introspective reports about mental events, since
these reports are notoriously unreliable, especially with regard to
existential commitment. But there is strong experimental evidence
for mental events that cannot be so readily dismissed. One type of
evidence, from within the neobehaviorist paradigm itself, concerns
experiments or pair-associated lists of words. Some lists are easy to
learn because of prior associations: for example, 'roving-nomad,'
'tranquil-quiet,' 'pious-devout.' Other lists are difficult to learn because of a tendency to confound pairs: for example, 'tranquil-placid,'
'quiet-double,' 'serene-headstrong.' Hull's theory predicts that individuals low in drive will perform worse than those high in drive on
the easy task; and those low in drive will perform better than those
high in drive on the difficult task. For an easy task the response is
dominant in the subject's response hierarchy, and thus the greater
the drive, the better the performance. But for a difficult task there are
competing responses, and thus when drive is high, chances for an
incorrect response are increased.[5] However, Weiner (1966) found
that these predictions can be negated by providing subjects with
false norms. For instance, telling subjects with low drive that they are
doing poorly and those with high drive that they are doing well on a
difficult task yields that subjects with high drive in fact perform
better than those with low drive, contrary to prediction. Weiner
concludes that "[t]he important determinants of behavior in this
situation are the cognitive and motivational consequences resulting
from success or failure at the task, rather than the individual's drive
level interacting with the structure of the task *per se*" (1966, p. 342; cf.
Weiner, 1972, pp. 50 ff., especially pp. 76 ff.). The subject's cognitive
awareness of success and failure, it would certainly appear, is best
understood in terms of mental happenings.

The second conceptual problem for Hull's drive construct and
Spence's incentive construct concerns planned activity. Folk psychology includes a distinction between intentional and nonintentional action. This distinction is to be unpacked in terms of planned
activity. Much of what persons do is planned in that it follows a
preconceived, stereotypic master representation. But Hullian Drive
Theory does not reflect this facet of the folk psychological picture.
Hull and his colleagues focused on the behavior of laboratory rats.
Some work was done on other species such as guinea pigs, cats,
dogs, monkeys, and even human subjects; but on the whole, the theory was generated from rat behavior. There may be good experi-

mental justification for this focus in that the behavior of laboratory rats is easily measurable and the conditions easily controllable. Nevertheless a consequence of it is that the conceptual framework of Drive Theory does not reflect the distinction between intentional and nonintentional action. Rats do not perform intentional actions.

Some Hullians distinguish between general activity and specific activity. General activity is described in the literature as aimless movement, for example, when a hungry rat runs in an activity wheel. In contrast specific activity is sometimes described as goal-directed, such as running toward food. This distinction, however, does not capture the difference between intentional and nonintentional action. First of all, the distinction is not as clear as once thought; some general activity is in fact learned, and not naive aimless movement. More important, 'goal-directed' and 'aimless' are not to be taken with their usual senses in the context of Hullian Drive Theory. That theory is an attempt to explain behavior *without* using 'goal-directed' in its folk psychological sense: Drive Theory is reductive in this respect.

In summary recall the Method of Case Studies. It is a reciprocal procedure. On the one side, commonsense notions are clarified and articulated by transformation into scientific concepts; and on the other side, the conceptual foundation of the scientific framework is secured by anchoring it to the well-grounded claims of common-sense, as formulated after critical appraisal. In both these respects Drive Theory is unsatisfactory. No progress can be made in clarifying and articulating the conative feature of intention in terms of drive, since that construct fails to serve a scientific explanatory role. It is as if an articulation of the commonsense notions of force and motion were attempted to be gained by transforming them into constructs within Aristotelian physical theory. There are in addition funda-mental conceptual gaps between the drive construct and the folk psychological notion of moving to act: the latter depends on there being mental events, whereas the former depends on there not being mental events; the latter presupposes a distinction between inten-tional and nonintentional action, whereas the former provides no ground for this distinction. Similar problems confront Spence's in-centive construct.

3. Expectancy Theory

Edward Tolman developed a system of behavioristic psychology— most fully presented in *Purposive Behavior in Animals and Men* (1932)—that differed in fundamental and interesting ways from Hull's. Tolman stressed the cognitive aspects of acting in contrast to

Hull who stressed the mechanical aspects. To be sure, Tolman's theory, like Hull's, is neobehavioristic, in that it presupposes that there are no mental events and that all intervening variables required in the explanation of motivated behavior are operationally definable in terms of observable stimuli and responses. For the moment, however, let us bracket this feature of Tolman's theory.

Tolman criticized Hull and his colleagues for taking the unit of analysis to be stimulus-response sequences. He spoke derogatorily of psychologists limiting their attention to muscle twitches. The unit of analysis, according to Tolman, should be molar behavior, such as a person's eating in a restaurant. Although molar behavior can ultimately be reduced to atomic S-R units, the large-scale units ought to be the objects of study, since the properties of molar behavior cannot be known by focusing exclusively on the constituent units. This approach is responsive to the criticism made of Hull that he ignores long-range, planned activity. Tolman's theory appears to have the resources necessary to distinguish between intentional and non-intentional action.

An accessible rendition of Tolman's system and one that reflects his considered opinion, appears in a late and little known paper "A Psychological Model" (1952). In brief summary Tolman holds there that a subject's immediate physiological condition and environmental situation, together with standing conditions such as genetic makeup, age, and so on, cause the arousal of needs. These needs contribute to the formation of a belief (expectancy)-value matrix, in which the subject weighs his beliefs (expectations) about what he can do and the values he places on each type of action. As a result of this process the subject restructures his thoughts about the available options. The process continues until he narrows the field to one. Thereupon, he acts. Figure 9.1 is Tolman's diagram of this situation. This figure depicts complex, intentional action. Simple, nonintentional action occurs presumably without all the depicted intervening events. Of those intervening events, the formation of a belief-value matrix is necessary for the performance of an action. Tolman's model bears striking resemblance to the folk psychological picture of action.[6] It is clearly a Causal Theory of Action. An event, or bit of behavior, is an action in virtue of its causal ancestry.

Several features of Tolman's model require additional explanation. Unlike Hull, Tolman makes a distinction between needs and drives. A drive is an antecedent physiological condition; a need is a disposition to undertake consummatory behavior. Tolman moreover forsakes Hull's idea of drive as a pooled energy source and thinks of it rather as multifarious causes of dispositions. There are as many

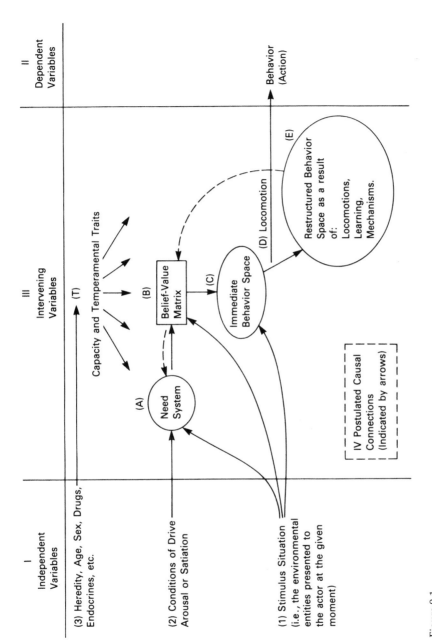

Figure 9.1
An expectancy theoretic model for intentional action. From Tolman, "A Psychological Model" (1952).

kinds of drive as there are consummatory behaviors. Needs are caused by drives and external stimuli; they are also affected by feedback from the belief-value matrix. Tolman holds that the Need System consists of specific needs and a libido need, which is undirected and tends to magnify other needs. Needs are not independent, and may influence each other positively or negatively. There seems to be some similarity between Tolman's notion of libido need and Hull's idea of drive.

The most noteworthy part of Tolman's model is its cognitive features. In the Belief-Value Matrix stage the agent considers types of activities open to him in virtue of his needs, the environment, and his standing abilities and temperamental traits. If the activity has any complexity, means-end beliefs are included in the matrix. Beliefs about types of events are paired with value assessments. If, for instance, the actor is hungry and has a choice between several foods, his consummatory behavior will depend on the positive and negative values placed on the kinds of food.

The subject's belief-value matrix, in conjunction with external stimuli, cause him to conceive of himself in a behavior space. Here Tolman borrows heavily from Kurt Lewin: "A behavior space," he says, "is . . . to be defined as a *particularized* complex of perceptions (memories and inferences) as to objects and relations and the 'behaving self,' evoked by the given environmental stimulus situation and by a controlling and activated belief-value matrix (or perhaps several such matrices)" (1952, p. 296). That is, the behavior space is the complex thought process by which the subject comes to be aware of the actions open to him given the environment, his needs, and his belief-value matrix. The belief-value matrix concerns general types of activities; the behavior space is a particularization of the belief-value matrix for the subject at the time. Though contrary to what Tolman suggests, the behavior space does not concern individual events: since these events are future, they must be types. The behavior space represents future action types as narrowly as the memories, inferences, and perceptions of the subject permit.

The intervening 'mental' representation undergoes transitions as the end and means of the activity become clear to the subject. The feature labeled 'Restructured Behavior Space' in the model represents the altered behavior space. As the subject forecloses some possibilities and opens others, the behavior space changes, that is, becomes restructured. The psychological change that takes place, according to Tolman, is locomotion. Locomotion is not itself observable behavior, but rather a series of selections that result in observable behavior. Locomotion in behavior space takes place because of perceptual discrimination, past learning, and psychodynamic mechanisms, such as repression and symbolic substitution. The immediate and restructured behavior spaces are a single feature of the model over time; the immediate behavior space provides the initial basis for selecting an activity and the restructured behavior space provides the terminal basis. The result of this complex process, from the need system to the restructured behavior space, is intentional action.

Hull (1943) held that there are two primary constructs necessary to take stimuli into responses, an associative one, habit, and a motivational one, drive. In most fundamental terms Tolman also held that there are two primary constructs that generate responses from stimuli: one is cognitive, belief (or expectancy), and the other is motivational, value (or valence). An expectancy is a disposition for there being processes of the form, S_1-R_1-S_2 (cf. MacCorquodale and Meehl, 1954; Tolman, 1955). Stimulus S_1 is the *elicitor* which can be an initial perception; response R_1 follows the elicitor; and the stimulus S_2, the *expectandum*, is the goal of the expectancy. Thus, for example, a subject sees the cupboard (S_1), opens the door (R_1), and thereby expects to see food (S_2). Expectancies need not be activated and can be stored in memory. They may be interlocked, one expectandum being the elicitor for another. A set of interlocked expectations serves to guide a subject through his environment. In that case the subject has a 'cognitive map' of the environment, where elicitors cue expectanda. Tolman's fundamental associative unit, S_1-R_1-S_2, differs from Hull's H in that connections between stimuli are essential to behavior.

The terminal stimulus (S_2) of an expectancy has a value or valence which can be either positive or negative. Similarly stimuli associated with S_2 have value. In instrumental learning, such as a chimp exchanging a token for a banana, the conditioned stimulus—the sight or feel of the token—acquires value. Tolman (1932) holds that needs do not directly activate responses, or even expectancies. Rather needs influence behavior by increasing the valence of terminal stimuli and associated stimuli. However, in his later model depicted by figure 9.1, Tolman allows that needs can affect value at all stages of the process leading to action. They alter the valences at the level of the immediate behavior space; but needs can also change valences directly in the restructured behavior space. In the latter situation they are called 'need-pushes.' Tolman says "I conceive a need-push as, so to speak, that of a drive which, under concrete stimulus conditions of the moment, gets into the behavior space" (1952, p. 318).

From our viewpoint the key feature of this model is the motivational construct, the valence of an expectandum. Unfortunately

Tolman never satisfactorily explicates this construct. At times he suggests that valence is determined by needs. However, as pointed out in the discussion of Hull's drive construct, there is little supporting evidence for the claim that behavior activation can be traced to homeostatic imbalance. More important, even if Tolman were correct about the source of value, it would remain unclear what value is. My conjecture is that value is the correlate of the folk psychological notion of wanting or desiring. Thus valence is a transformed notion of preference. If this conjecture is correct—and it certainly seems plausible—then valence cannot be used to understand the conative component of intention. As I argued earlier, preferring to do something does not initiate action, even under conditions of full cognitive awareness. Tolman seems to have succumbed to the same confusion as many philosophical action theorists in not distinguishing between attitudes expressing subjects' preferences (or desires) to do something and attitudes expressing the subjects' intentions to do it. Valence in short does not motivate action.

In recent years Tolman's stock has been rising. His views have not been adopted wholesale, since it is now widely agreed that neobehaviorism cannot be the conceptual basis for an adequate scientific psychology. But some of his leading ideas have attracted attention. In particular he has been followed in his turn toward molar behavior and his emphasis on cognitive processes. Unfortunately there has been an overemphasis on cognitive processes, to the neglect of conative ones. An extreme example is decision theory. Subjective probability and utility bear similarity to Tolman's notions of belief (expectancy) and value (valence). But where valence is intended by Tolman to have conative properties, utility does not. A subjective probability-utility matrix yields a judgment about the best course of action for the subject; but it says nothing about translating this judgment into overt activity. Even if Tolman misdescribes the conative feature of action, he does include a mechanism for activating decisions within his model. Contemporary decision theorists (e.g., Jeffrey, 1965) are not concerned with the psychology of decision realization.

Consider another approach that extends Tolman's work, one that is within the animal learning tradition. Bolles (1972) modifies Tolman's view in two respects: the behavioristic stance is eliminated and expectancy is construed as stored information; and the range of dispositions that count as expectancies is enlarged. An animal expects something when he has information about the way in which the environment will change. This information consists in some stimuli being cues for events in the near future. Learning occurs when an appreciation of environmental contingencies is acquired. Bolles formulates his 'Primary Law of Learning' as follows: "what is learned is that certain events, cues, (S), predict certain other, biologically important events, consequences, (S*)" (1972, p. 402). Thus in this primary sense an animal's making a response is not part of his having expectancy: for Bolles, unlike Tolman, an expectancy can be a direct connection between stimuli. Bolles also recognizes a secondary notion of expectancy that does involve responses. Here there is a predictive relationship between an animal's response (R) and other biologically important stimuli (S*), such as the smell of food or a route to safety. Bolles's theory, which includes two types of expectancies, is more flexible than Tolman's in accounting for learning, especially for cases in which no particular response is required by the subject, for example, Pavlovian conditioning.

We obtain an account of action, as contrasted with one merely of thought, when laws of motivation are included. According to Bolles the probability of a response increases with the strength of the S-S* expectancy, the strength of the R-S* expectancy, and the value of S*. He draws analogies between S-S* expectancy and incentive (K), between R-S* expectancy and habit (H), and between the value of S* and Hull's drive construct (D). With respect to the latter, he says "[T]he value of S* certainly must depend on the physiological state of the organism; thus it has some of the conceptual properties of Hull's D" (1972, p. 405).

Guthrie, an S-R theorist, once quipped that Tolman's rats are so immersed in thought at the choice points that they are unable to move. His point was that cognitive events, in particular, expectancies, are not sufficient for movement. Tolman, of course, was aware of this point. His system included a construct that was to have a motivational function. Unfortunately this motivational construct, the value of the expectandum, does not explain activity initiation. Bolles's account suffers a similar fate. Expectancies of the form S-S* and R-S*, like Tolman's S_1-R_1-S_2, are cognitive and do not explain the initiation of action. The only element in Bolles's account that has the prospect of being an action initiator is the value of S*. Unfortunately, to the extent it resembles Hull's D, it suffers from the same problems; and to the extent it is cognitive, it lacks properties that initiate action. In short, while Bolles has clarified the nature of the expectancy construct and its relation to response strength, like Tolman, he has not succeeded in clarifying response initiation.

Bolles's views are representative of the development of expectancy theory. The cognitive process of response selection has been the focus of attention. But the noncognitive process of response initiation has been treated as a peripheral matter; and as a result little progress in understanding it has been achieved. It is as if, having seen the enormous effort that went into clarifying and then defeating Hull's drive theory, safe ground is sought on cognitive issues. My complaint is not that work has been directed toward cognitive processes; surely these processes must be explained if action is to be understood. Rather it is that the noncognitive features of action initiation have been for the most part ignored.

4. Production Systems

The problem of transforming conation cannot be easily solved. But before undue pessimism sets in, let me offer some conjectures about future research that might lead to a scientific explanation of conation. It appears that part of the problem can be solved within the computational framework. In particular the theory of production systems explains the execution of action routines.

A production system is basically a series of conditional rules that codify procedural knowledge. Procedural knowledge is knowledge how to do something and stands in contrast to declarative knowledge *that* something is the case. The recent development of this idea within psychology is usually traced to Newell (1973; also see Newell and Simon, 1972). Various formulations have evolved, some of which differ in important technical respects. These differences reflect attempts to provide working simulations. For the purpose of illustration I will focus on Anderson's ACT (Adaptive Control of Thought) theory. That theory was first articulated in (1976) and revised in (1983).

The fundamental conceptual distinction here is between declarative and procedural knowledge. (See Ryle, 1949.) Suppose that you are asked who the thirty-seventh President was. You would recall this information from memory, perhaps by thinking of the current President and associating backward. Your response 'Nixon' confirms that you know that the thirty-seventh President was Nixon. This is a case of declarative knowledge. It is knowledge of a proposition. Many psychologists, including Anderson, have argued that declarative knowledge is stored within a network of propositional representations. (To be cautious, we should say only that this is a case of *de dicto* belief, since the epistemic credentials of the claim have not been established. However, let us follow the practice in the cognitive psychological literature and assume that claims of this type have been both originally evidentially grounded and veridically remembered.)

Suppose now you are asked how to knot a tie. If you are like me, you would not be able to articulate, at least easily, how to do it. You could *show* someone how to do it by actually knotting a tie, but you could not easily describe or state the procedure. This knowledge is not accessible in propositional form. As a consequence, it has been held that it is not embedded within a propositional network. The suggestion is rather that it is stored in the form of a list of procedures or rules for tie-knotting.

Notice that we are talking about an ability that a person already has, not the learning of an ability. The first stage in learning to knot a tie involves declarative knowledge (Anderson, 1982). A person learns a list of propositions that describe a step-wise procedure; he then encodes these propositions and recites them covertly. "Put the tie around one's neck; leave the wide side longer by one-third; and so on." But as the subject becomes proficient at tie-knotting, this declarative knowledge fades and is replaced by a list of rules, a production system. The rapidity of performance in skilled activities is a function of the form that a set of rules takes.

Fodor (1983) argues, as I pointed out, that central processes are unencapsulated. That is, they are global, each one connected with every other one. Anderson's picture of central processes is different. They divide into two irreducible types. One is based on storage of information by networks of propositional representations; and the other is based on storage of information by sets of production rules. In the former case the information is consciously accessible and plays a role in inference; in the latter case the information is not consciously accessible and plays a role in the performance of skilled activities. Fodor complained that cognitive science cannot explain central processes because, essentially, they cannot be isolated. To repeat an earlier point, though now in the context of the production system theory, if there is a distinction between those processes that involve propositional networks and those that concern production sets, some progress is possible. In particular central processes concerned with performance seem to be amenable to explanation— though the problem to which Fodor pointed, the frame problem, appears to remain for central processes involving propositional networks.[7]

There are several noteworthy features of sets of production rules. Consider two simple examples. The first is a production set for dialing a telephone number (Anderson, 1982, p. 383):

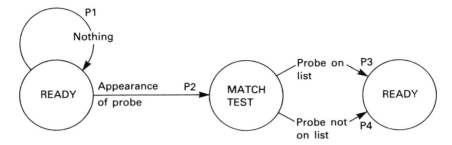

Figure 9.2
The flow of control for the Sternberg task. Based on Anderson (1976, p. 126).

(P1) IF the goal is to dial LVtelephone-number
& LVdigit 1 is the first digit of LVtelephone-number,
THEN dial LVdigit 1.

(P2) IF the goal is to dial LVtelephone-number
& LVdigit 1 has just been dialed
& LVdigit 2 is after LVdigit 1 in LVtelephone-number,
THEN dial LVdigit 2.

'LV' stands for 'local variable' and changes with each application of the Production rule. The second example is a production set for the Sternberg task. In these experiments subjects commit to memory a list of digits or letters varying in number from 1 to 4. They are shown a probe and must indicate whether the probe is part of the target set (based on Anderson, 1976, p. 127 and 1982, p. 385). The following is a simplified production set for this task:

(P1) IF ready,
THEN rehearse target list.

(P2) IF LVprobe appears on screen & LVprobe is an LVtype,
THEN test match of LVtype to LVitems in memory set.

(P3) IF memory set contains an LVitem of LVtype,
THEN press 'yes' & return to ready.

(P4) IF memory set does not contain an LVitem of LVtype,
THEN press 'no' & return to ready.

The system recycles in the ready position until the probe appears. The probe is then matched against the list stored in working memory, directing either a pressing of the 'yes' button or a pressing of the 'no' button. The primary result that a simulation of the Sternberg task must explain is that subjects take a constant additional time for each digit added to the target set. The model explains this result by means of the increased time required to apply (P3) and (P4). The list of digits is stored in working memory as propositions. Longer lists result in larger propositional structures, and hence a longer search time. Search consists in the spreading activation of a propositional network segment. Other production sets differ from these two examples primarily in the number of productions and loops.

Now note, first, that production sets interact with memory. The general picture is that there is a working or active memory connected both with declarative memory and production memory (Anderson, 1983, pp. 19 ff.). Antecedents of productions specify conditions that are true in working memory; and consequents specify sequences of changes to be made in working memory. In our second example (P3) applies only if the test digit is matched to one stored in working memory. If it does apply, the consequent is detached with the result that the 'yes' button is pressed, the proposition that it occurred is added to working memory, and the probe digit is deactivated.

Second, a production system itself does not yield action. Nor does it take in information. A production system is a set of rules that translate incoming information into a form that can be used by the motor systems. In our second example it is assumed that there is a perceptual parser that delivers the encoded probe digit in propositional network form, and it is also assumed that there is a motor system that takes the encoded response from propositional form into bodily button-pushing. Production sets are part of the central system; and while they interface with the input and output systems, they are distinct from them.

The third noteworthy feature is that a production system cannot begin its routine unless the antecedent of the initial production is satisfied. This is obvious, but quite important, and I shall return to it momentarily. The point is that production systems are not self-starting, but require input to run.

As Anderson observes (1976, pp. 81 ff., 1980, pp. 235 ff.), production systems resemble S-R mechanisms. They both enable the execution of sequential routines through intraconnections. In a set of productions the consequent of one production satisfies, or triggers, the antecedent of the next. Similarly in a series of S-R bonds, one response can be a stimulus for the next. When running a complex T-maze, a trace left by one turn serves as a stimulus for the next turn. One difference between production systems and S-R models is that only the former countenances mental events. Theoretically there are other, important differences. In a production system, activation of the intermediate steps in a behavioral routine depends on propositional representations stored in memory, whereas in S-R models they sometimes (at least) depend on external stimuli. Production systems in addition are often quite general; for instance, there can be a system for parsing ordinary speech, whereas S-R mechanisms are typically situationally specific.

I suggest that the production system theory provides at best a partial basis for the scientific transformation of conation. As pointed out in the opening section, there are several aspects of conation to be explained: being moved to perform an intentional action and being moved to perform a nonintentional action, and with regard to the former, being moved *to select* a plan of action and being moved *to follow* a plan. It is my contention that the production system theory is irrelevant to plan selection. In the other cases it is relevant, but only in that it explains the transmission of motivation, not its source.

A production set is activated only if the antecedent of the lead production is satisfied. For instance, in a production system for addition the lead production might read: "IF the goal is to do an addition problem, THEN the subgoal is to iterate through the columns of the problem" (Anderson, 1982). But this system itself does not make provisions for the satisfaction of the antecedent. The system does not include an explanation of why *this* system is run; that is, it leaves out of account the subject's being moved to solve an addition problem. In general there is no explanation of the selection of production sets.

It might be responded that one production set can be embedded in another, and that the satisfaction of the lead antecedent of one set depends on the satisfaction of some consequent of a more encompassing set. But there are two problems with this reply. First, it assumes that all activity is ordered in one or a few hierarchies of goals. And that appears to be false. Persons' activities are often independent of one another. It is a misplaced Aristotelianism that leads to the view that all of us have our goals nicely ordered in some hierarchy. Second and more important, this response pushes the issue of selection back a step but does not resolve it. Suppose that the lead production to do addition is embedded in a more encompassing production set for general problem solving. That set too must have a lead production, say: "IF the goal is to do a list of problems, THEN set as a subgoal to do the first problem on the list." But how is it that this antecedent gets satisfied? The subject must be moved to solve problems. Subjects might well be so moved, but that is not explained by the production system theory. Again the theory *assumes* that subjects are motivated; it does not explain it.

It would appear that the inability to explain plan selection is an inevitable feature of the production system theory itself. The theory is indifferent to the ontological type of the object instantiating sets of production rules. For example, with regard to doing addition it is irrelevant whether these rules are instantiated in persons or silicon Martians. Not all species or machines, of course, instantiate the same processes. But—and this is the main point—processes of the same kind are explained by a single production set, no matter their physical realization. However, plan selection, and motivation in general, is species-typical. Instantiation matters. Being moved to act by a need for affiliation, for example, varies among species, despite their relatively equal phylogenetic positions. Canines tend to be pack oriented; felines tend to be solitary. Suppose that silicon Martians replicated our cognitive processes. Even then it would be astonishing if they also replicated our motivational states. What would move a silicon Martian to select a course of action would likely be quite different from what moves a person to act.

A reasonable explanation why instantiation matters in the case of plan selection is that plan selection, and motivation in general, depends on physiology (or 'hardware'). It is clearly a difficult problem to specify the nature of this dependency. Hull thought that behavior was uniformly motivated by homeostatic imbalances. While hunger and thirst do sometimes move persons to act, they are also moved by the need to achieve, by pity, by guilt, and by greed, none of which is obviously connected with any physiological imbalance. In short the production system theory abstracts from physical realization, and hence identifies features of processes that are independent of the organism in which they are instantiated. But these are not the features that characterize motivation. Instantiation affects process.

We need to look elsewhere for an explanation of plan selection. But first, consider plan following, which does appear to be explicable in terms of the production system theory. The cognitive features of intentional action are basically explicable in terms of schema theories. An action is intentional in virtue of falling under a large-chunked, centrally located schema called a 'script' (or a 'MOP'). The motor activity involved in performing the action is guided to completion by a peripheral schema, not too different from a TOTE. Production systems, I conjecture, explain plan following by playing an intermediary and connecting role between these two types of schemata.

The picture of intentional action that emerges is this. Scripts are stored in declarative memory. A script is selected by means of a motivational system. (I will talk about motivation systems momentarily.) Each scene, or each segment of a scene, calls forth a production set stored in production memory. Production sets interact with working memory, which results in the activation of motor schemata. These motor schemata guide bodily movement.

Consider an example. My knotting my tie this morning, we can suppose, is intentional. I select a script from my repertoire, $Going to Work. That script, which is stored in long-term, declarative memory contains several scenes: say, Getting Up, Dressing, Eating Breakfast, Driving. When the scene Dressing is activated in declarative memory, the lead antecedent of a production set, stored in production memory, is satisfied. This production set is run. Contained in it is a subset for knotting a tie. As this subset is run, it triggers motor schemata for finger and hand movement. These schemata control the bodily activity by perceptual monitoring and feeding this resultant information back into working memory.

The conative aspect of an intentional action is inherited from its plan-following characteristics. Once a script is underway, the subject can be moved to perform each action automatically. Production sets channel the motivation of the initial selection into the individual activities. A production system takes scriptual knowledge and re-encodes it into a form that is usable by the motor systems. Metaphorically an initial impetus is required to set the script in motion. The complex script must be tracked: this is the function of declarative memory. But no additional impetus is required for the contained activities. Production sets transmit the initial impetus to the motor control schemata.

This picture is far from uncontroversial. From one quarter some would object to the inclusion of production systems. They would enlarge the role of peripheral, motor schemata so that they directly interact with declarative memory (see Norman, 1981 and Norman and Shallice, 1980). The primary reason is that they do not draw a distinction between procedural and declarative knowledge, but rather assimilate all knowledge to propositional knowledge (see Rumelhart, Lindsay, and Norman, 1972). My guess is that the difference between peripheral, motor schemata, and scripts is too great to proceed without an intermediate step, without, as it were, compilation. Suppose that that is right, that an intermediate stage is necessary. Norman and others would nevertheless maintain that that stage does not utilize production systems, but rather derives from declarative memory. It is not clear to me whether this point is forceful. In part it turns on the choice of formalism, and this type of issue is not subject to a definitive answer. Elegance seems to suggest that all internal representation be in the form of propositional networks;

but conceptual clarity seems to suggest that the distinction between procedural and declarative knowledge be reflected in the formalism. Incidentally, the production system formalism does not forsake reference to propositions. 'If . . . , then . . .' statements are propositions. Rather the main point is that the production system formalism does not reconstruct propositions into networks.

The picture I suggest might also be attacked from another quarter. Production systems might be thought to compete with scripts. Production systems typically chunk memory in smaller units than scripts (MOPs), though there is no reason why they could not chunk memory to the same extent (cf. Anderson, 1983, pp. 209 ff.). Scripts then would be superfluous. However, this objection misses an important differentiating factor between scripts and production sets. As Anderson put it at one time:

> Some people appear to view production systems as in competition with another kind of theoretical formalism variously called schemes, frames, and scripts. . . . It is my . . . view that the production system and schema formulations should not be viewed as competitors. Production systems are models for skills while schemas are patterns for recognizing recurring sets of features. (1980, p. 254)

Scripts, as I argued, need not be restricted to recognition of patterns of past events, but can also be used in plan formation. But in either case they are like generalized cognitive maps. Scripts are stored in declarative memory and hence are available for conscious decision making about possible courses of future action. But they are not procedural. Scripts do not transmit motivation. A set of interconnecting rules is required for that. Production sets by contrast are not representations stored in declarative memory. Hence they are not available for conscious decision making about possible courses of future activity. But they are procedural and do transmit motivation.

Suppose that I am correct in taking production systems to be intermediary transmitters of motivation between scripts and motor schemata. Then I will have explained the conative aspect of intentional action in virtue of being part of a plan. But the original source of motivation in a plan, plan selection, will not have been explained. In the next section I offer a conjecture about plan selection based on some ideas in animal learning theory. That conjecture is highly speculative. My original negative thesis remains: there is presently no extant theory (or theories) adequate to transform fully the folk psychological concept of conation into a scientific one.

5. Motivation Systems

The most extensive treatment of motivation has been by psychologists who focus on animal learning. Needless to repeat, there has been much controversy, and a consensus theory has yet to emerge. Nevertheless there is one idea that appears attractive, especially from the viewpoint of transforming the folk psychological concept of conation. That is that the initiation of a specific range of behavior can be explained by a *motivation system*. This is not a new idea, but rather one with a long history in psychology and ethology (cf. Gallistel, chapter 10). Interestingly it has recently been revived by Masterson and Crawford (1982) to explain avoidance behavior in rats. I will use their work as a point of departure to suggest how the idea of a motivation system might be generalized to persons.

An animal has an innate set of response patterns for a type of activity. There are sets of response patterns in rats for eating, for avoiding danger, for affiliation, and so on. In the case of avoiding danger a rat might respond to noxious stimuli by fleeing, freezing, fighting, or defensive burying. When confronted with an unfamiliar situation, or one previously associated with danger, a rat will become wary. Wariness consists in the priming or excitation of a response set. The entire set of responses is readied. Environmental cues then serve to activate one member of this set. For instance, an escape route will trigger flight, and an intruding conspecific will initiate aggressive activity.

The ability to rapidly change responses to danger has survival value; while aggressive behavior might be an appropriate initial reaction to a predator, flight might also be quickly required. On Masterson and Crawford's (1982) model the possibility of rapid changes among members of a response set is explained by the fact that the entire set is simultaneously readied. Moreover survival probability is increased if the response set for avoidance behavior is easily primed and extinguishes slowly. But it is counterproductive that a negative effect accompanies the excitation of the avoidance response set. The presence of an intense negative effect, panic or terror, is especially counterproductive in an attempt to avoid danger. Such intense reactions are best reserved in preparation for a traumatic experience, for cases when fleeing or freezing are ineffectual.

At times motivation systems can operate jointly. An alarmed animal can also engage in eating activity. This behavior might be described as 'wary eating.' But sometimes motivation systems compete for control. It remains an open question whether motivation systems compete on an equal basis, perhaps with rapid alternations between them, or there is some hierarchical structure that determines which motivation system dominates. The type of problem presented by competition among motivation systems is not unlike that presented by competing foci for attention.

An important feature of Masterson and Crawford's model of avoidance behavior is that it is attuned to the natural behavior of rats rather than highly contrived laboratory contexts. Diverse stimuli prime a range of innate responses, with response activation depending on the perceived environmental condition. This ethological approach contrasts sharply with the Hullian experimental paradigm in which specific responses are elicited by specific stimuli in a highly structured context. The ethological approach, it would seem, more easily permits extrapolation to human behavior.

Animals learn to produce stimuli necessary to activate a member of the primed response set. For example, a frightened rat can learn to press a lever that opens a pathway for flight. The stimuli engendered by flight (for instance, kinesthetic and visual feedback) serve as a reward and thus reinforce the instrumental behavior of bar pressing. This view contrasts with the widely held claim that the cessation of warning stimuli account for reinforcement in avoidance learning. If Masterson and Crawford are right about this, then they have found a way to unify avoidance learning with appetitive learning. For it has often been argued that in appetitive learning consummatory activity is reinforcing. In hunger brief exposures to pleasant tastes are rewarding. In both cases then, consummatory stimuli would serve to reward. Masterson and Crawford's view focuses both types of learning on the reinforcing effects of stimulus feedback.

So much for rats. Can this model help in understanding the conative features of human action? Maybe. Suppose persons have innate motivation systems. The range of these systems seems to include, but is not exhausted by, the systems for the rat. Persons have motivation systems for defense, for hunger, for sex, for affiliation, and so on. But they also have motivation systems for achievement, for, perhaps, moral fairness, aesthetic enjoyment, and so on. When placed in appropriate environmental conditions, one or more motivation systems become primed. Situational cues serve then to activate a type of response. Selection is based on past reinforcements.

Sometimes a motivational system directly leads to action. That is, in terms of our earlier picture, a motivation system provides satisfaction of the lead antecedent in a production set. This is motivated nonintentional action. Sometimes, however, motivational systems yield an output that filters through a stored, large-chunked schema. This is motivated intentional action.

Return to the example of the dastardly nephew who intends to kill his rich uncle in order to inherit the family fortune. He has constructed a plan, which includes his driving to his uncle's house, entering through the back door, and shooting him. He will act on this plan only when moved to do so. In terms of our model the nephew has a greed motivation system, which wins in the competition with other motivation systems such as the one concerned with moral fairness. As a result an entire range of greed responses is readied, including the newly constructed plan to kill his uncle. Since the environment is thought friendly to the conduct of this plan and since, let us suppose, it has the largest payoff among the greed responses, it is selected for execution. Once selected, the plan is followed, thereby generating a series of intentional actions.

Combining the motivation systems conjecture with the previous claim about production systems, a framework for motivated action emerges that is depicted by figure 9.3. Motivation systems either interact directly with production memory or initiate production system runs indirectly through declarative memory. A motivation system is not contained in memory, though it is linked to memory. It is a hardwired information processing module, dependent on the species to which the organism belongs. If this model is correct—or even approximately correct—it explains the conative features of nonintentional action and plan selection.

Production systems transmit motivation; they do not originate it. Motivation is generated by environmental stimuli operating on activated response sets. The model explains why motivation is affected by instantiation, by physical embodiment. Motivation systems are innate and species-typical. The achievement motivation system, for example, resides in persons (and perhaps higher mammals), but not in, say, pigeons. Persons come equipped, as it were, with motives to achieve. No doubt individuals differ among themselves with regard to the extent they are moved to achieve. But if there is an achievement motivation system in persons, there is a class of responses that are 'hardwired.' Various species can have the same motivation system; but the response set that such a system engenders depends on the range of activities available to the animal. For example, both rats and tigers have avoidance motivation systems; but the innate sets of available responses differ considerably. Tigers do not seek a burrow when danger is perceived.

As in the case of animals, persons learn instrumental behavior that serves to activate responses readied by a motivational system. These

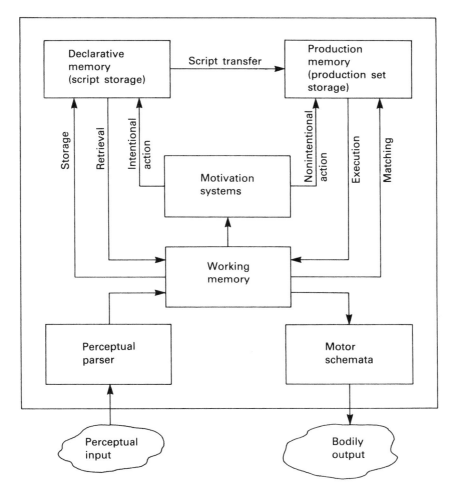

Figure 9.3
A possible framework for motivation and action.

instrumental responses are reinforced by feedback from activity leading to goal satisfaction. For example, suppose that a student's achievement motivation system readies a set of possible actions, which includes, for example, doing well in a test situation. He learns to study, which is instrumental in virtue of the rewards provided by feedback for studying, such as past perceived success. Presumably the range of learned instrumental behaviors for persons is enormous, when compared with phylogenetically lower species.

I do not pretend that this picture is unproblematic. One group of problems concerns the actual construction of a model. No formal structures have been articulated for motivational systems. One constraint on such structures is that information encoded in motivation systems interface with both declarative memory and production memory. Another group of problems concerns the motivation systems themselves. How are they to be individuated, and how many are there? The motivation system construct is not presently well defined. In some respects it is little more than a blackbox.

Another problem for this framework, and probably the central one, concerns the plasticity of human action. Suppose that there is in fact a greed motivation system. This system seems to differ from the defense motivation system of rats in an important respect. There is a small number of avoidance behaviors in rats. These can be topologically described and categorized. But there seems to be an enormous number of behaviors in persons that can count as greed. Indeed, under special conditions almost any physical action can be classified as greed. Unlike defensive behavior in rats, actions motivated by greed cannot be topologically described or categorized.

This last problem may be intractable. But even here there are possible responses. One such reply is that some motivation systems are essentially social constructs. Achievement, greed, and moral fairness are cases in point. Persons can be moved to achieve or to act from greed or from moral concerns only within a social context. Thus a psychological theory containing only natural kind terms referring to the topological behavior of single individuals cannot explain motivation. The 'joints' at which nature is cut in social behavior is mostly independent of physical, topological variables. If that is so, the borders between social psychology, and motivational and cognitive psychology are not sharp (cf. Cranach and Harre, 1982). This is an ethological approach on a grand scale. Notice incidentally that some motivation systems being essentially social does not necessarily preclude their being innate. In these cases the innate responses of a person are ones triggered in social situations.

But I speculate. The problems of the plasticity of human action and the difficulty in providing a formalism might defeat the motivation systems approach. Only attempts to construct working models can determine its plausibility in explaining action selection.[8]

Notes

Chapter 1 *

1 A similar comment applies to several other locutions that are commonly used in philosophical action theory, for example, *'performing* an action.'
2 I assume throughout that there are mental actions, such as intentionally thinking of one's favorite color or solving a mathematical puzzle 'in one's head.' The case for there being mental actions is well-made by Taylor (1970).
3 I detect traces of the Oldtime Volitional Theory in Toumela (1977) and Davis (1975). Davis (1979), however, advocates a Mental Action Theory.
4 See Brand (1970, pp. 3–21) for further discussion of the untenability of reductive accounts of human action.
5 I have offered my views about causation on a number of occasions (e.g., Brand and Swain, 1970, Brand, 1976, 1979). Basically I have serious reservations about a regularity approach, as well as the other main approaches current, such as the counterfactual approach, the probabilistic approach, and the necessary-sufficient condition approach. I suspect that some systemic view, one that does not attempt to reduce causality to any other category of phenomena, holds the most promise for success. For the present purposes all that is required is an intuitive grasp of the concept of causation, and that can be assumed. The views defended here can be supplemented with whatever explication of 'cause' is found acceptable on final analysis.
6 In Brand (1980) I argue that there must be some small but finite temporal overlap between a cause and its effect. I shall ignore this complication here.
7 These intermediate cases are discussed by Peacocke (1979). Peacocke's treatment is different; part of the difference is attributable to a difference in intuitions about the ordinary concept of action.
8 For the sake of clarity, note that it can be the case that $A_{i+1} = A$ and $A_i = A_n$.
9 Searle (1979) argues that not only is there a causal connection between the antecedent mental event—the intention—and the action, but in intentional action there is also a satisfactional relationship. The content of the mental event is satisfied only when there is a "world-to-mind" fit. Searle also holds that this content is characteristically self-referential: a person intends to A only if the content of his intention is that he A by way of carrying out *that intention.* That is, the intention is realized only when the action is in fact produced by that intention in the way specified by the intention. Carl's killing his uncle was not intentional because the intention did not include that that intention cause his killing his uncle by running him down.

By and large Searle is correct in all that he says. The main problem is that he does not say all that needs to be said. In particular a detailed account of the way in which intentions specify future courses of action is required. I take it that Searle's talk about the self-referentiality of intention is only a way of pointing to an account, not of providing one.

10 In order to sustain the claim that Carl's uncle dying is distinct from his cousin becoming an orphan, it is necessary to show that that claim follows from a tenable account of event identity. That issue is dealt with in chapter 3. Also see Kim (1974).

11 Goldman (1970, pp. 28–30) also claims that there is a fourth type of generation relation, namely, augmentative generation. This relation is meant to include, for example, that which

(a) Richard's saying 'hello'

bears to

(b) Richard's saying 'hello' loudly.

But the relation between (a) and (b) is not one of generation, on any intuitive construal of 'generation.' Generation relations, causal or otherwise, stand between distinct events. But the referents of descriptions (a) and (b) are not distinct. Generation relations are expressed by by-locutions. For instance, Carl orphaned his cousin *by* killing his uncle. The actions named by expressions before and after 'by' are distinct. But the augmentative relation cannot be expressed in terms of this type of by-locution: it is deviant to say, for example, that Richard said 'hello' loudly by saying 'hello.' Rather the descriptions (a) and (b) refer to the same action, with (b) making explicit the manner or way in which the action is performed. Adding an adverb of manner to an action description does not change the referent of the description.

12 Toumela (1977) claims that all cases of simple generation make implicit reference to rules. In the case of Richard's breaking his promise by coming home late the rule would be a meaning postulate saying that promising involves fulfillment. Toumela's thesis is strained; in any case it requires the addition of a theory about the extent of rule-governed behavior.

13 Two exceptions: Bach (1978 and forthcoming) argues against (IT); Meiland (1963) argues for it.

Chapter 2

1 Levison and Thalberg also broach this fundamental question (Thalberg 1972, chapter III); but they do so incidentally, since their main concern is to argue for the compatibility of causal and noncausal explanations of actions.

2 At one point Sellars denies that all immediate intendings issue from practical reasoning. He says "volitions [immediate intendings] are not tryings. To try to do *A* is to do one or more things which one thinks likely in the circumstances to constitute doing *A*. Nor are volitions choosings. One can will to do *A* without choosing to do *A* rather than something else. . . . Nor are volitions decisions: *a volition need not be the culmination of a process of deliberation or practical reasoning*" (1966b, p. 156; italics different in text). Thus, although his writings often suggest that immediate intendings always issue from practical reasoning and he is often interpreted as holding this view, I doubt that it is Sellars's 'official' position.

Chapter 3

1 One issue that this resolution to the problem of recurrence faces is stating the conditions under which two or more events are type-identical. I would contend that there is no uniform, abstract criterion, but rather, with respect to recurrence, type identity depends crucially on pragmatic or contextual features. Suppose that Gordon shot Jack and Pat shot Gordon. Did Gordon and Pat perform the same type of

action? It depends on the context. If the background concerned whether the killings resulted from stab wounds or gunshot wounds, the answer is 'yes'; but if the context makes it clear that Gordon shot Jack because of meanness but Pat shot Gordon as a matter of self-defense, the answer is 'no.' For a context-dependent account of recurrence on a particularist event theory, see Brand (1976).

2 For further discussion of the above issues, see Martin (1976), and Brand (1976b).

3 See Brand (1977), where I argued for a similar, though stronger thesis about identity conditions.

4 Tye (1979), for instance, in his comments on Brand (1977) does not draw this distinction (also see Brand, 1979).

5 'Leibniz's Law' is a proper name for this criterion, not an historically accurate description of Leibniz's view.

6 Strictly speaking, as Brody (1980) observes, '$(x)(x = x)$' must be added to Leibniz's Law for a complete theory of identity.

7 See Lombard (1979) for an interesting attempt to provide the additional necessary conditions. One problem is the following. Existent objects do not form an ontological kind; it is an 'unnatural' kind, constructed from others. In order to rule out these cases, Lombard requires that a nondisjunctive statement of identity be available for an ontological kind (p. 429). That is, F in (IC) is to be a nondisjunctive predicate. However, this resolution only pushes the problem back a step: predicates can be constructed that are logically nondisjunctive but equivalent to disjunctive ones—recall Goodman's "grue." Moreover this resolution precludes genuine ontological kinds from having disjunctive identity conditions, and that is a substantive matter, not to be ruled on for technical reasons alone.

8 Some philosophers have argued that there is no one best characterization of personal identity, that our intuitions on personal identity are not consistent (see, e.g., Parfit, 1971). I take it that these philosophers would deny the presumption that there is one best characterization of the ontological kind persons.

9 An interesting network of systems to consider in this regard are E. J. Lemmon's E-systems, which do not include the Gödel necessitation rule: see Lemmon (1957, 1966) and Brand and Swain (1976). At this point I do not rule out the possibility that a relevance logic would provide the best interpretation of the operator in (D3.2): see Anderson and Belnap (1975) and Walton (1979).

10 Refraining, omittings, and so on, which may seem to be negative events, are actually positive, ordinary events of a specific sort. Basically a person refrains from performing something just in case he does something else in order to prevent himself (that is, make it causally impossible) that he perform the original act. Thus the patrolman refrains from shooting the fleeing youth just in case he does something, say, keep his arm at his side in order to make it causally impossible that he shoot the fleeing youth. Related types of acts, such as omittings and lettings happen, can be defined in terms of refraining. See Brand (1971); cf. Walton (1980).

11 Davidson made this response in personal communication.

12 See Brand (1977) for a comparison of the *extension* of Kim's proposal and the necessary spatiotemporal coincidence one.

13 For simplicity I will often leave out the spatiotemporal components of an event-identity sentence.

14 Thanks to John Carroll for discussion of this and related points.

Chapter 4

1 There is some uncertainty in the philosophical literature about the use of the words 'object' and 'content' when talking about attitudes. Suppose that I desire to eat that

apple. Some philosophers (e.g., Castañeda, 1975, and Lewis, 1979) designate *what is desired*—or believed or intended—the *object* of the attitude. In the case of *de dicto* belief, for instance, the object is allegedly a proposition. Other philosophers (e.g., Chisholm, 1981) would say that the apple is the object of my desire and what I desire to do with the apple is the *content* of my attitude. I find neither usage wholly felicitous. Talk about the objects of attitudes seems more natural when the ontological status of what attitudes express is at issue. Talk about the contents of attitudes seems more natural when the semantic features of what attitudes express is at issue. For instance, if the issue is the truth conditions for ascribing an attitude to other persons, then the discussion is most naturally couched in terms of *contents*. Since the primary focus of this chapter is ontological, I shall mostly talk about the objects of attitudes. But when the focus shifts to semantical features of attitudes, I will shift to talk about contents. As far as I can tell, nothing substantive depends on whether 'object' or 'content' is used. I will, therefore, use that mode of expression which is most natural.

2 At least I take attitude-assimilationism to be Castañeda's 'official' position in his major work in action theory (1975). However, there are hints (1975, chapter 10) that his view is more complex than pure attitude-assimilationism; and in recent discussion and writing (explicitly, 1982), it is clear that he has given up pure attitude-assimilationism. See section 3 below. For additional discussions of Castañeda's views, see Bratman (1983), Chisholm (1979), and Gustafson (1980).

3 To avoid confusion, let us reserve 'transparent' and 'opaque' for talk about sentences and '*de re*' and '*de dicto*' (and '*de se*') for talk about mental states. I was alerted to these issues by Mike Harnish.

4 This is a simplifying assumption. There are difficulties for the view that propositions are ordered pairs of objects and properties, the major one being that it individuates propositions too grossly. Suppose that John = the least loyal person. Then

    (i) $\langle$John,λx(x is honest)$\rangle$
    (ii) $\langle$The least loyal person,λx(x is honest)$\rangle$

name the *same* proposition, since a single object is the first member of each ordered pair. But it is highly implausible to think that (i) and (ii) name the same proposition. Neither the orthodox nor the possible-worlds construals of propositions yields this result. The set of worlds in which (i) is exemplified is distinct from that in which (ii) is exemplified, since John is not the least loyal person in all the worlds in which he exists. There are various ways in which one might attempt to repair this view about propositions. One possibility is to make the proposition an ordered triple of a name or description of an object, a function f, and a property. The function f is to play the role of rigidly attaching the name to the object named. However, it is difficult to construct f in a nonquestion-begging way.

5 The principle required to make this argument sound is actually more complex than that given in the text. A reasonable approximation is:

If (i) F_1 and F_2 are species of F, (ii) F_1 does not cause G, and (iii) there is no F^* such that F_2 is a species of F^*, F_1 is not a species of F^*, and being a F^* is causally necessary for being a G, then F_2 does not cause G,

where the variables range over kinds of events that are distinct. For the argument at hand, let F_1 be believing, F_2 be intending, F be fully endorsing and G be action. Clause (iii) is needed to account for threshold properties (as Steven Lee has pointed out to me). Without (iii), a counterinstance could be generated by letting F_1 be being a quantity of water at 210°, F_2 be being a quantity of water at 215°, F be being hot water and G be being boiling water. In this case there exists an F^*, being water over 210°, such that (iii) is false.

Castañeda has two complaints about this principle. He says, first: "Here is a counterexample schema: Let a genus F have just two species F_1 and F_2; hence, conditions (i) and (iii) are satisfied; consider the causal effects depending only on the specific difference constitutive of F_2; hence, both (ii) is true and the consequent . . . false" (1983b, p. 414). But Castañeda underestimates the force of condition (iii). The final part of that condition serves to exclude cases of causal effects depending only on the constitutive differences of species of F. It does *not* follow from F's having just two species, F_1 and F_2, that there fails to exist a genus to which F_1 belongs but not F_2 (or conversely) such that being a member of this genus is causally necessary for being a G. To sustain his criticism, Castañeda would have to say that there is no genus distinct from F, to which F_1 belongs but not F_2 and conversely. There may be such cases when we reach the acme of the genus-species hierarchy, though that seems doubtful. But for cases of genus-species in the middle of the hierarchy, the type of case that concerns us, there will be genera, distinct from F, to which F_1 belongs but not F_2, and conversely.

Castañeda points out that intending and believing are not the only two species of endorsing; others are endorsing a command, forming a question, and so on. He then says: "Hence, condition (iii) of [the] causal principle is not fulfilled, since any effect issuing from the endorsing rehearsal of an intention will have as a necessary condition the presence of a middle generic property that has as species both intending and any other of the varieties just mentioned" (1983b, p. 414). That is, suppose again F_1 is believing, F_2 intending, F fully endorsing, and G acting. Now let F^* be intending *and* endorsing of a command. Thus (iii) is not satisfied, since being an intending and endorsing of a command is causally necessary for action. (Actually, Castañeda should say that F^* is a *disjunctive* generic property, say being an intending *or* endorsing of a command.) This point does not tell against the truth of the principle, but rather the soundness of the argument in the text. If the antecedent is false, the detached consequent would have been shown true, and thus the conclusion, that intending and believing are not species of endorsing, will not have been demonstrated.

This second complaint does require amendment of the principle. The range of the variables is to be restricted to natural kinds. Artificially constructed properties, including Boolean ones such as disjunctive and conjunctive properties, are thereby excluded. This reply is attractive since the principle talks about causal relations among instances of types; and thus these types (properties) would stand in law-like relations. Types that stand in law-like relations are plausibly construed as natural kinds.

6 An equivalent to (26) seems to be

(26a) Pat intends that Richard raise his arm.

7 In terms of strategy, if the reduction of *de se* to *de re* is feasible, it becomes worth-while to attempt to argue that *de re* attitudes are reducible to *de dicto* ones, perhaps in the manner of Kaplan (1968) or Plantinga (1974). Part of the motivation to reduce *de re* attitudes to *de dicto* ones is removed if *de se* attitudes are not reducible to *de re* ones.

8 This account is based on some of Perry's constructive remarks (especially, 1979, pp. 16-21), though judging from his critical comments in (1977) and (1979), it is a view that he would disown.

9 Other types of examples might seem more plausible, even if as fanciful. Richard might be a member of some primitive tribe of desert people who never see themselves in mirrors or reflected in water. Upon viewing himself in a mirror for the first time, Richard may well not realize that it is he who he is seeing. Or while recover-

ing from amnesia, Richard might be told that Richard has certain characteristics, such as a distinctive appearance. Richard might also think that he himself lacks these characteristics, and thus fail to realize that he himself is Richard when looking in a mirror.

10 It might be possible to affect such a reduction if the semantical resources were increased, say, to include person-dependent and context-dependent propositional-like objects. If so, the value of that 'reduction' would have to be assessed on the basis of the cost of these additional commitments.

11 Lewis (1979) talks about the subject S uniquely describing x, rather than there being an identifying relation R*. As a result this view has sometimes been labeled 'the description theory of *de re* attitudes.' There seem to be problems, however, for stating the view in terms of unique descriptions, rather than identifying relations. There may not be sufficient descriptions available; moreover, if this view is to be compatible with psychological reality, persons might not stand in relation to external objects by means of intermediary linguistic descriptions, but rather through icons or some other representational device. Talk about identifying relations leaves unprejudiced the way in which the subject represents his relation to the external object.

12 Lewis (1979) proposes to deal with *de dicto* attitudes without a commitment to propositions, only to properties. For belief the proposal is, roughly: S believes that p iff S self-ascribes the property of inhabiting a possible world in which it is the case that p. *De dicto* attitudes are reduced, then, to *de se* ones without the intermediate step of *de re* attitudes toward abstract entities. Lewis's proposal appears more parsimonious than the one offered in the text. But that is illusory. The ontological cost is the reification of possible worlds and that cost is too high.

13 For a contrary proposal that supports Fodor's identification of the objects of attitudes with events in one's head, see Stich (1982).

Chapter 5

1 Audi (1973) defends the amended version of (DB).

2 For some textbook details on scaling see Coombs, Dawes, Tversky (1970, chapter 3).

3 Bratman (1981) points out a related difference between desiring and intending: reasons generated by intending are distinct from reasons generated by desires. This difference is apparent when the individual intends to bring about the means to an end but does not desire to do so. He then has a reason to act generated by his intention but not by his desire.

4 There is also a technical problem for (8). The usual semantics for conjunction in first-order logic is between sentences, not singular terms.

5 For simplicity, the temporal parameters have been omitted from (D5.2) through (D5.6). Favoring and opposing are doubly temporally indexed.

6 Quantifying over linguistic items, 'physical impossibility' and 'logical impossibility' can be alternatively defined as follows: it is physically impossible for S to A at t if there is a statement of the laws of nature and the conditions at $t - \Delta t$ such that it is inconsistent with 'S A's at t'; and it is logically impossible for S to A at t if 'S A's at t' is inconsistent with the truths of logic and mathematics or with some analytic truths.

7 I thank James Hallmark for helpful discussion on this chapter.

Chapter 6

1 It is unclear whether the first conjunct in Davidson's (1978) proposal is purely cognitive or whether it makes reference to some motivational feature of intending. The text can support the interpretation that it is a judgment; it can be read as saying that the subject *believes that A*ing is desirable. In that case Davidson is proposing a purely cognitive account of intention.

2 The philosophical literature, surprisingly, has not always recognized that action involves monitoring and guidance of ongoing bodily activity. One exception is Bach (1978).

3 Notice that it will not do to object that someone can form arbitrarily complex beliefs by putting together extant ones. That objection rests on the principle 'if S believes that *p* and S believes that *q*, then S believes that *p* and *q*.' But this principle has counterinstances. A person might fail to put his beliefs together when, for example, they are garnered from different sources.

4 This example is related to ones that emerged as a result of discussions with Hugh McCann.

5 In this usage 'to naturalize N,' where the name of some philosophical area of inquiry replaces 'N,' such as 'epistemology,' or 'action theory,' means to show that that area is continuous with scientific theory. Not all persons who use this locution form agree. For example, it is sometimes held that an area is naturalized when it is given an analysis in purely causal terms. For example, to naturalize epistemology is to provide a causal analysis of belief, knowledge, perception, memory, and so on. This is epistemology without private mental representations. In my usage epistemology can be naturalized while including, for example, reference to private mental representations, if doing so makes epistemology continuous with science.

6 The folk psychological claim that some thinking is imagistic has received some recent experimental confirmation (see, e.g., Shepard and Podgorny, 1978, Kosslyn and Pomerantz, 1977, and especially Kosslyn, 1980). It remains an open question, however, whether imagistic thinking is functional. It might be that actual processing is nonimagistic: see Pylyshyn, 1973, 1978, 1981.

7 I am not unaware of the problem for Step (4) of how claims embedded in distinct theoretical structures are to be compared and contrasted. This problem is part of the general issue of meaning change within a theory (or sequence of theories) and of incommensurable predicates.

Chapter 7

1 But cf. Brand (1980).

2 Other authors have also observed that the event initiating action continues past the point of initiation. Bach (1978) speaks about receptive representations, which monitor activity, and effective representations, which guide it. These representations alternate throughout the duration of the activity. (Bach (1978, p. 378, n. 12) identifies effective representations with memory images.) Searle (1979, 1981) distinguishes between prior intentions and intentions-in-action. The former resemble representations of complex activity formed as a result of planning; and the latter resemble guidance and control mechanisms. I might add in passing that Bach and Searle seem to think that action initiation is purely cognitive, or at least these papers provide no unequivocal support for the claim that there is a noncognitive component in the cause of action.

3 That is, the subject can have no further control by means of the already initiated action. Of course he or she could perform *another* action that interrupts the effects of the first one.

4 Greenwald (1970) is aware that some activities are best explained by servo-mechanisms; Goldman (1976) does not discuss this possibility. For a good summary and historical perspective on physiological servomechanisms see Gallistel (1980).

5 The most extensive development of a dynamic action theory is by John W. Atkinson and David Birch, called 'The Dynamics of Action.' See Atkinson and Birch (1970, 1978) and Birch et al (1974); also see Brand (1980b) and Kim (1980), as well as Brandt (1979).

6 Attending involves perception and memory. If Neisser (1976) and others who claim that perception and memory involve the active formation and use of schemata are correct, then the evidence favors some sort of Cause Theory of attention, though not the version espoused by James.

Chapter 8

1 A distinction sometimes is made between computer simulation models and artificial intelligence ones: the former attempt to simulate, or copy, actual human processing, whereas the latter attempt to achieve the end result of the processing independently of the way humans do it. In practice no sharp distinction can be made. Simulation models do not copy, in every detail and on every level, human processing; and artificial intelligence models often copy human procedures, since that may be the only known way to achieve the end results.

2 See chapter 1, section 7.

3 Henceforth, unless otherwise stated, 'scripts' will be used to include I-scripts and 'plans' will be used to include I-plans. If only I-scripts or I-plans are at issue, 'I-script' or 'I-plan' will be used.

4 See Schank and Abelson (1977, chapter 5) and Wilensky (1978) for some discussion of these matters.

5 'Conceptual Dependency' is used ambiguously in Schank and Abelson (1977). It refers both to the goal side of representational structures and to the representational language. When talking about the artificial language used in the representational structures, I shall say 'CD.'

6 Cf. Dresher and Hornstein (1976). Although Dresher and Hornstein's criticisms of language study by AI is misdirected—they fail to see that the main interest is performance, not competence, and that performance is a legitimate 'scientific' subject—they raise some difficulties for the types of translations Schank requires (pp. 363 ff.). Cf. the replies by Schank and Wilensky (1977), Winograd (1977), and Lakoff (1978).

7 Thanks to Mike Harnish for this example.

8 Not all who hold that there are schemata for event sequences claim that they are serially ordered: see especially Rumelhart (1975, 1977).

9 Schank (1980b) suggests that there is an exception to this general claim. If some unusual event occurs during the conduct of a script, or if the order of scenes in the script is altered, the entire episode tends to be the focus of recall (cf. Graesser et al, 1980).

10 Some of the points discussed in this section derive from Brand (forthcoming).

11 Fodor's notion of information encapsulation resembles Pylyshyn's (1980) idea of cognitive impenetrability, except that Pylyshyn seems to limit the direction of impenetrability from the top down, whereas Fodor's idea of encapsulation excludes information from any direction. So for example, if two perceptual input subsystems

interact but are not directly influenced by central processing, they are not encapsulated but are cognitively impenetrable.

12 Fodor labels the property of central representations being interconnected on a global basis 'isotropic' and the property of central representations being dependent on features of the entire system of representations 'Quinean.' Fodor (1983, pp. 101 ff.) appears to agree that these global properties are independent and gradational.

13 Cf. Bratman (1981) on bootstrap rationality and intention.

Chapter 9

1 There is an additional motivational theory that I do not examine here, Atkinson and Birch's (1970, 1978, Birch et al, 1974) Dynamics of Action. This theory has some interesting conceptual features, such as being based on an ontology of dispositions rather than events; but it has not attracted a great deal of attention, probably because it does not generate an independent experimental research program. In Brand (1980b) I argued that this line of approach is promising. I am no longer convinced that that is the case primarily because, once stripped of its ontological commitments, it fares no better than Hull's or Tolman's neobehavioristic theories. Indeed Atkinson and Birch's Dynamics of Action is really a metatheory, a generalization of earlier neobehaviorist accounts. (See Kim, 1980.)

2 Some philosophers, for example, Bratman (1981, and in discussion and unpublished papers), claim that a person has a plan only if he is moved to act on it. If that is so, then one cannot *have* a plan to rob the bank without being moved to do so, and that surely is counterintuitive.

3 Rejection of (C) is, of course, not limited to psychologists. Philosophical action theorists have sometimes done likewise (e.g., Brandt, 1979).

4 J. B. Wolfe, "Effectiveness of Token Rewards for Chimpanzees," *Comparative Psychological Monographs* 12, Serial No. 60, 1936. Discussed by Bolles (1975, pp. 448 ff.).

5 Drive level in persons is commonly taken to be correlated with anxiety, which might be measured by a questionnaire designed to elicit how the subject responds emotionally to aversive stimuli (e.g., the Mandler-Sarason Test Anxiety Questionnaire) or behaviorally by, for example, the strength of conditioned eyelid responses to air puffs.

6 See *supra* chapter 5, section 3.

7 Anderson (1983, pp. 1 ff.) appears to misinterpret the modularity thesis, at least Fodor's version of it. He argues for a unitary theory of the mind, in contrast to the faculty approach of Chomsky (and historically, Gall). But Anderson is really defending only a unitary theory of central processes—and even here he thinks that there is an ineliminable dualism. Fodor (1983) does not see central processes as modular. Rather input processes, such as vision, are modular; and Anderson seems not to disagree with that claim. However, one point of controversy that does remain is whether there is an encapsulated language faculty: Fodor argues that there is one; Anderson assumes that there is not one.

8 Thanks to David Kieras for comments on a draft of this chapter.

Bibliography

Abelson, Robert (1981). "Psychological Status of the Script Concept." *American Psychologist* 36, 715–729.

Achinstein, Peter (1974). "The Identity of Properties." *American Philosophical Quarterly* II, 257–275.

Alston, William (1967). "Motives and Motivation" in *The Encyclopedia of Philosophy*, Paul Edwards, ed., pp. 399–409. New York: Macmillan Co.

Anderson, Alan Ross, and Nuel Belnap, Jr. (1975). *Entailment: The Logic of Relevance and Necessity*. Princeton, N.J.: Princeton University Press.

Anderson, John R. (1976). *Language, Memory, and Thought*. Hillsdale, N.J.: Lawrence Erlbaum Associates.

Anderson, John R. (1978). "Arguments Concerning Representations for Mental Imagery." *Psychological Review* 85, 249–277.

Anderson, John R. (1980). *Cognitive Psychology and Its Implications*. San Francisco: W. H. Freeman.

Anderson, John R. (1983). *The Architecture of Cognition*. Cambridge, Mass.: Harvard University Press.

Anscombe, G. E. M. (1963). *Intention*, 2nd ed. Ithaca, N.Y.: Cornell University Press.

Atkinson, John W., and David Birch (1970). *The Dynamics of Action*. New York: Wiley.

Atkinson, John W., and David Birch (1978). *Introduction to Motivation*, 2nd ed. New York: D. Van Nostrand.

Audi, Robert (1973). "Intending." *Journal of Philosophy* 70, 387–402.

Aune, Bruce (1975). "Sellars on Practical Reason" in *Action, Knowledge, and Reality*, Hector-Neri Castañeda, ed., pp. 1–25. Indianapolis, Indiana; The Bobbs-Merrill Co.

Aune, Bruce (1979). *Reason and Action*. Dordrecht, Holland: D. Reidel.

Austin, John (1873). *Lectures on Jurisprudence*, 4th ed. London: John, Murray Ltd.

Baars, Bernard J., and Mark E. Mattson (1981). "Consciousness and Intention: A Framework and Some Evidence." *Cognition and Brain Theory* 4, 247–263.

Bach, Kent (1978). "A Representational Theory of Action." *Philosophical Studies* 34, 361–379.

Bach, Kent (1982). *"De re* Belief and Methodological Solipsism" in *Thought and Object*, Andrew Woodfield, ed., pp. 121–151. Oxford: The Clarendon Press.

Bach, Kent (forthcoming). "Decision, Intention, and Practical Reasoning."

Bach, Kent, and Robert M. Harnish (1979). *Linguistic Communication and Speech Acts*. Cambridge, Mass.: The MIT Press.

Bartlett, F. C. (1932). *Remembering*. London: Cambridge University Press.

Beardsley, Monroe (1978). "Intending" in *Values and Morals*, Alvin Goldman and Jaegwan Kim, eds., pp. 163–184. Dordrecht, Holland: D. Reidel.

Berkeley, George. *The Principles of Human Knowledge*, first published 1710.

Berkeley, George. *Three Dialogues Between Hylas and Philanous*, first published 1713.

Birch, David, John W. Atkinson, and Kenneth Bongort (1974). "Cognitive Control of Action" in *Cognitive Views on Human Motivation*, B. Weiner, ed., pp. 71–84.

Black, John W., and Gordon H. Bower (1979). "Episodes as Chunks in Narrative Memory." *Journal of Verbal Learning and Verbal Behavior* 18, 309–318.

Block, Ned (1980). "What is Functionalism?" in *Readings in Philosophy of Psychology*, Ned Block, ed., pp. 171–184. Cambridge, Mass.: Harvard University Press.

Boden, Margaret (1977). *Artificial Intelligence and Natural Man*. New York: Basic Books.

Boer, Steven, and William Lycan (1980). "Who, Me?." *The Philosophical Review* 89, 427–466.

Bolles, Robert C. (1972). "Reinforcement, Expectancy, and Learning." *Psychological Review* 79, 394–409.

Bolles, Robert C. (1975). *Theory of Motivation*, 2nd ed. New York: Harper & Row.

Bower, Gordon H., John B. Black, and Terrence J. Turner (1979). "Scripts in Memory for Text." *Cognitive Psychology* 9, 177–220.

Bradie, Michael, and Myles Brand, eds. (1980). *Action and Responsibility*. Bowling Green, Ohio: Bowling Green State University Press.

Brand, Myles, ed. (1970). *The Nature of Human Action*. Glenview, Ill.: Scott-Foresman.

Brand, Myles (1970b). "Causes of Actions." *Journal of Philosophy* 68, 932–947.

Brand, Myles (1971). "The Language of Not Doing." *American Philosophical Quarterly* 8, 45–53.

Brand, Myles (1976). "Particulars, Events, and Actions" in *Action Theory*, Brand and D. Walton, eds., pp. 133–157. Dordrecht, Holland: D. Reidel.

Brand, Myles (1976b). "Reply to Martin" in *Action Theory*, M. Brand and D. Walton, eds., pp. 193–196. Dordrecht, Holland: D. Reidel.

Brand, Myles (1976c). "Defining 'Causes'" in *The Nature of Causation*, M. Brand, ed., pp. 1–44. Urbana, Ill.: University of Illinois Press.

Brand, Myles (1976d). Review of *New Essays in the Philosophy of Mind*. *Dialogue* 15, 679–685.

Brand, Myles (1977). "Identity Conditions for Events." *American Philosophical Quarterly* 14, 329–337.

Brand, Myles (1979). "Causality" in *Current Research in Philosophy of Science*, P. Asquith and H. Kyburg, Jr., eds., pp. 252–281. East Lansing, Mich.: Philosophy of Science Association.

Brand, Myles (1979b). "On Tye's 'Brand on Event Identity.'" *Philosophical Studies* 36, 61–68.

Brand, Myles (1979c). "The Fundamental Question in Action Theory." *Nous* 13, 131–151.

Brand, Myles (1980). "Simultaneous Causation" in *Time and Cause: Essays Presented to Richard Taylor*, P. van Inwagen, ed., pp. 109–135. Dordrecht, Holland: D. Reidel.

Brand, Myles (1980b). "Philosophical Action Theory and the Foundations of Motivational Psychology" in *Action and Responsibility*, M. Bradie and M. Brand, eds., pp. 1–19. Bowling Green, Ohio: Bowling Green Studies in Applied Philosophy, vol. II.

Brand, Myles (1981). "Review of Thomson's *Acts and Other Events*." *Philosophy of Social Science* II, 485–494.

Brand, Myles (1982). "Cognition and Intention." *Erkenntnis* 18, 165–187.

Brand, Myles (forthcoming). "The Human Output System," *Grazer Philosophische Studien*.

Brand, Myles (1983). "Intending and Believing" in *Agent, Language and the Structure of the World: Essays in Honor of Hector-Neri Castañeda*, J. Tomberlin, ed., pp. 171–193. Indianapolis, Indiana: Hackett Publishing Co.

Brand, Myles, and Marshall Swain (1970). "On the Analysis of Causation." *Synthese* 21, 222–227.

Brand, Myles, and Marshall Swain (1976). "Causation and Causal Necessity." *Philosophical Studies* 29, 369–379.

Brand, Myles, and Douglas Walton, eds. (1976). *Action Theory*. Dordrecht, Holland: D. Reidel.

Brandt, Richard (1979). *A Theory of the Good and the Right*. Oxford: The Clarendon Press.

Bratman, Michael (1981). "Intention and Means-End Reasoning." *Philosophical Review* 90, 252–265.

Bratman, Michael (1983). "Intention, Volition and Practical Reason," paper presented to the Twelfth Annual Philosophy Colloquium, University of Dayton.

Bratman, Michael (1983b). "Castañeda's Theory of Thought and Action" in *Agent, Language, and the Structure of the World: Essays in Honor of Hector-Neri Castañeda*, J. Tomberlin, ed., pp. 149–170. Indianapolis, Indiana: Hackett Publishing Co.

Broadbent, D. E. (1958). *Perception and Communication*. London: Pergamon Press.

Brody, Baruch A. (1980). *Identity and Essence*. Princeton, N.J.: Princeton University Press.

Browne, D. A. (1975). "Can Desires Be Causes of Action?." *Canadian Journal of Philosophy*, Supplementary Volume No. 1, Part 2 ("New Essays in the Philosophy of Mind"), 145–158.

Byrne, Richard (1977). "Planning Meals: Problem-solving on a Real Data-base." *Cognition* 5, 287–332.

Care, Norman, and Charles Landesman, eds. (1968). *Readings in the Theory of Action*. Bloomington, Indiana: Indiana University Press.

Castañeda, Hector-Neri (1966). " 'He': A Study in the Logic of Self-Consciousness." *Ratio* 8, 130–157.

Castañeda, Hector-Neri (1967). "Indicators and Quasi-indicators." *American Philosophical Quarterly* 4, 85–100.

Castañeda, Hector-Neri (1968). "On the Logic of Attributions of Self-Knowledge to Others." *The Journal of Philosophy* 65, 439–456.

Castañeda, Hector-Neri (1969). "On the Phenomeno-Logic of the I." *Akten des XIV Internationalen Kongresses fuer Philosophie*, Vol. III (University of Vienna), 260–266.

Castañeda, Hector-Neri (1975). *Thinking and Doing*. Dordrecht, Holland: D. Reidel.

Castañeda, Hector-Neri (1975b). "Some Reflections on Wilfrid Sellars' Theory of Intentions" in *Action, Knowledge, and Reality*, H-N Castañeda, ed., pp. 27–54. Indianapolis, Indiana: The Bobbs-Merrill Co.

Castañeda, Hector-Neri (1976). "The Twofold Structure and the Unity of Practical Thinking" in *Action Theory*, M. Brand and D. Walton, eds., pp. 105–130. Dordrecht, Holland: D. Reidel.

Castañeda, Hector-Neri (1979). "Intensionality and Identity in Human Action and Philosophical Method." *Nous* 13, 235–260.

Castañeda, Hector-Neri (1980). "The Doing of Thinking: Intending and Willing" in *Action and Responsibility*, M. Bradie and M. Brand, eds., pp. 80–92. Bowling Green, Ohio: Bowling Green State University Press.

Castañeda, Hector-Neri (1983). "Indexical Reference and Causal Diagrams in Intentional Action," paper presented to Twelfth Annual Philosophy Colloquium, University of Dayton.

Castañeda, Hector-Neri (1983b). "Response to Brand: Intentions, Properties, and Propositions" in *Agent, Language and the Structure of the World: Essays in Honor of*

Hector-Neri Castañeda, J. Tomberlin, ed., pp. 411–417. Indianapolis, Indiana: Hackett Publishing Co.

Chisholm, Roderick (1966). "Freedom and Action" in *Freedom and Determinism,* K. Lehrer, ed., pp. 28–44. New York: Random House.

Chisholm, Roderick (1970). "Events and Propositions." *Nous* 4, 15–24.

Chisholm, Roderick (1976). "The Agent as Cause" in *Action Theory,* M. Brand and D. Walton, eds., pp. 199–211. Dordrecht, Holland: D. Reidel.

Chisholm, Roderick (1976b). *Person and Object.* La Salle, Ill.: Open Court.

Chisholm, Roderick (1979). "Castañeda's *Thinking and Doing.*" *Nous* 13, 385–396.

Chisholm, Roderick (1980). "The Logic of Believing." *Pacific Philosophical Quarterly* 61, 35–53.

Chisholm, Roderick (1981). *The First Person.* Minneapolis, Minn.: University of Minnesota Press.

Chisholm, Roderick, and Ernst Sosa (1966). "On the Logic of 'Intrinsically Better'." *American Philosophical Quarterly* 3, 244–249.

Chisholm, Roderick, and Richard Taylor (1960). "Making Things to Have Happened." *Analysis* 20, 73–78.

Chomsky, Noam (1959). "Review of B. F. Skinner's *Verbal Behavior.*" *Language* 35, 26–58.

Churchland, Paul (1979). *Scientific Realism and the Plasticity of Mind.* New York: Cambridge University Press.

Churchland, Paul M. (1981). "Eliminative Materialism and Propositional Attitudes." *The Journal of Philosophy* 78, 67–90.

Clark, Romane (1970). "Concerning the Logic of Predicate Modifiers." *Nous* 4, 311–335.

Collier, G. H., E. Hirsch, and P. H. Hamlin (1972). "The Ecological Determinants of Reinforcements." *Physiological Review* 9, 705–716.

Coombs, Clyde, Robyn Dawes, and Amos Tversky (1970). *Mathematical Psychology.* Englewood Cliffs, New Jersey: Prentice-Hall.

Cranach, Mario von, and Rom Harre, eds. (1982). *The Analysis of Action.* Cambridge: Cambridge University Press.

Cummins, Robert (1977). "Programs in the Explanation of Behavior." *Philosophy of Science* 44, 269–287.

Danto, Arthur (1973). *Analytic Philosophy of Action.* Cambridge: Cambridge University Press.

Davidson, Donald (1963). "Actions, Reasons, and Causes." *Journal of Philosophy* 60, 685–700.

Davidson, Donald (1967). "The Logical Form of Action Sentences" in *The Logic of Division and Action,* N. Rescher, ed., pp. 81–95. Pittsburgh: University of Pittsburgh Press.

Davidson, Donald (1967b). "Causal Relations." *Journal of Philosophy* 64, 691–703.

Davidson, Donald (1970). "The Individuation of Events" in *Essays in Honor of Carl G. Hempel,* N. Rescher et al, eds., pp. 216–234. Dordrecht, Holland: D. Reidel.

Davidson, Donald (1970b). "Events as Particulars." *Nous* 4, 25–32.

Davidson, Donald (1971). "Eternal vs. Ephemeral Events." *Nous* 5, 335–349.

Davidson, Donald (1973). "Freedom to Act" in *Essays on Freedom of Action,* Ted Honerick, ed., pp. 137–156. London: Routledge and Kegan Paul.

Davidson, Donald (1978). "Intention" in *Philosophy of History and Action,* Y. Yovel, ed., pp. 41–60. Dordrecht, Holland: D. Reidel.

Davis, Lawrence (1975). "Action." *Canadian Journal of Philosophy,* supplementary Vol. No. 1, Part 2 ("New Essays in the Philosophy of Mind"), 129–144.

Davis, Lawrence (1979). *Theory of Action*. Englewood Cliffs, N.J.: Prentice-Hall.

Dennett, Daniel (1969). *Content and Consciousness*. New York: Humanities Press.

Dennett, Daniel (1978). *Brainstorms*. Cambridge, Mass.: Bradford Books.

Deutsch, J., and D. Deutsch (1963). "Attention: Some Theoretical Considerations." *Psychological Review* 70, 80–90.

Dinsmoor, James A. (1982). "Is this Defense Needed?" (Response to Masterson and Crawford, 1982). *The Behavioral and Brain Sciences* 5, 679.

Dresher, B. Elan, and Norbert Hornstein (1976). "On Some Supposed Contributions of Artificial Intelligence to the Scientific Study of Language." *Cognition* 4, 321–398.

Dresher, B. Elan, and Norbert Hornstein (1977). "Reply to Winegrad." *Cognition* 5, 379–392.

Dreyfus, Hubert L. (1979). *What Computers Can't Do*, revised edition. New York: Harper and Row.

Feldman, Richard, and Edward Wierenga (1981). "Identity Conditions and Events," *Canadian Journal of Philosophy* 11, 77–90.

Fitzsimons, J. T. (1972). "Thirst." *Physiological Review* 52, 468–561.

Fodor, Jerry (1975). *The Language of Thought*. Cambridge, Mass.: Harvard University Press.

Fodor, Jerry (1978). "Propositional Attitudes." *The Monist* 61, 501–523 (reprinted in Jerry Fodor (1981b) *Representations*, pp. 177–203).

Fodor, Jerry (1981). "Something on the State of the Art" in Jerry Fodor, (1981b) *Representations*, pp. 1–31.

Fodor, Jerry (1981). *Representations*. Cambridge, Mass.: The MIT Press.

Fodor, Jerry (1983). *The Modularity of Mind*. Cambridge, Mass.: The MIT Press.

Frankfurt, Harry (1978). "The Problem of Action." *American Philosophical Quarterly* 15, 157–62.

Galambos, James A., and Lance J. Rips (1982). "Memory for Routines: Just One Thing After Another?" *Journal of Verbal Learning and Verbal Behavior* 21, 260–281.

Gallistel, C. R. (1980). *The Organization of Action: A New Synthesis*. Hillsdale, N.J.: Lawrence Erlbaum.

Geach, P. T. (1960). "Ascriptivism." *The Philosophical Review* 69, 221–225.

Goldman, Alvin (1970). *A Theory of Human Action*. Englewood Cliffs, N.J.: Prentice-Hall.

Goldman, Alvin (1976). "The Volitional Theory Revisited" in *Action Theory*, Brand and Walton, eds., pp. 67–84. Dordrecht, Holland: D. Reidel.

Gould, Alan, and John Shotter (1977). *Human Action and its Psychological Investigation*. London: Routledge & Kegan Paul.

Graesser, Arthur C., Stanley B. Woll, Daniel J. Kowalski, and Donald A. Smith (1980). "Memory for Typical and Atypical Actions in Scripted Activities." *Journal of Experimental Psychology: Human Learning and Memory* 6, 503–515.

Greenwald, Anthony (1970). "Sensory Feedback Mechanisms in Performance Control: with Special Reference to the Ideo-Motor Mechanism." *Psychological Review* 77, 73–99.

Greenwald, Anthony (1970b). "A Choice Reaction Time Test of Ideomotor Theory." *Journal of Experimental Psychology* 86, 20–25.

Greenwald, Anthony (1970c). "A Double Stimulation Test of Ideomotor Theory with Implications for Selective Attention." *Journal of Experimental Psychology* 84, 392–398.

Grether, David M. (1980). "Bayes Rule as a Descriptive Model: The Representativeness Heuristic." *The Quarterly Journal of Economics* 95, 537–557.

Grice, Russell (1967). *The Grounds of Moral Judgment*. New York: Cambridge University Press.

Gustafson, Donald (1980). "Castañeda's Intentions: A Critical Study of Castañeda's *Thinking and Doing.*" *Synthese* 44, 247–284.

Hampshire, Stuart, and H. L. A. Hart (1958). "Decision, Intention, and Certainty." *Mind* 67, 1–12.

Hart, H. L. A. (1948–1949). "The Ascription of Responsibility and Rights." *Proceedings of the Aristotelian Society* 49, 171–194.

Hart, H. L. A. (1968). *Punishment and Responsibility.* Oxford: Oxford University Press.

Hayes, P. J. (1980). "The Logic of Frames" in D. Metzing, ed., *Frame Conceptions and Text Understanding,* pp. 46–61. New York: Walter de Gruyter.

Hilgard, Ernest R., and Gordon H. Bower (1975). *Theories of Learning.* 4th ed. Englewood Cliffs, New Jersey: Prentice-Hall.

Hobbes, Thomas. *Leviathan,* first published 1651.

Hochberg, J. E. (1970). "Attention, Organization, and Consciousness" in *Attention: Contemporary Theory and Analysis,* D. I. Mostofsky, ed., pp. 91–124. New York: Appleton-Century-Crofts.

Horgan, Terence (1980). "Nonrigid Event-Designators and the Modal Individuation of Events." *Philosophical Studies* 37, 341–351.

Hornsby, Jennifer (1980). *Actions.* London: Routledge & Kegan Paul.

Hull, C. L. (1931). "Goal Attraction and Directing Ideas Conceived as Habit Phenomena." *Psychological Review* 38, 487–506.

Hull, C. L. (1943). *Principles of Behavior.* New York: Appleton-Century-Crofts.

Hull, C. L. (1951). *Essentials of Behavior.* New Haven, Conn.: Yale University Press.

Hume, David. *A Treatise of Human Nature,* first published 1739.

Hume, David. *Enquiry Concerning Human Understanding,* first published 1748.

James, William (1890). *The Principles of Psychology,* vol. 2. Reprinted by Dover Publications (New York, 1950).

Jeffrey, Richard (1965). *The Logic of Decision.* New York: McGraw-Hill.

Kahneman, Daniel, Paul Slovic, and Amos Tversky, eds. (1982). *Judgment under Uncertainty: Heuristics and Biases.* Cambridge: Cambridge University Press.

Kaplan, David (1968). "Quantifying In." *Synthese* 19, 178–214.

Kaplan, David (1978). "Dthat" in *Contemporary Perspectives in the Philosophy of Language,* P. French, T. Vehling Jr., H. Wettstein, eds., pp. 383–400. Minneapolis, Minnesota: University of Minnesota Press.

Kim, Jaegwon (1970). "Events and Their Descriptions" in *Essays in Honor of Carl G. Hempel,* N. Rescher et al, eds., pp. 198–215. Dordrecht, Holland: D. Reidel.

Kim, Jaegwon (1973). "Causation, Nomic Subsumption, and the Concept of Event." *Journal of Philosophy* 70, 217–236.

Kim, Jaegwon (1974). "Noncausal Connections." *Nous* 8, 41–52.

Kim, Jaegwon (1976). "Events as Property Exemplifications" in *Action Theory,* M. Brand and D. Walton, eds., pp. 159–177. Dordrecht, Holland: D. Reidel.

Kim, Jaegwon (1980). "The Role of Intention in Motivational Psychology: Comments on Brand" in *Action and Responsibility,* M. Bradie and M. Brand, eds., pp. 20–26. Bowling Green, Ohio: Bowling Green State University Press.

Kimble, Gregory A., and Lawrence C. Perlmuter (1970). "The Problem of Volition." *Psychological Review* 77, 361–384.

Körner, Stephan (1976). *Experience and Conduct.* Cambridge: Cambridge University Press.

Kosslyn, Stephen M. (1980). *Image and Mind.* Cambridge, Mass.: Harvard University Press.

Kosslyn, Stephen M., and James R. Pomerantz (1977). "Imagery, Propositions, and the Form of Internal Representations." *Cognitive Psychology* 9, 52–76.

Kripke, Saul (1972). "Naming and Necessity" in *Semantics of Natural Language*, D. Davidson and G. Harmon, eds., pp. 253–355, 763–769. Dordrecht, Holland: D. Reidel.

Kripke, Saul (1982). *Wittgenstein on Rules and Private Language*. Cambridge, Mass.: Harvard University Press.

Lakoff, George (1978). "Some Remarks on AI and Linguistics." *Cognitive Science* 2, 267–275.

Lehrer, Keith, ed. (1966). *Freedom and Determinism*. New York: Random House.

Lewin, Kurt (1935). *A Dynamic Theory of Personality*. New York: McGraw-Hill.

Lewin, Kurt (1938). *The Conceptual Representation and the Measurement of Psychological Forces*. Durham, N.C.: Duke University Press.

Lewis, C. I. (1946). *An Analysis of Knowledge and Valuation*. LaSalle, Illinois: Open Court Publishing Co.

Lewis, David (1979). "Attitudes *De Dicto* and *De Se*." *The Philosophical Review* 87, 513–543.

Locke, John. *Essay Concerning Human Understanding*, first published 1690.

Lombard, Lawrence Brian (1979). "Events." *Canadian Journal of Philosophy* 9, 425–460.

MacCorquodale, Kenneth, and Paul E. Meehl (1954). "Edward C. Tolman" in William K. Estes et al, *Modern Learning Theory*, pp. 177–266. New York: Appleton-Century-Crofts.

Mackenzie, Brian (1977). *Behaviorism and the Limits of Scientific Method*. Atlantic Highlands, N.J.: Humanities Press.

Mackie, J. L. (1974). *The Cement of the Universe*. Oxford: The Clarendon Press.

Mandler, J. M., and N. J. Johnson (1977). "Remembrance of Things Parsed: Story Structure and Recall." *Cognitive Psychology* 7, 111–151.

Martin, R. M. (1976). "Events and Actions: Some Comments on Brand and Kim" in *Action Theory*, M. Brand and D. Walton, eds., pp. 179–192. Dordrecht, Holland: D. Reidel.

Masterson, Fred A., and Mary Crawford (1982). "The Defense Motivation System: A Theory of Avoidance Behavior" (with commentary). *The Behavioral and Brain Sciences* 5, 661–696.

McCann, Hugh (1974). "Volition and Basic Action." *The Philosophical Review* 83, 451–473.

McCann, Hugh (1983). "Comments on Brand's 'The Output System'," paper presented to the American Philosophical Association, Pacific Division.

Meiland, Jack (1963). "Are There Unintentional Actions?" *Philosophical Review* 72, 377–381.

Meiland, Jack (1970). *The Nature of Intention*. London: Methuen & Co. Ltd.

Melden, A. I. (1956). "Action." *Philosophical Review* 65, 529–541.

Melden, A. I. (1961). *Free Action*. London: Routledge & Kegan Paul.

Mill, John Stuart (1872). *A System of Logic*, 8th ed. Reprinted by Longmans, Green and Co., Ltd. (London, 1961).

Miller, George A., Eugene Galanter, and Karl H. Pribram (1960). *Plans and the Structure of Behavior*. New York: Holt, Rinehart, and Winston.

Miller, N. E. (1948). "Studies of Fear as an Acquirable Drive: I. Fear as Motivation and Fear-reduction as Reinforcement in the Learning of New Responses." *Journal of Experimental Psychology* 38, 89–101.

Minsky, Marvin (1975). "A Framework for Representing Knowledge" in *The Psychology of Computer Vision*, P. H. Winston, ed., pp. 211–277. New York: McGraw-Hill.

Moray, Neville (1969). *Attention: Selective Processes in Vision and Hearing*. London: Hutchinson.

Mowrer, O. H. (1960). *Learning Theory and Behavior*. New York: Wiley.

Neisser, Ulric (1976). *Cognition and Reality: Principles and Implications of Cognitive Psychology*. San Francisco; W. H. Freeman.

Newell, A. (1973). "Production Systems: Models of Control Structures" in *Visual Information Processing*, W. G. Chase, ed., pp. 463–526. New York: Academic Press.

Newell, A., and H. Simon (1972). *Human Problem Solving*. Englewood Cliffs, N.J.: Prentice-Hall.

Norman, Donald A. (1968). "Toward a Theory of Memory and Attention." *Psychological Review* 75, 522–536.

Norman, Donald A. (1969). *Memory and Attention: An Introduction to Human Information Processing*. New York: John Wiley and Sons.

Norman, Donald (1981). "Categorization of Action Slips." *Psychological Review* 88, 1–15.

Norman, Donald A., and Tim Shallice (1980). "Attention to Action: Willed and Automatic Control of Behavior." CHIP Technical Report 99, Center for Human Information Processing, University of California, San Diego.

Parfit, Derek (1971). "Personal Identity." *Philosophical Review* 80, 3–27.

Peacocke, Christopher (1979). "Deviant Causal Chains" in *Midwest Studies in Philosophy*, vol. iv, P. French, T. Vehling Jr., H. Wettstein, eds., pp. 123–155. Minneapolis, Minnesota: University of Minnesota Press.

Peacocke, Christopher (1979b). *Holistic Explanation*. Oxford: Clarendon Press.

Perry, John (1977). "Frege on Demonstrative." *Philosophical Review* 86, 474–497.

Perry, John (1979). "The Problem of the Essential Indexical." *Nous* 13, 3–21.

Peters, R. S. (1958). *The Concept of Motivation*. London: Routledge & Kegan Paul.

Plantinga, Alvin (1974). *The Nature of Necessity*. Oxford: Clarendon Press.

Pollock, John (1976). *Subjunctive Reasoning*. Dordrecht, Holland: D. Reidel.

Prichard, H. A. (1949). *Moral Obligation*. Oxford: Clarendon Press.

Pylyshyn, Zenon W. (1973). "What the Mind's Eye Tells the Mind's Brain: A Critique of Mental Imagery." *Psychological Bulletin* 80, 1–24.

Pylyshyn, Zenon W. (1978). "Imagery and Artificial Intelligence" in *Minnesota Studies in the Philosophy of Science* Vol. 9, Wade Savage, ed., pp. 19–55. Minneapolis, Minnesota: University of Minnesota Press.

Pylyshyn, Zenon W. (1980). "Computation and Cognition: Issues in the Foundations of Cognitive Science." *The Behavioral and Brain Sciences* 3, 111–169.

Pylyshyn, Zenon W. (1981). "The Imagery Debate: Analogue Media versus Tacit Knowledge." *Psychological Review* 87.

Quine, W. V. O. (1956). "Quantifiers and Propositional Attitudes." *Journal of Philosophy* 53, 177–187.

Quine, W. V. O. (1960). *Word and Object*. Cambridge, Mass.: The MIT Press.

Rosch, E., C. B. Mervis, W. Grey, D. Johnson, and P. Boyes-Braem (1976). "Basic Objects in Natural Categories." *Cognitive Psychology* 3, 382–439.

Rumelhart, David (1975). "Notes on a Schema for Stories" in *Representation and Understanding*, D. G. Bobrow and A. M. Collins, eds., pp. 211–236. New York: Academic Press.

Rumelhart, David (1977). "Understanding and Summarizing Brief Stories" in *Basic Processes in Reading: Perception and Comprehension*, D. Laberge and S. J. Samuels, eds., pp. 265–303. Hillsdale, N.J.: Lawrence Erlbaum Associates.

Rumelhart, David, Peter H. Lindsay, and Donald A. Norman (1972). "A Process Model for Long-term Memory" in *Organization of Memory*, E. Tulsing and W. Donaldson, eds. New York: Academic Press.

Rumelhart, David, and Donald A. Norman (1982). "Simulating a Skilled Typist: A Study of Skilled Cognitive-Motor Performance." *Cognitive Science* 6, 1–32.

Ryle, Gilbert (1949). *The Concept of Mind.* London: Hutchinson.

Schank, Roger (1972). "Conceptual Dependency: A Theory of Natural Language Understanding." *Cognitive Psychology* 3, 552–631.

Schank, Roger (1975). *Conceptual Information Processing.* Amsterdam: North Holland.

Schank, Roger (1979). "Reminding and Memory Organization: An Introduction to MOPs." Research Report #170, Yale University, Department of Computer Science.

Schank, Roger (1980). "Language and Memory." *Cognitive Science* 4, 243–284.

Schank, Roger (1980b). "Failure-Driven Memory." *Cognition and Brain Theory* 4, 41–60.

Schank, Roger (1982). *Dynamic Memory.* Cambridge: Cambridge University Press.

Schank, Roger, and Robert Abelson (1977). *Scripts, Plans, Goals and Understanding.* Hillsdale, N.J.: Lawrence Erlbaum Associates.

Schank, Roger, and Robert Wilensky (1977). "Response to Dresher and Hornstein." *Cognition* 5, 133–145.

Searle, John (1979). "The Intentionality of Intention and Action." *Inquiry* 22, 253–280.

Searle, John (1981). "Intentionality and Method." *Journal of Philosophy* 78, 720–733.

Sellars, Wilfrid (1963). *Science, Perception and Reality.* London: Routledge and Kegan Paul.

Sellars, Wilfrid (1966). "Thought and Action" in *Freedom and Determinism,* K. Lehrer, ed., pp. 105–139. New York: Random House.

Sellars, Wilfrid (1966b). "Fatalism and Determinism" in *Freedom and Determinism,* K. Lehrer, ed., pp. 141–174. New York: Random House.

Sellars, Wilfrid (1967). *Science and Metaphysics.* London: Routledge and Kegan Paul.

Sellars, Wilfrid (1973). "Action and Events." *Nous* 7, 179–202.

Sellars, Wilfrid (1976). "Volitions Re-affirmed" in *Action Theory,* M. Brand and D. Walton, eds., pp. 47–66. Dordrecht, Holland: D. Reidel.

Sellars, Wilfrid (1981). "Mental Events." *Philosophical Studies* 39, 325–345.

Sen, Amartya Kumar (1970). *Collective Choice and Social Welfare.* San Francisco: Holden Day.

Shaffer, L. H. (1976). "Intention and Performance." *Psychological Review* 83, 375–393.

Sheffield, F. D. (1966). "New Evidence on the Drive-Induction Theory of Reinforcement" in *Current Research in Motivation,* R. Haber, ed., pp. 111–122. New York: Holt, Rinehart & Winston.

Shepard, R. N., and L. Cooper, eds. (1982). *Mental Images and Their Transformations.* Cambridge, Mass.: Bradford/MIT Press.

Shepard, R. N., and J. Metzler (1971). "Mental Rotation of Three-dimensional Objects." *Science* 171, 701–703.

Shepard, R. N., and P. Podgorney (1978). "Cognitive Processes that Resemble Perceptual Processes" in *Handbook of Learning and Cognitive Processes* vol. 5, W. K. Estes, ed., pp. 189–237. Hillsdale, N.J.: Lawrence Erlbaum Associates.

Smith, Edward E., and Douglas L. Medin (1981). *Categories and Concepts.* Cambridge, Mass.: Harvard University Press.

Spence, K. W. (1956). *Behavior Theory and Conditioning.* New Haven, Conn.: Yale University Press.

Stich, Stephen (1978). "Beliefs and Subdoxastic States." *Philosophy of Science* 45, 499–518.

Stich, Stephen (1982). "On the Ascription of Content" in *Thought and Object,* A. Woodfield, ed., pp. 153–206. Oxford: Clarendon Press.

Stoutland, Fredrick (1970). "The Logical Connection Argument." *American Philosophical Quarterly* Monograph No. 4, pp. 117–130.

Strawson, P. F. (1959). *Individuals.* London: Methuen & Co. Ltd.

Suppe, Frederick, ed. (1975). *The Structure of Scientific Theories*. Urbana, Illinois: University of Illinois Press.

Suppes, Patrick (1970). *A Probabilistic Theory of Causality, Acta Philosophica Fennica* Fasc. XXIV. Amsterdam: North-Holland.

Taylor, Charles (1964). *The Explanation of Behavior*. New York: Humanities Press.

Taylor, Richard (1966). *Action and Purpose*. Englewood Cliffs, N.J.: Prentice-Hall.

Taylor, Richard (1970). "Thought and Purpose" in *The Nature of Human Action*, M. Brand, ed., pp. 267–282. Glenview, Ill.: Scott-Foresman.

Taylor, Richard (1974). *Metaphysics*, 2nd ed. Englewood Cliffs, N.J.: Prentice-Hall.

Thalberg, Irving (1972). *Enigmas of Agency*. London: Allen and Unwin.

Thalberg, Irving (1976). "How Does Agent Causality Work?" in *Action Theory*, M. Brand and D. Walton, eds., pp. 213–238. Dordrecht, Holland: D. Reidel.

Thalberg, Irving (1977). *Perception, Emotion and Action: A Component Approach*. Oxford: Blackwell.

Thomson, Judith Jarvis (1977). *Acts and Other Events*. Ithaca, N.Y.: Cornell University Press.

Tolman, E. C. (1932). *Purposive Behavior in Animals and Men*. New York: Appleton-Century-Crofts.

Tolman, E. C. (1952). "A Psychological Model" in *Toward a General Theory of Action*, T. Parsons and E. Shils, eds., pp. 279–361. Cambridge, Mass.: Harvard University Press.

Tolman, E. C. (1955). "Principles of Performance." *Psychological Review* 62, 315–326.

Toumela, Raimo (1977). *Human Action and Its Explanation*. Dordrecht, Holland: D. Reidel.

Toumela, Raimo (1981). "Comments on Brand's 'Cognition and Intention'," presented at the 1981 Philosophy Colloquium, University of North Carolina, Charlotte.

Treisman, A. M. (1964). "Effect of Irrelevant Material on the Efficiency of Selective Listening." *American Journal of Psychology* 77, 533–546.

Treisman, A. M. (1969). "Strategies and Models of Selective Attention." *Psychological Review* 76, 282–299.

Tye, Michael (1979). "Brand on Event Identity." *Philosophical Studies* 35, 81–89.

Vendler, Zeno (1967). "Causal Relations." *The Journal of Philosophy* 64, 704–713.

Vermazen, Bruce (1980). "Occurrent and Standing Wants" in *Action and Responsibility*, M. Brand and M. Bradie, eds., pp. 48–54. Bowling Green, Ohio: Bowling Green Studies in Applied Philosophy, Vol. II.

Walton, Douglas (1980). "Omitting, Refraining and Letting Happen." *American Philosophical Quarterly* 17, 319–326.

Weiner, Bernard (1966). "The Role of Success and Failure in the Learning of Easy and Complex Tasks." *Journal of Personality and Social Psychology* 3, 339–344.

Weiner, Bernard (1972). *Theories of Motivation*. Chicago: Rand McNally.

White, Alan R. (1968). *The Philosophy of Action*. London: Oxford University Press.

Wilensky, Robert (1978). "Why John Married Mary: Understanding Stories Involving Recurring Goals." *Cognitive Science* 2, 235–266.

Wilson, Neil L. (1974). "Facts, Events and Their Identity Condition." *Philosophical Studies* 25, 303–321.

Winch, Peter (1958). *The Idea of a Social Science*. London: Routledge and Kegan Paul.

Winegrad, Terry (1977). "On Some Contested Suppositions of Generative Linguistics about the Scientific Study of Language." *Cognition* 5, 151–179.

Wittgenstein, Ludwig (1953). *Philosophical Investigations*, G. E. M. Anscombe, trans. New York: Macmillan.

Wright, Georg Henrik von (1963). *Norm and Action*. New York: Humanities Press.

Index

Abelson, R., 201, 203–222, 225–227, 234–235, 276
Achinstein, P., 70
Action: according to plan, 241; basic, 223–225; compared with intentional action, 31, 39, 209, 239–240, 248–250; compared with mere doing, 4; computational analysis of, 184; as decision, 197–198; deviance, 17–30; dynamics of, 277; by fiat, 193, 195–196; focal, 28; as following a rule, 10, 240, 257; functional accounts of, 9, 182; ideo-motor, 193–194; initiation, 94–97, 184, 187, 197, 238–239; mental antecedent to, 45, 237–239; moral responsibility for, 6, 13–14; nonintentional, 240–242, 248–250, 260, 265; and preferring, 139; reasons as causes of, 33, 274; substitution, (defined) 28–29, 215; TOTE analysis of, 182–191; types, 174, 218, 240, 252. *See also* Action Plan; Action Theory; Guidance and Monitoring; Intentional Action; Waywardness
Action Plan: branching structure in, 26; causal role of, 25; definitions of, 23, 24, 27, 216; following an, 240, 260–261; having an, (defined) 24; hierarchical order in, 26, 240, 260; improvisation, (defined) 29, 215–217; and intentionality, 27–28, 183, 240; interruption, (defined) 29, 216–217; as program (TOTE unit), 183–185; selection, 240–241, 260–261, 266, 268; substitution, (defined) 28–29, 215–216. *See also* Causal Theory; Scripts and Plans
Action Theory: causal, 3; dynamic, 183–184, 276; and events, 55;

fundamental problem, 33–48, 94, 186, 237; history, ix–x; and mental events, 42–45, 79; naturalized, x, 46, 158, 169, 192, 199, 238, 275; and psychology, x, 46, 204, 277; reduction in, 7, 249; static, 184. *See also* Action; Agency Theory; Causal Theory; Double Action Theory; Mental Action Theory; Oldtime Volitional Theory; Social Context
Act Sequence: 193–195; folk psychological model of, 127–131
Agency Theory, 9–10, 36
Alston, W., 133
Anderson, A. R., 271
Anderson, J. R., 238, 257–260, 263, 277
Anscombe, G. E. M., ix, 4
Aristotle, ix, 129–130
Artificial Intelligence (AI): xi, 46, 166, 169, 201–203, 227, 229, 276; and CD, 218; high-level languages in, 218; top-down model, 202, 228
Atkinson, J. W., 276, 277
Attention: 108, 194, 265, 276; as causal, 116; as cognitive, 45; effect and cause theories of, 196–198; as fiat, 45, 195–196. *See also* Selective Consideration
Attitude-Assimilationism: (defined) 86, 87–90, 96–97; psychological attitude in, 88, 96; and self-referentiality, 93–94. *See also* Mental Attitude; Object-Assimilationism
Audi, R., 121, 274
Aune, B., 8, 14, 37, 38, 39
Austin, J., 8
Austin, J. L., ix

Intentional Action: 5–6, 23, 46–47, 215–218, 253; cognitive antecedents of, 201, 203, 208, 210, 234, 239; conative antecedents of, 239–242, 262–263, 265–266; definitions of, 25, 28, 204, 216; focal, 28; as future-directed, 208, 214, 252; intended consequences of, 14; legal and moral responsibility for, 32; as past-directed, 208; plans in, 27–30, 173, 183, 201, 208, 215; satisfactional relationship in, 269. *See also* Action; Immediate Intention; Scripts and Plans
Intentionality Thesis, (defined) 31, 32, 39, 183, 209, 270

James, W., x, 45, 173, 176, 180, 191–199, 239
Jeffrey, R., 131, 254
Johnson, N. J., 228

Kahneman, D., 139
Kant, I., ix
Kaplan, D., 75, 273
Kim, J., 51, 52, 67, 69–73, 78, 270, 271, 276, 277
Kimble, G. A., 195–196
Knowledge: procedural and declarative, 256–257, 263
Körner, S., 140
Kosslyn, S. M., 178, 219, 275
Kripke, S., 10, 75, 240

Lakoff, G., 276
Landesman, C., ix
Language of Thought: 115–117. *See also* Mental Attitude; Psychological
Lehrer, K., ix
Leibniz's Law, 61, 63, 68, 271
Lemmon, E. J., 271
Levison, A., 270
Lewin, K., 183
Lewis, C. I., 43
Lewis, D., 47, 85, 90, 97, 103, 118, 272, 274
Lindsay, P. H., 262
Linguistic Phenomenalism, 43
Locke, J., ix, 9, 60
Logical Behaviorism, 103
Lombard, L. B., 57, 271
Loving, 144–145
Lycan, W., 100, 103

McCann, H., 13, 275
MacCorquodale, K., 253
Mackenzie, B., 242
Mackie, J. L., 134
Mandler, J. M., 228
Martin, R. M., 271
Masterson, F. A., 264–265
Mattson, M. E., 239
Medin, D. L., 111, 223
Meehl, P. E., 253
Meiland, J., 150, 270
Melden, A. I., ix, 10, 13, 34
Memory and Recall: (defined) 110, 163, 239, 252, 266, 276; computational, 184; declarative and production, 259, 261–262, 268; episodic, 223; as images, 174–175, 192–196; with scripts and plans, 208, 213, 225–226, 228; self-referentiality, 210; of sensations, 194; trace, 193; working, 260, 262. *See also* Scripts and Plans
Mental Action Theory: 6–9, (defined) 7, 12–15, 197–198; immediate intention in, 36; and moral responsibility, 13–14
Mental Attitude: (defined) 85, 85–118, 208; and abstract entities, 111–112, 115–117, 131; content, 105, 151–152, 271–272; focusing, 111–112; as full or partial endorsement, 88, 95–96, 273; object, 85, 90–94, 100, 117, 124, 136, 271–272; other than intending, desiring, and believing, 140–145; and possible worlds, 274; practical, 87; and properties, 85, 97–105, 274; semantical value, 124; self-referentiality of, 90–94, 98, 131–132, 211, 213. *See also* Attitude-Assimilationism; Believing; Concepts; De Dicto; De Re; De Se; Desiring; Intending; Object-Assimilationism; Property; Propositional; Semantics
Mental Event: 36, 38, 79–83, 123, 134; as action, 12–15, 36, 175; antecedent to action, 45, 127, 152, 168, 173–174, 179, 192, 208, 238–239; as function, 100–101; identity with physical event, 44, 116; as imagistic, 163, 219, 275; as representational, 116–117, 152, 153–154, 156, 163, 183, 196, 208, 222, 241, 252; spatiotemporal location of, 81–83;